The Anarchist Cookbook

by William Powell

with a prefatory note on
Anarchism Today by
P. M. Bergman

BARRICADE BOOKS, INC.
P.O. BOX 1401
SECAUCUS, N.J. 07096

The
Anarchist
Cookbook

Contents

Illustrations

A prefatory note on Anarchism today

by P. M. Bergman

We live in an age of anarchy both abroad and at home.

—President Richard M. Nixon

Confronted with a choice, the American people would choose the policeman's truncheon over the Anarchist's bomb.

—Vice President Spiro T. Agnew

The revolutionary reaches beyond dissent to nihilism and anarchy.

—Mayor John V. Lindsay

This is a brutal book—sensual, rude, coarse, and cruel. However, it is timely and well-written, even witty. Professionally and painstakingly, all possible informative instructions for individual actions of destruction having a presumably social effect are detailed here.

There is no political merit in publishing this book; it is not a call to action. For the real Hippy and Yippy, especially for the rebellious student, it hardly contains anything basic that he does not already know. I believe that it is usually the "square guy" who wants to know what is going on, though (or because) shocked and even tantalized by such subjects. More often than not it is the subscriber to *Reader's Digest* and *Time* who constitutes the literary market for such boring commodities as, for example, *Games People Play*.

Still, the present book is an important reflection of American Anarchism. It has its historical precedent in a similar "Cookbook" which was published in many editions and sold openly around the turn of the century (by the Anarchist headquarters, at the time in New York City, 167 William Street). Its title was *Science of Revolutionary Warfare—A Handbook of Instruction regarding the Use and Manufacture of Nitroglycerine, Dynamite, Gun-Cotton, Fulminating Mercury, Bombs, Arsons, Poisons, etc.* The book was written by the Anarchist J. H. Most, who was the teacher of Emma Goldman.*

I believe it to be very characteristic that such a book appeared only in this country. The same is true of the present "Cookbook." One might think this is because of the American constitutional "freedom of speech." But in other countries even the clandestine literature does not, so far as I know, show any similarities to such a "Cookbook." Blanqui's famous "Instructions for Insurrection" concentrates on mass actions (even if initiated by élites) like the building of barricades—something which neither Most's *Science* nor the present "Cookbook" gives any attention to. And this, in fact, expresses the basic difference—I think the only difference, even—between what is usually called Anarchism and revolutionary Marxism. I would like to go further and emphasize the specific nature of American Anarchism without denying that this local form still is Anarchism.

The word "Anarchism" as used in the present book might be somewhat misleading, even a misnomer. As often happens, it is confused with "Nihilism"—a word which Wendell Phillips favorably used after it was introduced by Turgenjev in *Fathers and Sons*. It frequented Russian literature until the time of Artzybashev. The chapter on narcotics, therefore, belongs to the present book. "Free Love"

*Johann Joseph Most (1846-1906), a bookbinder by trade, was one of the first Marxist deputies to the German Reichstag. He wrote the first popularization of *Capital*. For his very radical publications against religion and patriotism, he was several times imprisoned, and in 1878 had to flee Germany. In England, because of his extreme Anarchist views, Most broke with Marx and, after serving eighteen months at hard labor for advocating regicide, he emigrated in 1882 to the United States. Here he was, at the time of the Haymarket Square riot, considered the inspiration of radicalism throughout the country, but later, during the Homestead strike, Most spoke out against Berkman's assault on Henry Clay Frick. He was imprisoned for alleged sedition after the assassination of President McKinley.

(also religion) is missing here, for the good reason that it lost its sensational popularity in the Anarchist kitchen. Thus the popular synonymous use of Anarchism for Nihilism is understandable: Dostoyevsky's Netshayev was, after all, an important collaborator of Bakunin.

Nihilism *is* Anarchism, and Nihilism *is* revolutionary although it is an aberration of Anarchism. Like *all* other modern revolutionary tendencies, it is based philosophically on the Hegelian axiom: "Negation of Negation," which Friedrich Engels approvingly resolved with Goethe's words: "All that exists is worth perishing"; or, as recently expressed more simply in a note left in a bank burned by Anarchists in West Berlin: "Make *kaputt* what makes you *kaputt*."

Not only Anarchism, but any other real revolutionary movement is dragged into some forms of Nihilism. This understandably occurs especially in the formative stages as well as sometimes in the declining, depressive stages. Who can deny the historical importance of the wrecking of machinery by the Luddites (though today we are so clever that we tell them what they should have done instead)? There is no doubt that the assassination of czars and Russian governors effected, if nothing else, different treatment of political "criminals"—something which still has not been achieved in the "free" United States. Without denying the truly revolutionary character of the Palestinian commandos, their newest weapon, hijacking, is surely an aberration in their struggle for recognition. But the taking of hostages is nothing new in revolutionary history. The Paris Commune did it, as well as such partisans as the Titoists in Yugoslavia, the Maquis in France, and, before them, the Max-Hoelz Brigade in Weimar Germany.

"Putschismus," as it is called in German, or *"coup de main,"* in French, is not limited to Anarchism. In the early twenties in Germany, attempts at bombing of public toilets and of the victory memorial in Berlin, or the famous bombing of the cathedral in Sofia (1923), and many other such "actions" were tacitly approved and initiated by Communists, especially at the time of their decline.

The main aspect of Anarchist actions, which surely do not conform with the civilized rules of politics and warfare (no government abides by them either, by the way) is to draw attention more to the existence of the movement than to its ideas. The attempt to free prisoners by taking hostages, or to reduce mistreatment of prisoners by individual attacks on officials and by bomb scares, will not create sympathy. However, it might lead to a "giving-in" by the government, forcing it to recognize the existence of the illegal Anarchist movement. As a matter of fact, the government itself commits an illegal act by "giving-in" to the assault. Usually a government fares better by "giving in," but, on the other hand, one of the criteria of a revolutionary situation is that a stage is reached where the government feels it can no longer give in.

Calling a policeman a "pig" seems silly and must antagonize the very people the revolutionaries want to win over or to neutralize. But the actual relationships of power are such that name-calling is the only weapon available at the moment. Besides, name-calling is an emotional outlet (and revolutionaries also have emotions). "Pig" is an assault, no doubt—an assault against the uniform which, though a fetish, is in itself a power, an assault against the whole power structure. It is an assault—and a crime punishable by law. Here is the strong policeman, heavily armed, with the entire physical and ideological power of the state behind him, and he is attacked by a word—by a word only, but it is still an attack.

What will the "pig" do? In the last analysis it is not up to the policeman, who, though having a loaded gun in his hand, has in fact no power; it is up to the state to give the answer. It might not be "smart" of Bobby Seale to provoke his jailers by repeatedly calling them "pigs," therefore getting brutally beaten and put in isolation. But "pig" is his only means of defense against the attacks upon his humanity at the moment and gives him a chance to get recognition for his beliefs and as a human being.

Basically what applies to the silly "pigs"-calling is also valid for the often Hollywoodlike hijackings, the taking of hostages, and even for the more harmful "Anarchist cooking." These methods are not "smart"; they are aberrations which sometimes border on insanity. But these methods of the revolutionary struggle of today are here and existing and real and, in the philosophical sense, reasonable. They reflect the true stage of the revolutionary struggle in the whole world. Its stage is today again embryonic.

In describing the American Revolution, history textbooks tell us only of such great episodes as the Boston Massacre, which unlocked the revolutionary spirit of the people; of the Boston Tea Party, which contested the power of the British parliament; or of the Battle of Bunker Hill, which took on the form of a real revolutionary war. The history textbooks, however, fail to describe the "Anarchist cooking" and innumerable sabotage actions which surely were going on in the several decades *before* the actual revolution. One cannot doubt that the Hessian mercenaries were called names.

The author of *Anarchist Cookbook* does not see in the individualistic acts of terror he describes the *ultima ratio.* He emphasizes that the real revolution will require the American people, and he has trust in them, but still he is not scared by the anger of short-sighted liberals and sensitive quasi-revolutionaries. However, I believe in the approach that Marx took toward the different forms of revolutionary struggles. This approach was not at all abstractly "theoretical," but very concrete and practical. It was limited to one question: "Whom does this serve?" But before dealing with this question, in regard to the "cooking," it seems to me necessary to consider the all-important question: What is Anarchism?

Anarchism as an idea is *nonviolent*. Its philosophy is Spinozan, ethical, and nature-loving. Anarchism in modern times began under the intellectual and spiritual influence of the French Revolution and the late stage of Enlightenment of the young-Hegelian school.* The progenitor of Anarchism is generally considered to be the German philosopher Max Stirner (Kaspar Schmidt, 1806-56), who in the tumultuous 1840's came out with the obviously neurotic form of Individual Anarchism. Except in England, an industrial proletariat hardly existed at that time but, seemingly without communication with each other (the telegraph was just invented), students in Paris and Rome, in Vienna, Berlin, and Madrid became rebellious. Interestingly, the only connection between the different places where students rioted was among the governments in suppressing these riots—the "Holy Alliance." Even at that time, it was the "foreigners" who misled these boys from nice families, as Heinrich Heine's verses satirically remind us. And, just as today, these students "never had it so good." They were mostly sons of the new and prosperous middle classes. Many of these "bums" received scholarships and the "best education ever," no doubt scholastically superior to the one Nixon in his ignorance is raving about today.

The idea of Anarchism already existed more universally when Stirner's confused writings appeared. American Anarchism began as far back as the 1820's with Josiah Warren, a New England Yankee of early colonial stock and a descendant of the famous Warren of Bunker Hill, who was followed by Ezra Heywood, William Greene, Lysander Spooner, Joshua Ingalls, Stephen P. Andrews, and later Benjamin Tucker. Thoreau is considered the American Anarchist *par excellence,* and, if we can believe Vernon Louis Parrington, all of the Adams family—from the two presidents to the brothers—wished nothing more than the burning of State Street, the site of Boston banking. (Parrington quotes that Henry Adams was held back from Marxism by "some narrow trait of the New England nature.")

Years before the Haymarket Riot, Wendell Phillips—this old-fashioned Yankee soul who was of the opinion that "if it must be bullets, so be it"—addressed the respectable Phi Beta Kappas at Harvard University with the words:

Nihilism is righteous and honorable. Nihilism is evidence of life. The last weapon of victims choked and manacled beyond all other resistance. I honor Nihilism, since it redeems human nature from the suspicion of being utterly vile, made up only of heartless oppressors and contented slaves. This is the only view an American, the child of 1620 and 1776, can take of Nihilism. Any other unsettles and perplexes the ethics of our civilization.

Anarchism in America, as an idea as well as a movement, was much stronger and more conspicuous than Marxism, even though Marx moved the headquarters of the First International to this country. The "Wobblies," who were the only ones representing the revolutionary labor movement, especially in the western United States, were undoubtedly mostly Anarchists.* Later the impact of the Bolshevik revolution dominated and bureaucratized here all radical thought (the Communist Party in America was something like a slap in the face to Marx's suggestion that "every revolution will bear the birthmark of the old society from whose womb it sprang"). Again, today, while in Europe and Asia the revolutionaries agitate in the name of Marx (and Lenin), in the United States Mao, Ho, Guevara, Castro, etc., are the ones who are worshiped.

Anarchism as an idea reached its highest motives through the Darwin-Haeckel-inspired observation of *Mutual Aid* by Kropotkin. It also found strong support in Tolstoy's Christianity of Civil Disobedience. Anarchism as a theory of political science, however, as founded by Proudhon and Bakunin, has exactly the same goals as Marxism: abolition of private property, the basis of economic exploitation; and abolition of the state, the institution of social oppression. In this sense (and, after all, herein lies the premise of all revolutionary argument) Marx and Lenin consented to be true Anarchists. "As long as there is the state there is no freedom; when there is freedom there will be no state." (Lenin)

The formula of Blanqui (who was called by Marx "the heart and brain of the French proletariat") was the connecting word of Communism and Anarchism in the First International: "ni Dieu—ni Maître." Together, Proudhonists, Bakunists, Blanquists, and Marxists in the Paris Commune wrote, as Wendell Phillips said, "the grandest declaration of popular indignation on the pages of history in fire and blood." (Phillips added, "I honor Paris as the vanguard of the Internationals of the world.") And in the very beginning of Lenin's Third International, up till the Kronstadt episode, Anarchists from France, Italy, Germany, and also from America (Emma Goldman and Alex-

---

* Hegel introduced the idea of *freedom* into philosophy. Much clearer than in his pedantically obscurantist philosophical writings, which often looked as if he favored the existing Prussian King, Hegel unmistakably expressed in his private letters the true meaning and the revolutionary character of his philosophy. For example, in a letter to Schelling: "The people will learn to feel the dignity of man. They will not merely demand their rights which have been trampled in the dust, but themselves will take them—make them their own."

* From the beginning, no other political idea was so severely persecuted in this country as Anarchism. Aside from the Chinese Exclusion Act, the only immigration restriction which existed up to the introduction of the quota system in 1924 was the law of 1901 forbidding Anarchists (and prostitutes) to enter the United States. The most renowned expression of American judicial murder was the case of the Anarchists Sacco and Vanzetti.

ander Berkman) took part in the Comintern at Moscow.*

Anarchism is *anti-parliamentarian*. So, in fact, is Marxism. The only difference is that Marx and Engels, Lenin and Rosa Luxemburg believed in making use of Parliament against the power of the existing government. They never allowed active participation in any but a revolutionary government. The Paris Commune was surely not a parliament, and the Soviets of 1905 and 1917 came about as anarcho-syndicalist forms of free association completely independent from political parties.

Participation at elections is a purely tactical question. Anarchists in Romance countries sometimes took part in elections. Lenin was ambivalent toward elections to the Czarist Duma, and the first Communist Party Congress in Germany voted against participation (though their leader Rosa Luxemburg was for it). Today's students in America, diligently canvassing for politicians, are in for disillusionment, if their campaign for Gene McCarthy has not already disappointed them. The surprising fact that in this freest democratic country there are millions of conscientious non-voters (more than anywhere else in the world) is evidence of an interesting mass basis for "Anarchist cooking." It is a good sign for the ripening of revolutionary consciousness that, as James Reston reports in the *New York Times,* "all the excitement last spring about mounting a successive campaign by students to help elect peace candidates in the November elections has dwindled to a whisper."

Anarchism differs from Marxism in that the basic premise of Marxism is the class struggle of the proletariat against the capitalistic form of production. Therefore, society's taking possession of the means of production is, according to Marx, "the last act" the state fulfills. This state ("which is no longer a state") is identical with the dictatorship of the proletariat. By virtue of its permanent revolutionary character, the dictatorship of the proletariat consciously brings about such a condition that the state in any form *withers away.*

Anarchism wants the abolition of the state *out of hand,* since neither economic change in general nor the proletariat as such seems to guarantee freedom and humanity. Marx's whole revolutionary theory is based on his economic critique of bourgeois society—on what he regards as the all-decisive conflict which exists between private ownership and social production. Only as a result of this struggle on the part of the very often lethargic proletarians, caused by "objective" economic conditions, among which the most

important is the periodicity of crises, does true Communist society become possible and even unavoidable—while Anarchism simply does not need a theory of economics. The same is true of all new revolutionary philosophies. Neither Sartre nor Marcuse bothers about economic theory, while for Marx and Lenin it was of the utmost importance.

It is absolutely not true that Marx favored-state socialism, as the social democrats and Soviet economists want us to believe. On the contrary, *Capital* characterizes *all* governmental economic measures—and especially state ownership of industry—as "feudal-reactionary."* By the way, almost all criticism of Soviet Russia is limited to the political and cultural brutality of its system. When it comes to economics, this system rectifies itself shamelessly by Marxist phraseology. Even revolutionaries believe it is a great thing that the Soviet state owns the means of production.

Criticism of the Soviet Union almost never touches the main and real Marxian point that all the economic terms which, according to Marx, characterize capital, like "wages," "profit," "accumulation," and especially "value," are officially recognized by the Soviet regime as valid for a socialist economy. Marx's genial conception of the fetishism of commodities and the secret thereof, described in the first pages of *Capital,* is completely ignored.

Of even greater importance is the so-called role of the proletariat. The proletariat is the main social contradiction of capitalist society. This postulate united German Communists, French Socialists, Russian Anarchists with English Chartists around the *Communist Manifesto* in 1848 during and after the student revolts all over Europe initiated mass insurrections. The proletariat was declared the gravedigger of capitalism, whereas the students were criticized as "utopian," "reactionary," and "petit bourgeois."

But whenever Marx came into contact with the real facts of the organized proletariat, his and Engels' whole political life, as later that of Lenin and Rosa Luxemburg, was a constant struggle which resulted dialectically from the general role of the proletariat. Capitalism does create through the proletariat its own gravedigger, but the proletariat is an integral part of capitalism. The well-being of capitalist economy is, in any existing conditions, the best possible condition for the material well-being of the pro-

---

* Lenin's *Left-Wing Communism—an Infantile Disorder* was an opportunistic pamphlet that paved the way for the Rapallo policy, which introduced the Soviet foreign policy of "co-existence." Probably Lenin himself did not realize that this booklet would help the Comintern bureaucracy get rid of the radical critics in the international revolutionary movement—among them many of his closest friends outside Russia. It is interesting that today the foreign visitor will find at the bookstall in the Moscow airport huge stocks of this pamphlet in all languages, but *State and Revolution* is usually "out of stock."

* In his criticism of the German Social Democratic Party program (Erfurt, 1891), Engels very sharply said that Marxism "has nothing in common with the so-called State Socialism, that system of nationalisation which puts the state in place of the private owner and by so doing concentrates the power of economic exploitation and the political oppression of the workers in one hand."

There is no difference at all between Marxism and Anarchism in regard to the economics of Socialism. In the famous closing statement of the first volume of *Capital,* where Marx predicts "the expropriation of the expropriators," he makes it clear that the Negation of Negation will not reestablish *private* property (which in fact is being destroyed by corporate capitalism). He observes, however, that it will "certainly establish *individual property,* based on *cooperation* and the *possession in common* of the land and the means of production."

letariat. Marx was completely aware of this decisive contradiction and therefore emphasized the position which his Communists take toward the proletarian masses.

The proletarians are interested in economic affluence in its simplest form—dollars and cents—regardless of whether capitalism is private or state or semi-socialistic. In some ways they are even more interested in, and very apologetic toward, any militaristic-industrial establishment which guarantees employment, health insurance, and wage levels which can be attained without costly strikes. As long as there is affluence which provides even a measure of freedom of competition among "equals," as long as increased productivity and a "just" distribution of produced wealth let the proletarian have a share (its relative size—an important factor in Marx's analyses—is unimportant to him), what logical interest can he have in economic recession, depression, slumps, and crises, about which old Marx was so avid in his letters and which were once so ardently desired in the reports made up by the Comintern-economist Varga? On the contrary from a simple, logical point of view, the leaders of trade unions and of established Socialist and Communist parties became the healers of society's economic and social sicknesses. Their bureaucratic degeneration is only part of their function—and secondary. Their corruption is only a symptom which helps, as in any state system.

Interesting in this connection is W.E.B. DuBois's analysis of the English and German Socialist immigrants who came here as political refugees and first blurted out their disapprobation of Negro slavery on principle. Later they found they could increase wages and regulate working conditions much better in the United States than in Europe. This happy discovery, instead of increasing sympathy for the slave, turned the attitude of the immigrants directly into rivalry and enmity. "The wisest of the leaders," DuBois observed, "could not clearly envisage how slave labor in conjunction and competition with free labor tended to reduce all labor toward slavery. For this reason, the union and labor leaders gravitated toward the political party which opposed tariff bounties and welcomed immigrants, quite forgetting this same Democratic party had as its backbone the planter oligarchy of the South with its slave labor." This was and still is the role of organized labor with regard to the Negro question and party politics. It has been true even in those cases when organized labor was committed to Socialism and Communism. Needless to say, this attitude was always heavily criticized by Marx.

Thus the organized proletariat became in fact a *conditio sine qua non* for existing society. Without social democratic bureaucrats and without Communist *apparatshiks,* European capitalism could hardly have survived after the First World War. Even more so everywhere today, including in the so-called "developing countries," classical capitalism has no chance whatsoever without social democracy and

Communist bureaucracy. Look at India—this greatest wonder of misery in the whole world is held together today by Liberal, Socialist, and even Communist bureaucracy. It is perhaps more corrupt than anywhere else in the world. Preaching nonviolence, it is in actual practice very violent toward its dissenters. It is only proper that India is the ideal of the liberals, such as John Kenneth Galbraith.*

Marx emphasized that it is not the worker's consciousness that leads him to revolution. It is the "objective situation" which will drive him to his historical role. In May, 1968, the students of Paris realized that they needed the help of the workers—that no revolution is possible without the proletariat. Remaining a rebellion of students, it can never become a revolution.

What do these naughty, ill-behaving, and ungrateful students want? We could quote Marx and Bakunin and Blanqui and Lenin and Rosa Luxemburg and Trotsky. I prefer to mention a recent resolution passed by students of the very "square" Harvard Business School and published as an ad in the *Wall Street Journal:*

> We condemn the administration of President Nixon for its view of mankind and the American community which . . . is unwilling to move for a transformation of American society in accordance with the goals of maximum fulfillment for each human being and harmony between mankind and nature.

This is not only the idea, it is even the language, of Hegel and Marx. Those students have already passed the stage of protesting against the obscene war in Vietnam and the stage of the silliness of Hickel's "Earth Day." No student in America (and in Russia) believes any more that the Second World War was fought because Hitler killed six million Jews, but the textbooks, written by Liberals and Socialists, still say it. These students are now on the way to finding out that basically everything Lenin wrote about the First World War can be applied to the Second World War as well as to the conflict in the Near East. They are discovering, too, that what he wrote on imperialism is still valid for state capitalism, which must lead, if left to its "natural" development, to planned barbarism.

After so much costly confusion created mostly because the Russian Marxists were not able to cope with internal and international conditions, and after their intellectual fellow travelers covered up every Robespierian terror (and now *after* the "Gods have failed them" are angry about the Egyptian expedition of the little Napoleons in the Kremlin), the writings of Marx were put on the highest

---

* Significantly, there are hardly any Anarchists (or Nihilists) in India. It is also interesting that ideologically Anarchism, even in its individualistic forms, has never been "Faustian" or Nietzschean or Spenglerian. Philosophically, today's Hippies and Yippies, though a number of them are somehow "mystic," are in complete contrast to the Jeremiad of the decline of the world. Toynbee does not interest them.

pedestal of modern philosophy, called psychology and sociology (whatever that means). At the same time only naïve "Anarchists" and incorrigible "dogmatists" still dared to believe in the great Marxian perception that the social destiny of man is his own work and that his goal—the solution of his fundamental historical 'problem, of his misery—can only be the abolition of state, of government in any form. And thus the emancipation of humanity requires revolution. This is the real principle of Anarchism. It is the quintessence of Marx and Bakunin and also of Tolstoy. What have the Liberals, Socialists, and Communists to offer instead?

When the students became more and more disturbed as they saw the illusory and contradictory conditions around them and throughout the world, with no solution in sight (as did the students in the times of young Marx), the psychology and sociology professors in Heidelberg, Paris, and Boston and also in Warsaw and Zagreb came out with a word which they found in the newly discovered early philosophical manuscripts by Marx. (He himself said that he preferred to leave those early manuscripts to the "gnawing critique of the mice.") The word was *Alienation*. Alienation *is* the basic evil of the world. So is "Pollution," the newest fashionable word in politics. "Alienation" is class-less, and that is why it became a shibboleth of the critical minds of the philosophers. Although it really is revolutionary (after all it *is* Marxist), "Alienation" became fashionable and perfectly legal, in Poland as well as in Spain. This was for the very same reason that Marx 125 years ago had no more use for it from the moment he gave up the narrow academic life and began to take an active part in the real movement in France. It was then he turned from Hegelian philosophy, aesthetics, and psychology to revolution, and said: The philosophers are trying to *interpret* the world differently—what matters is to *change* the world.

It is tragic that those professors whose learned efforts in the fields of sociology and history, and in a wider sense of philosophy and psychology, bring them nearest to the real facts of life, which one would think are forcing them to make the jump to revolution (it can only be a jump!)—that those professors especially are most alienated and are left behind by the students. Those rebellious students are so nasty that they show them the behind (imagine, to those well-meaning professors!). Thus we learn from a report in the book publishers' trade weekly that Nixon's "bums" have stopped reading books. What books? Symptomatically, the same periodical reports that in Germany the students are reading mostly nineteenth-century books.

Interestingly, it is different in the field of the sciences, where there is a more real connection with production and business and where the students acquire something like the role the highly qualified worker used to have. (It is well-known that this worker was the intellectually advanced,

class-conscious stock of the old revolutionary movement in Europe.) This also might explain why frequently Nobel prize winners like Szent-Gyorgyi, Wald, and Pauling (to mention only American ones) are sympathetic toward the rebellious students—in fact, most of those scientists condone Anarchist "cooking" all the way, starting with the first chapter on dope. Today, an Einstein (who, by the way, was a pronounced Anarchist) would probably not go to the president to draw his attention to the military meaning of a discovery like the one by Hahn-Meitner. He would probably go with his information to the Anarchists. How frightening to think that among today's Italian students there might be a new Enrico Fermi!

The students are warned by Bruno Bettelheim, by Irving Howe, by Arthur Schlesinger, Jr., and by the established head of the emptiest philosophy in America, the Social Democrat Professor, Sydney Hook, that "Anarchist cooking" will lead to the situation that prevailed in Italy and Germany before Mussolini and Hitler took over. The "backlash" argument is as old as written history—even biblical—and could be chewed on endlessly. It would doubtless be a waste' of space to quote what Marx and Lenin had to say about, "They should not have taken up the arms." Aside from all that, the historical analogy which Liberals are warning the students about is rubbish. Historical comparison is certainly necessary and for good reasons plays a big part in revolutionary literature. But no comparison with the pre-Hitler period can be proven by one single social, economic, political, or cultural event (aside the fact that Hitler could not have come to power without the tacit support of the Vatican, the Quai d'Orsay and the Foreign Office figuring that Hitler would fulfill his *Drang nach Osten*—something similar to the newest desire for a war between Russia and China).

When Hitler came to power, no war was going on, labor did not ask for higher wages, prices were deflating. Surely there was no "affluence." Students were not shaking the educational system. Racial or national minority struggle for equality did not exist. (Anti-Semitism did not arise because Jews asked for equal rights.) *All* such things happened, however, in Russia in 1905. One more interesting criterion: Unlike Italy and Germany, Russia at that time, like this country today, had no labor movement to speak of.*

---

* It is true that, in the immediate pre-Nazi period, the German Communist Party—on instructions from Moscow—"cooked anarchistically," throwing bombs, killing policemen, and initiating acts of senseless terror, even in cooperation with Nazi gangs. But it is false and only a legend that the transfer of power to Hitler by the German industrialists and the military was a "backlash from the Bolshevik danger." All the documents which have come out since the collapse of the Nazi regime, among them reports on conferences within the Hindenburg clique and the circles of big business and Prussian Junkers, do not even mention any serious concern about Communist activities. Rather, we find that breaking the power of the Social Democratic Party and the big trade unions was the foremost consideration of the Hindenburg-Papen-Schleicher group and of big business. In fact, the decisive act in paving the way for the

Dr. Bettelheim refers to the noisy, nauseating students at the Vienna University giving him a traumatic experience, and without a blink he—as a scientist—simply equates "students" with "students." One hopes that this therapist does not in his profession treat all children alike. Aside from the decisive fact that those Vienna students Dr. Bettelheim berates were supported (and not only tacitly) by the half-fascist government which they wanted to be more fascist, doesn't the child therapist Bettelheim look at the faces of the children? One can proudly see the difference between the *teutsche* students and today's rebellious boys and girls in this country, in France, and, yes, in Germany, simply by looking at their faces. What Dr. Bettelheim says is an insult—at least an insult to the intelligence of his readers.*

Just as false, of course, is the "radical" rationalization that today's American government is equal to Fascism— an argument which might "constitutionally" help to justify "Anarchist cooking." The irony is that William Kunstler uses basically the same analogy to Germany as Irving Howe does, only for divergent reasons.

Though also ignoring the parliament, Nixon is not a Hitler and not even a Hindenburg. Only as a joke one could make an analogy, since there are so many Sauerkraut-names in the Nixon entourage. And, to facetiously stretch the analogy further, one might say that the "decent" conservative Nazi supporters tried to persuade Hitler to curb the offensive tone of his "African" (Goebbels), as the good Americans wish Nixon would do with his "Greek," but here the analogy really ends.

Rather, Richard M. Nixon is—*cum grano salis*—a Czar Nicolas II, and Attorney General John Mitchell is his Plehve.**

What went on in Kent, Ohio, and elsewhere is a small

but true copy of Bloody Sunday in January, 1905, when the guards "felt threatened" by the petitioners led by the priest Gapon (who, it was revealed a year later, was in the service of the Russian police). At that time, all-mighty Czarist Russia was involved in a bitter and costly and hopeless war with a second-rate, little, aggressive Asian country; it was bothered by racial and minorities' demands, by stone-throwing bearded students, by bomb-fabricating boys and girls from good and even aristocratic families. Plenty of dope was used, also (not only by rebellious students who, as today, did not get drunk as did their fathers). The list of striking similarities could be much extended.

The "backlash" reaction to "Anarchist cooking" in Russia was not from S.S. and S.A. Storm Troopers or Fascisti, but such well-established income-earning people as today's construction workers. In old Russia, it was especially the poultry traders who broke up student meetings, while the police looked on. Those were the most active Jew-beaters also, because of the competition at the open street markets. After all, the hard-hats feel threatened by Negro demands for job opportunities. That these construction workers will become the nuclei comparable to the "Black Hundreds" in Russia I doubt very much. They are not the Ku Klux Klan type, of which this country has plenty, to be recruited for "White Hundreds"—even at the universities.

On the other hand, there were many Hickels in the Russian government and among the nobility, who pleaded for "understanding" of the rebellious students and their causes, and criticized the educational system.* Millionaires gave money to the revolutionaries. The great opera singer Chaliapin arranged parties to collect for the imprisoned "Panthers" of that time. And also an impetuous women's liberation movement appeared.**

It is hard to leave this historical "necromancy" because it is, besides amusing, very helpful in analyzing the present political situation and its probable perspective. It is amusing to observe the way in which Nixon "hawks and spits" (if a phrase by Schiller may be used) like Nicolas II. The Czar was also a great friend of peace conferences, and this especially used to enrage old Tolstoy. It was the same Czar who initiated the World Court of Justice in The Hague. And Nixon now tries to do in reverse what Nicolas II did by getting an American president to settle his war in Asia in 1905. (Why not? The Russians are our oldest "imperial friends." They were called that a long time ago when we engaged them as umpire to get back our slaves according to the terms of the Treaty of 1783.)

What wonderful "generation of peace" this could be if only Czar Nixon and President Kosygin would get together

Nazi regime was Papen's "backlash" against the Social Democratic government in Prussia, which capitulated to this illegal act, although the Social Democrats not only had organized labor behind them, but also the Prussian police force. The next and final "backlash" by the Nazis was caused by the readiness of the leadership of the German trade unions to put themselves at the service of the Nazi-Arbeitsfront. Thus, if the Nazi regime was a "backlash," then it came not as a move against revolutionary activities. Rather, it clearly resulted from the impotence of the liberals who were afraid of a "backlash." Such an attitude of course, directly led to the erosion of all the power the German liberals had.

* The percentage of the students within the whole Nazi movement before 1933 was minute. Symptomatically, the bulk of the Nazi students were law students preparing themselves for administrative and judicial posts in the government—thus the real law-and-order people. Many of them would have gone to officers' schools, but there were none in the Weimar Republic, and the regular army was restricted by peace treaty to 100,000 men. That sociologists and historians can neglect such important differences is hard to believe.

** Tom Wicker in the *New York Times* compares Mitchell with Rasputin. He is, of course, mistaken. Rasputin was not a member of the Czarist government and became prominent years after the 1905 Revolution. Rather, Billy Graham is Nixon's Rasputin. Nevertheless. Wicker's remark is discerning, because it draws attention to similarities between Nixon and Czar Nicolas II.

* See Lenin's works, English edition, vol. 7. Excellent for the description of the student movements and their potencies; it offers some interesting analogies to today's events at the universities.

** The women's liberation movement was a serious aspect of the Russian Revolution. Its achievements in the first five years after the and continue where their counterparts Eisenhower and Khrushchev left off because of the damned U-2 incident! This was a time when the Anarchist Bertrand Russell was so frightened by the nightmare of Russian-American co-operation (just as frightened as Tolstoy was when he learned that the visiting Czarist fleet in Nantes played the "Marseillaise" and the republican French navy of Liberté, Egalité, and Fraternité responded with "Long Live the Czar") that he expressed the crazy wish that the Pentagon should throw atom bombs on the Kremlin.

History proves that it is not the antagonism which leads to wars, but paradoxically the *modus vivendi,* when, to paraphrase Heinrich Heine, they will both understand each other and promptly find themselves in the mud. (Bismarck and Louis Bonaparte, so also Stalin and Hitler.)

Moscow does not have to worry any more about NATO (if it ever seriously did). The drag on European economy by the American "stagflation" makes it probable that the successor of Willy Brandt may throw the American army out of Western Europe if the Federal Reserve should resist the return of the gold bullions (instead of paper dollars) it owes Germany. But what worries Moscow is the coming crisis of world economy; that might make the Kremlin's readiness for "co-existence" more palatable and stop its support of "anti-imperialist forces." Stalin's policy of "Socialism in one country" by exploiting the fellow-travelers of the Communist parties and national revolutionary movements in the world was in general very successful. Today, the Kremlin still keeps to this very profitable policy. To give up that policy—as was partially done during the Roosevelt-Stalin honeymoon—would require that American capital is ready to pay for it and to give much better trade conditions than Western Europe and Japan. Soviet Russia has a very substantial reason, one can call it an "imperialist" reason, for supporting the Arabs, the Vietcong, and Cuba—and to that degree Russia is a true ally of the revolutionary world. (Somehow similar to Napoleon's revolutionary role in Europe.) The trade figures for the last decade speak a clear language: The substantial surpluses that Russia earns from trade with the so-called developing countries cover its trade deficit with the Western industrial suppliers. Of course, there might arise the great problem of indebtedness, which the "aid" given so graciously by Russia creates, with all its eventual consequences—like Western

revolution were more progressive than anywhere else in the world.

It is interesting that such a good observer as Kurt Vonnegut, Jr., prognosticates that today's Women's Lib movement will have a greater revolutionary impact than that of the "kids."

As expressed by the best-selling book *Sexual Politics,* the basic theories of the new movement are not any longer the liberal ones, but the revolutionary opinions of Friedrich Engels' *Origin of the Family.* Author Kate Millett rightly criticizes the liberal and "free" sex literature of Norman Mailer and Henry Miller. Our objection is only that, by reproducing extensively the cheap filth, she seems to have fallen for the same old tricks as have other "unhurried viewers of Erotica."

"aid" already does, especially in South America where constant *coup d'états* are partially motivated by the desire to get rid of the indebtedness to the Chase Manhattan and by the same token to get new "aid" from the First National, or else from Russia.

The Smart Alecs at the *New York Times* advise Nixon to make use of the existing conflict between China and Russia to get out of Vietnam. The conflict between China and Russia really exists, but it is naïve to think that Peking and Moscow do not know what Washington wants. There is no doubt that Stalin was a neurotic and therefore he did it in his peculiar way, but his pact with Hitler threw off the Daladiers and Chamberlains, who wished that the Nazis would go against Russia and gain enough *Lebensraum* that France and England would be spared. And it is just because of the conflict between themselves that Russia and China desire that Nixon stay as long as he can in Vietnam, and go deeper and deeper into Cambodia, Laos, Thailand, Burma, and, if possible, again into Korea.

Nixon wants to get out of Vietnam; one can believe him. (It is anyway not the "right" war as Korea was, and not as "popular" as, for example, an invasion in the Near East could be.) It is not the war Congress does not like (the Tonkin resolution was almost unanimous), but the unpopularity of the war in Vietnam. Nixon is right when he says that ending the war in Vietnam would not stop the student movement and solve the decisive internal problems. The internal policy of a big power is never dependent on its foreign policy. Rather, it is the reverse. Otherwise revolutionaries would wish nothing better than wars. It is not true that wars are the fathers of revolutions. Rosa Luxemburg and Lenin thought at the outbreak of the First World War that the chances of proletarian revolution were delayed and not progressed, and that the war brutalities would destroy the international spirit of the proletariat. What revolution resulted directly from the Second World war? Not even Stalin could say that the invasions by the Red Army were revolutions. But it is true that wars, even victorious ones, often add decisively to internal difficulties and therefore ultimately may lead to revolution.

Wars break out for economic reasons. We are told that the war in Vietnam damages the economy. Yes, but whose economy? Adam Smith argued correctly that slavery is unrentable, while he must have seen how Liverpool flourished as the mecca of the international slave trade. George Washington, the biggest slaveholder in Virginia, used to complain bitterly that he lost money on slaves. At the same time, he bought new ones (secretly, so that his good northern friends should not know). It is true that Wall Street protested strongly against the Cambodia invasion, and it is known as a historical fact that every time a war starts the stock market goes down, while peace or peace rumors usually bring the shares up.

We are told that economically the United States did not

win World War II, especially because of U.S. generosity in foreign aid and because the losers (Germany and Japan) are prosperous. Never mind that the bulk of our aid consists of armament which is not productive. Only one look at the list of American investments in Europe and at the interest obligations of the so-called undeveloped countries suffices to show that imperialism pays. Ford's newly negotiated participation at the automobile factory in—what irony!—Hiroshima alone will pay off more than the cost of the first atom bomb which was thrown on this town.

It is true that the military has its own interest, and so has every other branch of the ruling class—the banks, the insurance companies, the agrarian conglomerates etc., etc. The special interest of the military is a pretty old one, older than capitalism. Campanella nearly four hundred years ago complained that the Spanish commanders prolonged the war so that their pay as well as their authority might also be prolonged.* There is no need for the special term "military industrial complex," since *Imperialism* characterizes sufficiently the stage of capitalism in which we live.

The military does not live in a vacuum. No doubt, American capitalism can exist without South America, without Arabian oil, and even without investments in Europe, though those alone are a greater investment than the British Empire ever had. But when those "third persons" (as Lenin called them) are once available, capital necessarily is somehow driven to exploit them and to swallow up the surplus profit the "help"-needing countries provide. About one quarter of India's, Brazil's, Argentina's, and Mexico's exports go for covering of the interest debts on foreign loans. This is the economic explanation for imperialism and war.

The economic difficulties of American capitalism were not created by the Vietnam war. In capitalism industry produces commodities, no matter whether industry is applied to production or destruction of things. True, military production does not create wealth. Neither does advertising. It is waste, overhead, misused capacities, and loafing that characterize cooperative capitalism, so that any wage demands threaten the rate of surplus value toward capital's point of no return so much that inflation becomes, in fact, the main source of profit. But profits are high. Look at the growth of American banking. Stopping the Vietnam war will not change inflation and improve employment. Acheson, the protagonist of the Pentagon, is right that it does not mean much if all that the U.S. military spends is hardly seven percent of a national growth amounting to a trillion!

All governments shed crocodile tears about inflation. Even the Thieu gang does it, while sucking dry the Americans with black-market operations. Who else but govern-

* General Douglas MacArthur became seriously worried that the invention of atomic weapons, and thus wars of very short duration, might shake the whole idea of the military.

ments create inflation? There are no private money-printing presses. It is a pretext that welfare and education are the real causes of inflation. American industry has reached such capacities and productivity that, even with very high wages, prices could go down instead of up. Inflation is economically nothing but a method of avoiding the commercial crisis which, under normal capitalism, usually appeared periodically after the growth of industry reached a certain high point. The practical social effect of inflation is the same as Depression and Recession, but with other means. The pockets of labor and the middle classes are emptied, while their nominal earnings even increase. Unemployment, a typical result of Depression, disappears, while pauperism is growing. ("It is estimated that each year a million people become poor," says Columbia Professor Etzioni.) Surely inflation has its dangers and, like a Depression, it is threatening the existence of the capitalist system. No wonder that every measure Nixon is taking (or pretending to take) to stop inflation brings about "normal" depressing results: reduction of capital investments, a bear market, unemployment—all the symptoms of a regular economic crisis.

Looking at the economic and social realities, there is no reason to believe that any other government could do better than Nixon's—even if the computer could give the right answer—avoiding the catastrophe that Herbert Hoover did not foresee. Hoover kept saying, "Everything is so good." What else should he have done? Suppose Hoover had known what all the economics professors (who claimed that American ingenuity had abolished the normal business cycle forever) did not know—that the 1929 crash was coming? What nonsense to have expected him to tell the people to stop buying stock and to withdraw their bank deposits! What in all honesty should Nixon do now?

The first solution of (at that time) "free enterprise" American capitalism to the Depression was the classical one: mass unemployment, low wages, pauperization. That is the normal capitalist solution, which Nixon would like and for which the new economics genius Milton Friedman invented a formula of "government interference by government noninterference" (fits Nixon so nicely). One is reminded of the wizard of the German economy, Hjalmar Schacht, who was also strictly "free-enterprise" oriented, but managed the Weimar economy as well as Hitler's. (*Le Monde,* Paris, calls the Nixon economic policy "Friedman's paradox.")

There is always a way out for a capitalist economy as long as there is no revolution. In the heights of the Depression, President Franklin D. Roosevelt lowered the value of the dollar by the rate of 40 percent (a drastic inflation) and introduced Social Security and public works, thus government interference. Still the Depression was practically holding on till American business got the big push caused by the outbreak of the Second World War. By "giving-in" to labor and farmer, Roosevelt succeeded in ameliorating the Depression and avoiding the revolutionary consequences of capitalist crises.

It is not possible to foresee the solution of today's Recession. But it seems probable that Nixon will "give-in." That will mean—as paradoxical as it sounds—more inflation and more taxation, higher interest rates and increased money liquidity, with all of which labor and big business can be neutralized. Or will he continue to follow the Friedman-paradox which claims that a big unemployment now will avoid a bigger unemployment later?

Nixon *is* in trouble. The present economy has made a shambles of the impressive computer-built "econometric" forecasts which were made for 1969. Still we have forecasts for the seventies with doubling and tripling of production (for the computer industry tenfold, I believe). The interesting thing is that, if the analysts would not predict these tremendous amounts of growth, they logically would have to prognose crisis.

The trouble Nixon faces is economic and quite normal, conditioned by the capitalist system in its imperialist stage. The situation parallels that of the British Empire, whose role has now been assumed by the United States. The British also used to invade the so-called undeveloped countries "solely" to protect lives and "to get our citizens out." To prove his theory of imperialism, Lenin quoted Cecil Rhodes, the main initiator of the Boer War who, as early as 1895, said: "If you don't want civil war, you have to become imperialists."

Like any other phenomenon of capitalist economy, which is solely motivated by divergent and competitive interests, imperialism has its contradictions. Only in the night do all cats look gray. The closing of the Suez Canal has hurt, but the owners of the big tankers, which could not use this shorter route anyway, now get the business.

Nixon, whose Republican Party traditionally has been for tariffs, now fights the protective measures which the Democratic-controlled Senate passed in the interest of the shoe and textile industries. High or low interest rates, inflation or price and wage controls, taxation or spending reduction are claimed to be principles. They are only interests, because a simple principle of economics is: What one loses another gains. Even in a bear market, every stock that is sold has a buyer.

Wall Street felt angry about Cambodia—but the real reason for the bear market is not Nixon's blundering in Cambodia. Ask any businessman, and he will always blame bad business on politics. While the government made inflation (which is always a swindle because the additional money supply does not really represent the volume of actual capital growth), the bull market was Wall Street's private inflation. Theoretically the average price of shares should be determined by the balance of activities—that is, by the earnings, like prices of any other commodities oscillating around their real value. The bull market went much further than was justified by real growth plus inflation. The shares went much higher than the earnings and potentials of the companies allowed. They even went up for stocks of companies which were bankrupt or near bankruptcy like Penn Central, Lockheed, and Chrysler. It is "normal" today that many companies are paying prevailing interest rates of 10 percent while earning only 6 to 8 percent of their investment.

In addition to the blunders within the American economy, there is a crisis in the international capital market, where the U.S. dollar plays a dominant role, with inflationary effects. McNamara, who learned at the Pentagon that disagreeable events often repeat themselves, is now as president of the World Bank busy avoiding a new attack on the gold swindle of the Federal Reserve. An American Depression will undoubtedly drag in the European and Japanese economies which already are suffering under their own inflations. An international collapse is in the making, but when it will come and what form it will take depends on so many imponderables that nothing can be predicted about it. A world economic crisis will surely make acute the situation which already bears a revolutionary character. But permanent crises do not exist. There is always an escape hatch.

All governments are interested in avoiding economic crises, even such with a "principle of noninterference" (which is itself a contradiction and no principle at all). Nixon is trying very hard to prevent the Depression which has been threatening since he came to Washington. Nixon truly represents the interests of avoiding bad business *in general,* and he would like to represent the economic interest of the silent majority, if possible. However, the intricacy of the matter is that capitalism is a competitive system and acutely so in depressive situations, when the whole pie gets smaller. And since what one gains the other loses, government interference becomes increasingly directed by the most powerful interest groups. What follows is usually that the interests of the silent majority are neglected and even antagonized. Additionally, all governments have Bonapartistic tendencies and often follow their own interests, as constantly increasing its own financial power, which might temporarily conflict with pure economics.

Obviously, in the face of the vast complexity of world political and economic affairs, it is impossible to predict when a revolution may occur.

The students are told that the time is not ripe. Ripe for what? If the actual revolution is meant, then even the great master of revolution, Lenin, did not prognosticate the revolution in 1905 until it really happened. A few weeks before the February revolution, in a speech to Swiss students, he told them it would be them, not him, who would live in the time of the coming revolution. The character of a revolution implies its timely indefiniteness. Eldridge

Cleaver's perspective of a right-wing *coup d'état* in the United States by 1972 which will trigger a mass eruption with the revolution victorious in the end sounds fine, but it reminds one too much of the 1932-33 Stalinite Comintern policy that "after Hitler come we." "It has to get worse before it can get better," is a banality. "The dawn of the morning does not appear again until the darkness of the night has completely broken" sounds like a Greek classic, but it is not a revolutionary thought. Sure, the Stalinites were "right" and it is true that they came after Hitler, but how and to what? "Perspectives" like the one by Cleaver lead only to illusions.

Anarchists have no "perspective." Mao had no "perspective." As he described it to Malraux, even if the revolution, which came as a "ripe fruit," had not come at all, the "long march" by itself had tremendous value: in the education of the masses, in developing the farms, in constantly breaking the power of the enemy.*

Nobody can know how the revolution in America will come about. Impressed by the Emancipation war and Reconstruction period, even Marx thought about the probability of a peaceful (by-election-achievable) revolution in this country. He did not live long enough to see that all tendencies which he described in the theoretical analyses of "Capital," especially the one leading to monopolism and corruption, would, beginning with the 80's find their excessive and brutal triumph here, more than anywhere in the world.

American historians always avoided raising the question of what a conviction of President Andrew Johnson by the Senate after the impeachment by the House would have led to. Only one vote more for the constitutional two thirds required for removal and Reconstruction would have been the revolution the Anarchists Thoreau, Parker, Emerson, Phillips and Garrison were longing for!

All we can know of the near future is that the riots will multiply—the riots on the campuses, in the ghettos, in the jails; people will burn their apartments to get rid of the bedbugs, set fire to the garbage on the streets because the Sanitation Department cannot cope with the waste of affluence; the cops who are already more afraid than the people they are supposed to protect will be more scared to walk alone in the streets; people will put more iron bars and locks on the doors and windows of their homes. Who knows where the riots will break out next: in the high schools, in the plants, in the armed forces? By squatting

---

* In *Man's Fate,* the greatest novel of our time illustrating the realities of the revolutionary movement, Malraux provides a masterly description of the relationship between Anarchists and Marxists in China. Significantly, it is Ch'en, the Anarchist, with whom this novel starts. Later, in his talk with Malraux, Mao emphasizes that the revolution took power while Hankow, the most industrialized city in all China, was quiet. Mao did not even properly inform the Stalinite Communists in the cities. The same is true of Castro—the Cuban Communist Party was surprised when the revolution came.

---

against speculating landlords, by jumping the subway turnstiles, by beating up dope pushers, by looting stores as the symbols of price inflation, by sit-ins as answer to unemployment and in support of wildcat strikes, by directing doctors in hospitals and teachers in schools to do what the people want them to do or get out, by wrecking draft boards and military installations, etc. etc., people will take their fate in their own hands. All such "Anarchist Cooking" represents good American tradition. "Anarchist Cooking" and self-protection are taught to American children by the Western movies.

Cui bono?

> Every Negation contains an Affirmation, Citizen Procurator.
> —Bukharin to Vishinsky at the trial of the "Block of Rightists and Trotskyites"

Who are these revolutionary students? What do they want? And whom do they serve?

It is a lot of fun to see the play about Marat with the long-winded title, which reveals to us the great wisdom that the whole world is crazy. We learn that, because the People's Friend was irritated by a skin disease, he bloodily called for heads. Thus, Kropotkin's and others' efforts to find the reasons for and explain the terrorism of the French Revolution—which symbolized more than any other in history the eternal contrast between the goal of humanity and the means of violence—were in vain, since it is so simple. That Marat wrote his *Philosophy of Man,* wherein he proclaimed an extreme materialism almost twenty years before the Revolution even began, and that he vented his hatred not only against the king but also against Liberals like Voltaire, Mirabeau, and Lafayette, and *therefore* had to go into hiding in the sewers of Paris, where he contracted the disease, seems not to be relevant. The play is the thing!

A growing body of literature tries to explain the spreading of violence and drug addiction in our present society from the psychological viewpoint. And it is a fact that to hardly any other expression of human behavior can the fashionable term "Oedipus Complex," "Castration Anxiety," "Libido," "Aggression," "Rejection," etc., etc., be so impressively applied as to revolutionary movements and their protagonists. But even when this is done by serious analysts, such explanations often lead to silliness. For example, four decades ago Wilhelm Reich, who with Otto Fenichel was among the first politically oriented Freudians,* came out with the most simple explanation for fascism, namely, "lack of a healthy orgasm."

---

* Freud considered himself apolitical. He was very conservative until his later years, when his friendship with Romain Rolland began. In his letters, Freud clearly expressed sympathy toward the Kaiser and for Hindenburg's war successes (in which he believed up to the very end).

On a similar level, psychologists today are taking part in commissions set up by Nixon and Lindsay to explain the causes of addiction, violence, and crime among youth; and just as simple are the corrective gadgets these commissions propose.

We know that Anarchism is antiauthoritarian (a statement which is hardly more than a tautology). Hence it seems that Anarchists are like adolescents. They are—we are told—rebelling against the authority of government as young people do against the authority of the father. The comparison of the family with the state, though it has a certain historical juncture, cannot be taken seriously. But, for reasons of clarifying what Anarchism really is, let's deal with the analytic vulgarism which says that all these young people want is to do what their fathers are doing. Those bums do not want to go to school; and therefore they attack the educational system. They want to sleep with their mothers; therefore they kill their fathers. They want to be seductive and to addict themselves; their fathers talk big, get drunk, and become violent. If Father Nixon is allowed to play with B-52s in the Far and Near East, they see nothing wrong with planting a bomb in a department store. They also seem to subscribe to juridical logic: If surface atomic tests are outlawed, let's go underground. . . .

Such simplified psychoanalytic nonsense, which reduces the predestined disharmony of the state to seemingly the same for the family tends *ad absurdum*. The conservative, the liberal, and the status-quo solutions to the problem are: Agnew is for more spanking, Hickel for more love, and Nixon (by custom required to be the responsible father), for both.

The undoubtedly skillful handling of wayward and aggressive youngsters by August Aichhorn cannot be applied to today's student revolts. By disregarding the decisive political and ideological character of youth movements all over the world, valuable psychoanalytic observations on delinquency become psychological crap.

This is not to say that a serious psychological approach does not have its merits. After all, those rebellious boys and girls are human. They are very human indeed. In a highly interesting, recently published book *(In the Service of Their Country: War Resisters in Prison)* Dr. Willard Gaylin, a practicing analyst and professor of psychology at Columbia Presbyterian Medical Center and at Union Theological Seminary, supplies analytical case studies of nonviolent draft resisters. He shows how it is the treatment by the government as well as the experiences with the penal system which change their emotions and thoughts into real revolutionary ones. Especially interesting is what Dr. Gaylin has to say about the reaction of his analyst colleagues, to whom he tried to transmit the results of his knowledge, efforts, and time: "They [the students] are masochists"; "they have deep-rooted guilt"; "they are psychotic. . . ."

There is undoubtedly a gap between the generations, expressed by different behavior from that which goes on in daily life. For example, a report by the Internal Revenue Service says that more than one out of every three American doctors appears now to be cheating on his income tax. While the affluent doctor is thus in constant fear of the government authorities, his sons and daughters are also affected, but in a peculiar way. The parent taught them not to cheat, and that this government is a sublime one. The father actually has good reasons for approving the government, one reason being that it gives him all the political freedom he wants, as well as the best freedom a liberal bureaucratic system can offer, namely the possibility of cheating. His children are less "objective" toward the state that threatens their father. They also have other and better reasons to become antagonistic to the father than that he sleeps with the mother: They are experiencing the hypocrisy and immorality of that father. They often see him in his so highly ethical profession put money interests above the interests of his patients "because," they hear him say, "I want to give my children a good education." (The morale of the son is not enhanced by his feeling imprisoned in college because of a 2-S draft classification.) Numerous examples like this can be cited, especially from the daily life in affluent circles of our society where many of the students in revolt come from. The "gap" is there and incomparable to the usual one between fathers and sons.

But what is socially redeeming about this conflict between father and son is that in general the strong human quality of mutual respect between father and son proves strongest and the idealism of the young is forced upon the old generation.

The point is this: the psychological makeup of individuals is not the determinant of real social movement. Even the most deep rooted customs and forms of relationships are steamrollered by participation of individuals in mass movements, which cannot wait on neuroses and complexes and which contrary to being based on the common psychological makeup of many in fact transcends such as a basis for unity or disunity, as a basis for action. It would seem that if anyone is hung up on unresolved problems of adolescence it is these same people who can only understand others in these terms. These are the alienated ones.

Why is it especially the student rather than youth in general? It is because the intellectually (and often also pecuniarily) privileged student, as any talented individual, develops an urge to communicate his knowledge and other gifts to the less privileged, to the poor, to the Blacks. This is a living process of learning in itself, far superior to any that formal education can offer. This urge will lead the fine mind to recognition of and involvement with others, an involvement which, if successful, will go beyond the narrow intellectual frame and become the real life. It was so with the students of the 1840's when, to meet the demands of industrial development, mass education started. It was so before 1905 in Russia. And it is so with much greater quantitative and qualitative force now all over the world (very much also in the developing countries). Innumerable stories are told that during the strict Black Laws in the South, daughters and wives of slave holders had that motivation which knowledge usually awakens, and taught Negroes to read and write. Again those girls and women were often led, at great risk to themselves, to more manifest breaches of law and order when they supported the Underground Railroad.

It is often such involvement which shakes illusions about the established order—about the state, about religion, about conventional habits, among them especially sex and race prejudices. Contesting illusions leads to radicalism. To become radical—to question the existing system at its roots—requires a certain degree of consciousness. It is the same process of consciousness which Lenin's theory of class consciousness expected of the revolutionary worker: He reasoned that, through involvement in demands for pennies and other Sisyphean improvements which the masses raise naturally, the worker becomes conscious of the contradiction that the real producer is not the owner of his product, that the illusory and inhuman commodity relationships among men are conditioned by the political power of the state, and that therefore taking control of social production will mean Socialism.

No wonder that, as the degree of consciousness which leads to radicalization increases, students become more and more the real enemies of Liberalism, and vice versa. Liberalism is based on principles. Radicalism is based on consciousness and has no principles. Political Liberalism is based on the principle of majority rule—a wonderful principle, no doubt, but illusionary, since the majority can only be achieved by power. (In democracies, it is also the power of illusion and of organization which creates majorities.) Baffled by the fact that Hitler, together with reactionary splinter groups, actually had the majority before Hitler took over the government, German Liberalism either had to stick to its principle and accept Hitler (which in the beginning it did) or to give up its principle, fight him *illegally,* and even to propagandize war against him (which at the end it also did). (That Hitler started that war is in this context irrelevant.)

Radicalism cannot respect Voltaire's principle to fight with all his power for the right of his adversary to express his opinion—it is a falsehood, and was used by Voltaire for opportunistic reasons.

To demonstrate the practical consequences of Liberalism for the actual example of fighting the war in Vietnam, let us for a moment consider the conflict between the two branches of Republican government: The Liberals contest the right of the president to make war without the consent of the Senate. But to defend that constitutional principle (which is circumvented anyway by the argument that this is not a "war" but only an "action" to save the lives of our soldiers) in the face of an existing law passed by Congress that the president has the autonomous right, without asking anybody and when only *he* feels it necessary, to press the button to atomic holocaust, is a blatant absurdity.

There is for the Liberal senators the legitimate parliamentary method of filibustering to prevent the continuation of the Vietnam War. This could be effected by far fewer than the some forty Senators who claim to be for immediate withdrawal. But the principle of Liberalism is against filibustering, although it is perfectly legal.

When the government finally allowed the impressive anti-war demonstrations and even "gave-in" to some disturbances, although the government had the legal right to suppress them violently, Liberalism was stuck with the dilemma: "What do we do next?" Another peaceful demonstration, which would play on the nerves of the government as well as the nerves of the demonstrators? One of the answers was given by the nervous guards in Kent, Ohio. Such an answer, given by the government when it feels it cannot "give-in," creates a revolutionary situation and thus the challenge for which radicalism consciously and admittedly is waiting (as happened in one of the best examples in history, 1905 in Russia). Exactly the same kind of answer is given by radicalism—one might call it Marxism, Anarchism, or whatever. Radicalism by its very definition is always provoking the establishment with the clear intent of creating a revolutionary situation (as happened in 1917 in Russia).

At the beginning of this process, which in the end looks like the natural catastrophe of an avalanche (though in fact it never comes by "itself"), there is always the tendency of a seemingly similar interest between the establishment and its radical adversary. This "mutuality" of interest finds its most practical expression at the beginning of the process, and very often also occurs when the revolutionary process decays. A "mutual" interest among the voluntaristic arms of government *and* of radicalism, namely the police and the Anarchists.

Anarchist cooking contributes to the disrupting and weakening of the establishment. It is a response to the realities of the existing social forces and their legal institutions. It is also a response to the realities brought about by the alienation, with its accompanying illusions, phantasies, confusions, and its isolation from the real world. It responds to these as self-defense, but in its practical effect it could seem to be an invention of the police. The "cooking" is mostly done by confused (in fact, unpolitical) desperadoes with good ideas and intentions, and from good families, and by criminal neurotics who want to take from the rich and give to the poor. But soon the police—also interested in disruption, which is after all their *raison d'être*—make use of Anarchist cooking. One method is to use the very same people who get caught whom the police get in the squeeze, as they still believe that they can dupe the police and achieve their aim—disruption of society. Classic is the case of the famous spy Azov who, with Savincoff, was leader of the terrorist wing of the Russian Social Revolutionaries. For a long time Azov successfully arranged most of the terrorist acts against the Czarist government with the direct help of the *Okhrana* (the Czarist FBI). Historians are still in dispute as to whether these secret police manipulations damaged or helped the revolutionary cause in Russia.

This system of *agent provocateurism* is nowhere so much in practice as in the United States, supported by the unique legal institution which lets a "state's witness" (though an active participant and even the initiator of the crime) go free. The American Communist Party was always infiltrated by the FBI, in some localities to such an extent that without this infiltration the CP would hardly have had any members. It is well known that presently the FBI and state and local policemen appear as Hippies with long hair, smoke pot, etc. In many countries a spy is considered even among conservative people the lowest wretch of society. In Pilsudski-Poland, it once happened that the man who killed an infiltrator into the illegal Communist Party was acquitted by a judge, who asked: "What else could they have done to such scum?"

There is hardly a police department of any American city today which does not hire and train agents who are supposed to live and behave as hippies among hippies. They grow beards and long hair, and, since they have one of the best available sources of dope and any kind of weapons, they easily become influential within Anarchist circles.

The natural emotional reaction to discovering a spy or *agent provocateur* is to kill him—more so when he was a trusted friend—as a punishment and revenge. But there is not only the emotional side to it, which has an individualistic character, the punishment becomes a political and organizational question. Killing a spy seems to be the only way to save the organization, but it also puts the organization in jeopardy.

In many cases where assassination and bombing had considerable political after-effects, history could never ascertain whether these terrorist acts were committed by desperate radicals or by government agents. Characteristically even the best and most thorough investigations could not solve this riddle. And in most of these cases of "Anarchist cooking," the established government was the gainer. We still do not know if Goering or the demented Dutch Anarchist Van der Lubbe set fire to the Reichstag, which triggered the Nazi terror. We still do not know if it was Mussolini who hired the Croatian terrorist to assassinate Alexander of Yugoslavia and Barthou, who as a man of letters was pleading for Liberalism in the Balkans. We

still do not know if Stalin organized the killing of Kirov, following which the novelty occurred that Bolsheviks were not only fired from their positions but executed *en masse*. Khrushchev in his four-hour-long speech about Stalin's crimes was silent about the killing of Kirov, who was considered the most conciliatory among the Stalinists. And last but not least, we still do not know who killed President Kennedy, of whom it was said that he had just planned to recognize Castro's Cuba. (That does not conflict with the fact that President Kennedy discussed with the Senator from Florida a plan to have Castro assassinated.)

Who was really behind the killing of Malcolm X, who had just achieved for himself a radical orientation similar to the Panthers? Who financed the killing of Martin Luther King, Jr., who, as is now known, intended to ignore the FBI threat to release telephone buggings which would allegedly show his "immorality," if he were to give up his policy of nonviolence?

It was this dilemma inherent in individual terrorism—and *never* theoretical or political differences—which motivated Marx to dissociate himself from the French Blanquists (he always adored the courageous Blanqui) and to break abruptly with the "World Society of Revolutionary Communists." It was also only the Nihilist machinations of Netshayev that made him break with Bakunin and led to the de facto liquidation of the First International.

Since the attitude of Marxism toward "Anarchist cooking" plays such an important role in the heads of radicals, I believe it necessary to add here a corrective picture of Marx and Engels as it was distorted by German Marxists. Marx and Engels always, from the beginning to the end of their political life, had great admiration for the Russian revolutionary activists. This was in clear contrast to their —often even personal—aversion toward their German followers, whose parliamentarian cretinism and revolutionary sounding programs they detested. They approved unequivocally that the tactic of a "party of action at the moment in Russia should be to bring about such strong disturbances which could intimidate the ruler." A report to Maria Oshanina, the leader of the conspiratorial "People's Will," about conversations with Marx and Engels (the authenticity of this report is confirmed by Engels' approval of its publication in 1893) leaves no doubt that Marx agreed to the assassination of Alexander II in 1881, which occurred on the same day the Czar signed a liberal constitution. Since Alexander II was a "liberal" Czar, who emancipated the serfs and introduced local self-government, the terror act undoubtedly served the reaction. Still Marx and Engels encouraged the Russian conspirators "to disturb as much as possible," "to bring about un-order," "to knock down the fatalistic power of inertia," and "to shake society out of its indolence and immobility." "Worldly wisdom" and "grand" were the words Marx used about the letter of the terrorists written to the new Czar announcing they would not kill him if he amnestied all political prisoners.

Lenin's older brother who as we know was already influenced by Marxist literature hesitated to take part in the terrorist attempt against Alexander III, but finally he involved himself in it as the leading spirit and was executed.*

It is silly to think that any revolutionary supposes "Anarchist cooking" could get rid of the government. One of the oldest devices of the state is: "The King is dead—long live the King!" Even ten blowups similar to the one at the University of Wisconsin could not destroy the military research for the Pentagon. It can only express the degree of radicalization. This process of radicalization is not the same as Socialist propaganda. It is not a step to organization. "Anarchist cooking" *is* destruction. It does not "build." It is not enlightenment through programs, opinions, and debates. It is real practical movement. Whoever is involved in it has radically broken with the rotten society of oppression, racism, war, and pollution. He is "out of it" as much as can be. "Anarchist cooks" do not build organizations. The campus, the neighborhood, and the street are their field. Any organization they could build by and for themselves would isolate them, as the tendency to isolation and sectarianism is always implied in radicalism. And, as we can see from the experiences at the campuses in the last years, their radicalism continues even when they get older—in contrast to the previous generation which kept switching in fellow traveling from Stalin to Roosevelt, from Castro to Kennedy, and back.

What will "Anarchist cooking" achieve? If bluntly put or in the sense of the bombasting goals Socialist educators used to close their lectures with, the answer is: *Nothing.* Today's rebellious youth are not bothered by the old question: Does the end justify the means? In fact, the end is already included in the means they use. These students do not break away and isolate themselves from society and from the family. On the contrary, they are very active—too active from the viewpoint of the establishment and their fathers. What they instantly achieve by their actions is liberation, the opposite of alienation. In using and tasting the "recipes," the joy is already there. It is a similar experience to the one of the old-time class-conscious worker who liberated himself from the dullness and alienation of the factory treadmill by joining his organization, by being active, and even risking his life for it. This was already Socialism for him, as much as it is possible within this world around him; here he achieved real human freedom. His motivation was not to provide for his children "a

* Lenin in the later years, describing his sharp fight against the Russian Anarchists before 1917, says: "Naturally, only for opportunistic reasons (not for principled reasons) did we not approve of individual terror."

better world," as the devout sisters of Socialist or Communist churches believe.

"Anarchist cooking" can be as liberating to the student as participation in the Palestinian Liberation movement is to the Arab women who through it can for the first time rise up from the backwardness which has for centuries covered their faces and kept them home after 6 p.m.

The Anarchist achieves "better living through chemistry." His is not a protest movement, as liberals would like it to be. Anarchists are not much interested in strengthening the legal opposition against war and poverty or perhaps transitions to an economy of peace, to "normal capitalism," to a better education. Their aim is, indeed, disruption, confusion, undermining, and destruction—the most realistic and adequate aim in a world of organized chaos. "Positive" critique and opposition would make them a part of this world. Anarchists are not politicians, they are realists. Only they really can identify the means they are using with the goal they want to achieve. Since they do not know where to go, every way is the right one. The construction of the future is not their thing. (It is different with such movements as the Panthers, but even their strength evidently lies not in improving the lot of the poor Blacks, in "peace," in "equal rights," in "equal opportunities," in "desegregation" or "Black capitalism," but lies in "Anarchist cooking," which develops their personal dignity, holding their heads high as an answer to the drudgery into which not only birth but "benign neglect" forces them.)

When, after the Second World War, the mainstream of revolution had shifted from highly industrialized countries to underdeveloped ones like the Congo, Guatemala, Algeria, there seemed for a very long time to be no "Marxian" (i.e., economic and social) basis for class struggle and Socialist revolution. In this vacuum, Herbert Marcuse in the best German philosophical tradition was the first who conceived a new Hegelian theory of the "Dialectic of Liberation," a theory of "the Great Refusal" against the intellectual and sexual repression of modern industrial society. Marcuse, in combining Marx with Freud, became for a while the apostle of a new Anarchism (even Nihilism).

The newest development of this "Great Refusal" after the events of May and June, 1968, in France expressed the trend to a new recognition of class struggle and therefore the recognition of the role of the proletariat which, as the strongest link in the chain of exploitation, is where the break must come. Freed from his esoteric language, this meant—never mind sex, pot, and bombs—the *return* to Hegel and Marx. But is it?

In an earlier day, the old Marxists and Leninists became impressed by the growing propaganda power of mass movement, and interpreted, constructed, and applied "realistically" or "dialectically" the universal perception of human freedom, which is *Negation of Negation*. As they did so, they were immediately confronted with a demand to state the *"Concrete alternative."* Today Herbert Marcuse, whose theories have gained new attention as a result of the impressive events of 1968 in France and the nearly universal antiwar and antipollution movements in the United States, feels confronted with the same demand. The term *concrete alternative* came up at the Warsaw University, and was frequently used by legitimate Marxist professors after strict adherence to the party line was no longer demanded. Politically, *concrete alternative* means for them nothing more than the return to the France-oriented *Little Entente*. This time the *Entente* would consist of Dubcek, Tito, and Ceausescu, as an alternative to Russia and America.*

Marcuse is a serious thinker and knows that all Utopians were authoritarian prophets who wanted to force their system on the people. Marcuse is moreover a man of integrity, not a politician, and agrees that "the demand is meaningless if it asks for a blueprint of the specific institutions and relationships which would be those of the new society: they cannot be determined a priori." "However," Marcuse says now, "the question cannot be brushed aside by saying that what matters today is the destruction of the old, of the powers that be, making way for the emergence of the new. Such an answer neglects the essential fact that the old is not simply bad, that it delivers the goods, and that the people have a real stake in it. There can be societies which are worse—there are such societies today. The system of corporate capitalism has the right to insist that those who work for its replacement justify their action."

Is this the newest Hegelian interpretation of "Negation of Negation"? Our answer is that the old is not only simply bad, but hopelessly rotten. This old is not like "the good old days," which old people always find better or at least "not simply bad." Today's world has reached that stage where its gradual development can only be, as Rosa Luxemburg called it, Civilized Barbarism. To get such a barbaric society, an eruptive event, as transformations from one society to another in history used to require,

would not be necessary any more. It is true that the world is pregnant with all the material and technical conditions of a better world. But these conditions, prerequisites of Socialism, are already beginning to die; they are rotting and decaying. Mass transportation, one of the first requirements of advanced (and not so advanced) industrial society, often supported by the state, is now in this country systematically, and with the help of the government, destroyed in the interest of real estate speculation and automotive and oil capital. The progress achieved by the reduction of the working day to eight and even to six hours is annulled by a travel time to work of two to four hours in conditions which are more miserable than the factory and office work itself. The "good old days" were undoubtedly better. This part of Marx's description of capitalism is no longer valid, since the "dialectic of its progress" is disappearing.

The threat to society becomes even greater because everybody sees the madness, but lives and even becomes affluent with it. To use Marcuse's words, "People have a real stake in it." Lewis Mumford mentions the fact that only those who are over fifty can remember many features of that older world that now seems ideal, including travel without a passport.* I would like to add that only those of us who are over sixty can remember that Anarchists and revolutionary Marxists from all over the world exiled without trouble to Switzerland, held openly their conferences there, and printed clandestine literature destined for their home countries. Today, under a supposedly more liberal government, the Swiss police often do not hesitate to practice their no-knock right, molesting harmless refugees at dawn even though passport and registration are in order, only under suspicion that they might be politically active.

In general, the majestic equality before the law which Anatole France once satirized has become in practically all countries so "democratic" that the poor do not suffer less, but the privileged also experience bureaucratic and police chicanery.

When Marcuse says, "there can be societies which are much worse—there are such societies today," he is even more indefinite than his peculiar esoteric language should allow. What can be "much worse"? And why not name "such societies"? Does Marcuse mean that it is Russia which is "much worse"? We do not agree. Such an opinion is just as wrong as the Stalinist theory that Social Democrats are "social fascists" and *worse* than Nazis.

With the reasoning that "the Czar is worse than the Kaiser," *all* Socialist members of the German Reichstag (with the only exception of one extreme radical) voted for

---

* Dubcek, this new hero of world liberalism, is the symbol of avoiding a "blacklash." He, in fact, betrayed the Czech people. He seems to have been scared by the famous Czech "backlash of 1618," when the Emperor's delegation in Prague was thrown out of the window, thus starting the Thirty Years' War in Europe. For the next 350 years the Czech nation played the typical liberal role best expressed in literature by the good soldier Schweik. The "backlash" against Dubcek came just the same, although he avoided the *levee en masse* for which all conditions existed in 1968. He did not resist, because he fancied the idea of good old liberalism to which today the bureaucracy of the Communist parties and trade unions all over the world subscribes. His goal was that program which Jaroslav Hasek, the author of Schweik, once jokingly for his Socialist friends invented—the program's goal was "to achieve progress in the framework of the existing."

* Such restrictions hurt only the law abider, since the criminal or Anarchist can easily produce false identification papers. Similarly, gun control laws have the effect that only criminals can own certain kinds of effective weapons.

the first war credits in August, 1914. And with the reasoning that Hitler is much worse than Stalin, radicals all over the world (with very few exceptions) supported the Second World War. Such was always the trap of the "Alternative."

The *Great Refusal,* yes. But *Concrete Alternative,* no. Because where "the alternative" comes from, it means the "Third World" of Mrs. Gandhi, Tito, and Nasser (and also of Moshe Dayan). It is the acceptance, not the refusal, of the harmony of "co-existence" by Khrushchev and Kennedy. This is what we have, adapted by Nixon and Kosygin. It is the pitiful world of Trade Union bureaucratism.

*   *

*

Anarchism, Marxism, Leninism, Maoism—whatever one wants to call it—they all are the real and concrete Refusal, as formulated by Marx in the moment he broke with abstract Hegelianism and made his great jump to the real, radical, and concrete Negation which justifies without "ifs and buts" *all* revolutionary action:

The construction of the future and the completeness for all times is not our task. What we at present have to do is the *reckless* critique of all the existing—reckless in the sense that the critique is not afraid of its results and likewise not afraid of conflicts with the existing powers. Thus we do not approach the world doctrinairily with a new principle: "Here is the truth, here kneel down!" We do not tell the world: "Let go of your fights, they are silly stuff. We wish to cry out to you the true password of the struggle." We only show the world why it really struggles, and that consciousness is a thing which it *must* acquire, even if it does not want to. Then it will become obvious that mankind for a long time had the dream of a cause of which it only needs to possess the consciousness, to really possess this human cause.

Foreword

This book is for the people of the United States of America. It is not written for the members of fringe political groups, such as The Weathermen, or The Minutemen. Those radical groups don't need this book. They already know everything that's in here. If the real people of America, the silent majority, are going to survive, they must educate themselves. That is the purpose of this book.

In this day and age, ignorance is not only inexcusable, it is criminal and perhaps fatal. *The Anarchist Cookbook* is not a revolutionary work in itself, just as a gun cannot shoot, but I have a sincere hope that it may stir some stagnant brain cells into action. If the people of the United States do not protect themselves against the fascists, capitalists, and communists, they will not be around much longer. Do I sound like an alarmist? Follow the process of disintegration: from the most immediate capitalist pollution; through the rising inflation, which is creating an atmosphere ripe for communism; to the final repression of the people by the fascists in power.

Maybe I use the term revolution too frequently in this book, without really defining it. I will do so here. I do not particularly like any form of government but, if the majority of the people seem to think that they are incapable of governing themselves and want a government, then I think the principles the United States was born with are about the best there are. So now revolution comes to mean re-vitalization, bringing America back to where she was two hundred years ago. This is the first time I've thought of myself as a reactionary.

I believe that the people in power—not only political power, but also economic and social power—will not non-violently give up that power to the people. Power is not a material possession that can be given, it is the ability to act. Power must be taken, it is never given.

I hope that, by the time the two hundredth anniversary of The First American Revolution rolls around, we will be able to look back at the sixties and early seventies as a dark era in the great history of a free nation.

Introduction

The human race, throughout its long history, has always tried to uncover the meaning or essence of certain ideas or concepts according to their particular frames of reference. This is also true of the twentieth century, but man is traveling so fast and his frame of reference is becoming so large that it is almost impossible to keep up with it. Throughout history, persons have attempted to redefine and put dated definitions to currently prevalent questions: This also has become increasingly difficult in this age of massive technological discoveries coupled with a perpetual information and propaganda bombardment by the media. So I feel that an attempt on my part to redefine anarchy in terms of the twentieth century would be a pointless task. Such a pastime is best left to the politicians and the academicians.

This is not the age of slender men in black capes lurking in alleyways with round bombs, just as it is not the age of political discussions in a Munich beer hall. This is a truly unique age, where the individual has become the supreme agent of anarchist theory, without his even being aware of it. Anarchy can no longer be defined as freedom from oppression or lack of governmental control. It has gone further than that. It has become, especially in the young people today, a state of mind, an essence of being. It can be expressed as "doing their own thing," or maybe just simply having the choice to do or not to do.

Anarchy or anarchistic theory is the only ideology that is in the least bit optimistic. It places the full weight of responsibility where it should be—on the shoulders of all the people, not just the select few. Its basic premise relies on an unshakable faith in human nature, and the primary goodness of the human race.

Today, young people are not blind idealists. They are perhaps the most rational and practical generation this country has ever seen. There is no great movement comparable to the Russian or French revolutions. There are just a great many individuals working as entities unto themselves, to create a new world order. Today has brought forth a great revival of anarchy in all fields: politics, arts, music, education, and even to a small degree in business. Although this surge of individualism is present, you won't find too many people willing to call it anarchy. But that's just terminology.

An anarchist is not necessarily a revolutionary, although it is more common than not that a person who has attempted to rid himself of exterior controls, for the purpose of developing his own philosophy, will find himself oppressed. This oppression may lead the individual to formulate ideas of insurrection and revolution.

This book is for anarchists—those who feel able to discipline themselves—on all the subjects (from drugs, to weapons, to explosives) that are currently illegal and suppressed in this country. It is my firm belief that the only laws an individual can truly respect and obey are those he instills in himself. This is not a revolutionary book in any traditional sense, but its premise is the sanctity of human dignity. If this human individual dignity and pride cannot be attained in the existing social order, there is only one choice for a real man, and that is revolution.

There will never be a traditional revolution in this country, in the sense of the Russian or French revolutions. The revolution in this country has already started. It is a multi-faceted battle on many different fronts. It is a battle politically between the young freedom fighters in Chicago and the stagnant system, represented by arthritic old men making laws they do not understand, and making wars they have no feeling for. It is a battle between the poor blacks and the rich employers. It is a battle between the artists and the censors. It is a battle between the Black Panthers and the police. It is a battle between the welfare mother and the bureaucracy of the city, and surprisingly enough it encompasses the yearly battle between the taxpayer and the Internal Revenue Service. All these battles are but part of a larger war, being fought to liberate the minds and bodies of the people who feel freedom is the most important concept in their lives.

If I could come out in this book and advocate complete revolution and the violent overthrow of the United States of America, without being thrown in jail, I would not have written *The Anarchist Cookbook,* and there would be no need for it.

Read this book, but keep in mind that the topics written about here are illegal and constitutes a threat. Also, more importantly, almost all the recipes are dangerous, especially to the individual who plays around with them without knowing what he is doing. *Use care, caution, and common sense.* This book is not for children or morons.

chapter one: Drugs

Freedom will cure most things. . . .

A. S. Neill, *Summerhill*

Drugs are not central to anarchy, have nothing to do with politics, and may be considered the opposite of revolution, since their use tends to create apathy. I believe basically that this country is going through two revolutions: On one hand there is the political struggle, and on the other we are witnessing a cultural renaissance. The use of drugs comes under the birth of a new culture. After all the political battles have been fought and won, then will come the most difficult time of all. This is the time when the entire population—black and white, right and left—must move together to form a new society. This new society is being written about, talked about, planned by everyone. It will have to be a type of society completely devoid of the repression that is so present today. It will have to be based on respect, since the churches have a monopoly on trust.

The use of drugs in this new culture will be free. There will be no more political arrests for pot or acid, for who will arrest whom? There will be no more black kids in jail, on trumped-up charges, for there will be no more jails.

"Pot is central to the revolution. It weakens social conditioning and helps create a whole new state of mind. The slogans of the revolution are going to be POT, FREEDOM, LICENSE. The BOLSHEVIKS of the REVOLUTION will be long-haired pot smokers." A quote from Jerry Rubin, who was sentenced early in 1970 to over five years for effectively speaking his mind.

Certain drugs affect the mind and allow the individual, for the first time, to see the world freely, without enforced values and rituals. For the first time the person can see clearly the real inequities and the farcical absurdities. The antiquated drug laws and the archaic lawmakers have given us an underground. Now it is our job to make good use of it.

Pot

Pot, grass, or marihuana is available anywhere in the country, as the black market is widespread and thriving very well. Marihuana goes under a whole slew of names, such as Acapulco gold, Panama red, Vietnam green, and New York white. All of these names depict the potency and place of natural origin. Mexican and Vietnamese marihuana are probably the best on the American market. Middle Eastern grass is also highly prized, but not so readily available. There is no way of knowing what you are buying, without first trying it, as most grasses look alike and smell very similar regardless of potency. The most interesting of all the different types of grasses is New York white, as it is a natural growth of high potency in a large metropolitan city. It is often found in vacant lots, growing by the side of alleys, and in schoolyards; but, strangely enough, the place where it has cropped up in abundance is in the sewers. The Department of Health and Sanitation have attempted to explain this phenomenon in several published reports. They have stated that the practice by illegal users of dumping marihuana seeds down the toilet, to prevent arrests, has resulted in massive subterranean growths. These growths were held directly responsible for many floods and blocked sewers. Apparently, according to the report, the conditions in the sewers are ideal for the growth of marihuana. It is damp and warm, and there is enough debris lying around to make good fertilizer. The sewer plants usually reach a height of between 12 and 15 feet and are bleached white because of the lack of sunlight. This could answer a lot of questions—such as what the rats were doing in the middle of the Park Avenue mall.

There are many different methods of growing grass, and it seems that everyone has just discovered the best fertilizer. I could not relay all of the methods in five books, so I have settled for two techniques which have proven extremely successful for me.

First Method

Most seeds are fertile, but the best are from Mexico. Never in any circumstances throw seeds away, since marihuana is a weed and will grow almost anywhere. The first step is to soak your seeds overnight in clean, lukewarm water. Your container should be a standard planter box. If this is not available, a plastic dish tray about two inches deep will serve just as well. Fill the container with washed fine sand and shredded sphagnum moss. If this is not readily available, you can use regular soil. The soil should be packed firmly, and watered well so that the excess water is allowed to run off. Dig furrows the full length of the container about one-half-inch deep. Now you are ready to sow your seeds. Do so every inch. Fill in each furrow with soil, sand, moss, and water. Cover the container with a clear plastic sheet, and place it in a warm location where there are at least six hours of sunlight a day. The plants now remain on their own until they develop their first true leaves.

Even if the material mentioned above is not available, almost the same degree of success can be accomplished by placing the seeds on several layers of water-soaked paper towels. Now cover the seeds with a plastic sheet just as above, and expose to sunlight.

In about one week, signs of life should start to appear. Within two weeks, definite little leaves should be present. This is the time to transplant. The plot you intend to use for your transplant should be carefully prepared. Manure should be used for at least one week in advance of the actual transplant. The soil should be similar to the original soil used in the germinating box. All other weeds, in the general area of your plot, should be pulled up to allow your plant as much freedom of growth as possible.

The original germinating box should be watered the day before you are going to transplant, so as to make the move easier on the plants, and cut root damage to a minimum. The plants should be placed in holes two to three inches deep, depending on the size of the plant. The earth around the plant should be loose, and, if possible, some earthworms should be added. If there is a lack of sunlight, a simple ring of tin foil around the plant can be very helpful. The first few days are the most critical after the actual transplant. If the plants survive the shock, there should be no reason why they shouldn't grow into healthy, fully grown plants (which means, in certain climates, fifteen to twenty feet high).

Care:

Very little care is needed after this stage, with the exception of fertilization. For fertilizers, one can use manure, soluble nitrogen, nitrate of soda, sulfate of ammonia, or rotting garbage (which has always been popular). To produce a stronger plant, one can clip off the lower leaves; do this only when the plant reaches a height of at least three feet. The ground surrounding your plant should be kept clear of other weeds but, strangely enough, insects ignore marihuana and do no harm.

Harvesting:

As a rule, it is better to wait until the plants have gone to seed before they are cut, but, if you're greedy, you can kill the goose that laid the golden egg. The best agent for drying is the sun, but if you live in the city it could prove embarrassing and dangerous to have five- or ten-foot marihuana trees on your fire escape—in this case a sun lamp can be used. When using the sun, drying usually takes about two weeks. With a sun lamp, the pot is smokable after only three or four days. When drying is done, separate the leaves and crush them. This will be the finest smoke, unless you have a female plant. If so, save the blossoms for the most potent smoke there is. The stems and twigs can be chopped up and smoked in a pipe, or sold to a friend.

Grass is basically a weed and can be grown anywhere, including indoors with artificial light. A sun lamp works well from a distance of two to three feet. For an interesting experiment, use infra-red light on part of your crop and a sun lamp on the other part, then compare. A bathtub or cement mixer is an ideal planter for the city dweller.

Second Method

This method is slightly more complicated than the last, but has achieved really good results.

First of all, you need a germinating box. This is constructed as follows: Take one wooden milk crate and cut away the sides to six inches from its bottom (check the bottom diagram in Figure 1). Cover the opening with clear plastic, leaving one flap open. Nail a strip of wood across the top and fix to it a sixty-watt light bulb. Now you have your germinating box. You will need Kitty Litter and milorganite. Take one part manure or milorganite and mix with five parts Kitty Litter, and fill the germinating box with two or three inches of this mixture and saturate with water. Now, place seeds, 20 to 30 per square inch, on top of the soil and cover with a quarter inch of milorganite and Kitty Litter. Keep the sixty-watt light bulb on twenty-four hours a day. When the seeds have broken the surface, use the bulb only as a supplement for regular sunlight.

The plants should be grown in the germinating box for one month, and then transplanted. To transplant, select a spot with reasonably fertile soil, and of course reasonably safe from being discovered. When this is done, dig a hole about one foot deep and as wide as necessary. Leave each seedling room enough to grow; in other words, don't crowd them together.

To help stimulate growth, use peat, milorganite, manure, or any of the fertilizers mentioned in the first method, before planting. After planting, water your plants, and use about a cup of hydrated lime per square yard of your plot.

Marihuana usually takes four to eight months to mature, but it does adapt amazingly well to almost any growing season. You can usually tell the female plant, as it will be the smaller of the two. It should be treated with special care.

To cure your crop, the ideal method is to hang the plants upside down in a barn or similar structure, where the ventilation is good. Now let the crop take its time. If you are in a hurry for some reason, and do not have a barn available, you can dry your crop in the oven at a temperature below 200 degrees. A sun lamp can also be used as in the first method.

Grading marihuana goes as follows: The most potent type of all is the female blossom tips (the sticky cluster of small leaves and seeds just at the tip of the female plant). The small female inside upper leaves are also very potent. They are often found covered with resin and are considered the second grade. The third grade of marihuana is the upper female leaves, which are potent but not as much as the first two grades. The fourth and final grade is made up of the male blossoms and all the male leaves on the upper half of the stem.

If you decide against growing your own pot, for one reason or another, you still should have no difficulty in obtaining grass. When buying grass, or anything illegal, there are several important things to remember. First, and probably most important, is not to buy on the street, and in no circumstances buy from a stranger. Believe it or not, the cops are paying out millions of dollars a year to keep plainclothesmen wandering around the streets trying to bust people. There is another reason that buying on the street is a bad scene: You don't get a chance to try the stuff before you buy it. The chances will be very good that when you get home, you will find that you have bought some of the best-tasting parsley or oregano that you have ever smoked.

Cooking with pot

Many people after cleaning their grass throw away the seeds, stems, and twigs. I would highly recommend that you save these, as there are many recipes for these odds and ends. A tasty hot drink that resembles tea can be made very simple by tying up all the waste from your stash into a muslin ball or into a piece of cheesecloth. Use the quantity you have on hand, as the quantity will determine the strength and potency. Now, drop the cheesecloth containing the grass into a kettle of water, and bring the water to a boil. Allow the kettle to boil for a few minutes, and then remove it from the flame and let it steep for another five minutes with the grass still inside. After this, the drink is ready. Just add sugar and lemon to taste.

If you decide against growing pot, and want to eat your seeds, there is an interesting recipe for "seed pancakes." It is prepared by lightly toasting a quarter of a cup of seeds into a large frying pan. Now, take the seeds from the frying pan and add them to a mixture of one cup of pancake mix, one egg, a quarter cup of milk, and one tablespoon of butter. Beat this mixture until it is smooth and creamy. Heat a frying pan with a small amount of butter, then pour in pancake batter. Turn the pancakes as they start to look done, or when the edges begin to turn brown. Repeat procedure until all the batter is used. Serve pancakes with butter, maple syrup, and honey.

For a stimulating drink (sounds like all the rest of the cookbooks) place eight ounces milk, a few spoonfuls sugar, a tablespoon malted milk, half a banana, a half tablespoon grass, and three betel nuts in a blender. Keep

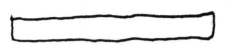

2-inch container (plastic or wood)

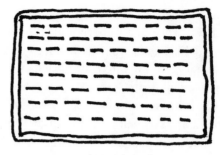

Container showing ½-inch
furrows

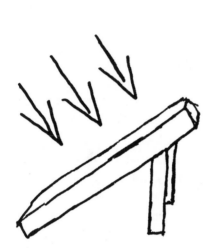

Germinating box covered with
a sheet of clear plastic, receiving
sunlight

Plants ready for transplant

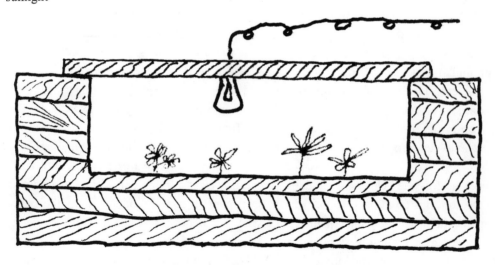

Germinating box for second method

Figure 1. Methods for growing marihuana.

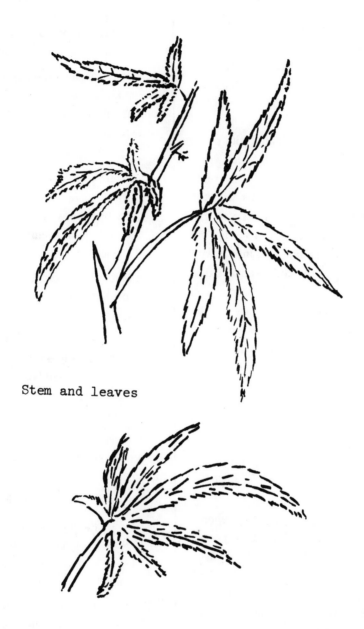

Stem and leaves

Leaves

Figure 2. A mature marihuana plant.

the blender working full speed for a few minutes, then strain and serve.

If you like candy, it's very simple to make some using pot. Take a quarter cup of powdered grass and add water until it equals a full cup. Mix this with four cups sugar and two and a half cups corn syrup. Now heat in a large pot to 310 degrees, and add red food coloring and mint flavoring. Remove the pot from the stove, and allow the mixture to cool a little, before pouring it onto wax paper. When the candy's cool, cut it into squares and eat.

One of the most common recipes for cooking with pot is spaghetti. This recipe doesn't take too much special preparation: Just when you add your oregano, add at the same time a quarter cup grass, and allow it to simmer with the sauce. Be sure to use well-cleaned grass, unless you can get into eating twigs and stems. Another way of serving pot with spaghetti is to grind it up very fine and mix it with some ground cheese. Then sprinkle the cheese-pot mixture over the sauce just before eating.

Dessert is probably the most important stage of the meal, since it will be the last thing your guests remember before they pass out all over your table. For an interesting dessert, grind a quarter ounce of grass very finely, and add enough water so it forms a paste. Now separately dissolve one and a half cups sugar into two cups milk. Add to this your pot paste and one lemon rind grated. Beat in a half cup heavy cream, until the mixture is firm and thick. Now pour the mixture into ice cube trays and freeze. Just before you're ready to serve, rebeat the frozen mush until it becomes light and fluffy.

Since everyone else has a private recipe for an aphrodisiac, why shouldn't I put one in here? I've heard people tell me, in all seriousness, that they believe the only true aphrodisiac is a case of beer in the back seat of a '56 Chevy. Well, if you're not into that, you might as well try this recipe, because it's got to work better than a case of beer. Pound one tablespoon unground mace, two cantharides beetles, one teaspoon fresh red saffron, and one teaspoon of the best quality grass you can find. Pound all the ingredients together until they form a powder. Now add one pint of water and heat to boiling point. After boiling for a few minutes, reduce the heat and simmer for 45 minutes or so, until the liquid is reduced to about a quarter of a cup. This can be served as a drink or over brown rice. I have not tried this recipe, as I have been unable to locate any cantharides.

On the following pages are some additional recipes for cooking with pot.

Acapulco Green

3 ripe avocados	3 tablespoons wine
½ cup chopped onions	vinegar
2 teaspoons chili powder	½ cup chopped grass

Mix the vinegar, grass, and chili powder together and let the mixture stand for one hour. Then add avocados and onions and mash all together. It can be served with tacos or as a dip.

Pot Soup

1 can condensed beef broth	½ can water
3 tablespoons grass	3 tablespoons chopped watercress
3 tablespoons lemon juice	

Combine all ingredients in a saucepan and bring to a boil over medium heat. Place in refrigerator for two to three hours, reheat, and serve.

Pork and Beans and Pot

1 large can (1 lb., 13 oz.) pork and beans	½ cup light molasses
½ cup grass	½ teaspoon hickory salt
4 slices bacon	3 pineapple rings

Mix together in a casserole, cover top with pineapple and bacon, bake at 350 degrees for about 45 minutes. Serves about six.

The Meat Ball

1 lb. hamburger	¼ cup bread crumbs
¼ cup chopped onions	3 tablespoons grass
1 can cream of mushroom soup	3 tablespoons India relish

Mix it all up and shape into meat balls. Brown in frying pan and drain. Place in a casserole with soup and ½ cup water, cover and cook over low heat for about thirty minutes. Feeds about four people.

Spaghetti Sauce

1 can (6 oz.) tomato paste	1 can (6 oz.) water
2 tablespoons olive oil	½ clove minced garlic
½ cup chopped onions	1 bay leaf
½ cup chopped grass	1 pinch thyme
1 pinch pepper	½ teaspoon salt

Mix in a large pot, cover and simmer with frequent stirring for two hours. Serve over spaghetti.

Pot Loaf

1 packet onion soup mix	2 lbs. ground beef
1 (16 oz.) can whole peeled tomatoes	1 egg
	4 slices bread, crumbed
½ cup chopped grass	

Mix all ingredients and shape into a loaf. Bake for one hour in 400-degree oven. Serves about six.

Chili Bean Pot

2 lbs. pinto beans	½ clove garlic
1 lb. bacon, cut into two-inch sections	1 cup chopped grass
2 cups red wine	½ cup mushrooms
4 tablespoons chili powder	

Soak beans overnight in water. In a large pot pour boiling water over beans and simmer for at least an hour, adding more water to keep beans covered. Now add all other ingredients and continue to simmer for another three hours. Salt to taste. Serves about ten.

Bird Stuffing

5 cups rye bread crumbs	⅓ cup chopped onions
2 tablespoons poultry seasoning	3 tablespoons melted butter
½ cup each of raisins and almonds	½ cup chopped grass
½ cup celery	2 tablespoons red wine

Mix it all together, then stuff it in.

Apple Pot

4 apples (cored)	4 cherries
½ cup brown sugar	⅓ cup chopped grass
¼ cup water	2 tablespoons cinnamon

Powder the grass in a blender, then mix grass with sugar and water. Stuff cores with this paste. Sprinkle apples with cinnamon, and top with a cherry. Bake for 25 minutes at 350 degrees.

Pot Brownies

½ cup flour	1 egg (beaten)
3 tablespoons shortening	1 tablespoon water
2 tablespoons honey	½ cup grass
pinch of salt	1 square melted chocolate
¼ teaspoon baking powder	1 teaspoon vanilla
½ cup sugar	½ cup chopped nuts
2 tablespoons corn syrup	

Sift flour, baking powder, and salt together. Mix shortening, sugar, honey, syrup, and egg. Then blend in chocolate and other ingredients, mix well. Spread in an eight-inch pan and bake for 20 minutes at 350 degrees.

Banana Bread

½ cup shortening	1 cup mashed bananas
2 eggs	2 cups sifted flour
1 teaspoon lemon juice	½ cup chopped grass
3 teaspoons baking powder	½ teaspoon salt
1 cup sugar	1 cup chopped nuts

Mix the shortening and sugar, beat eggs, and add to mixture. Separately mix bananas with lemon juice and add to the first mixture. Sift flour, salt, and baking powder together, then mix all ingredients together. Bake for 1¼ hours at 375 degrees.

Sesame Seed Cookies

3 oz. ground roast sesame seeds	¼ cup honey
3 tablespoons ground almonds	½ teaspoon ground ginger
¼ teaspoon nutmeg	¼ teaspoon cinnamon
	¼ oz. grass

Toast the grass until slightly brown and then crush it in a mortar. Mix crushed grass with all other ingredients, in a skillet. Place skillet over low flame and add 1 tablespoon of salt butter. Allow it to cook. When cool, roll mixture into little balls and dip them into the sesame seeds.

If you happen to be in the country at a place where pot is being grown, here's one of the greatest recipes you can try. Pick a medium-sized leaf off the marihuana plant and dip it into a cup of drawn butter, add salt, and eat.

Hashish

Hashish, or hash, is nothing more than the essence of the marihuana plant extracted and hardened into a block. Hash is usually smoked in a pipe, although there are many recipes that employ it as an ingredient.

I have heard people say that hash has a different effect

than marihuana. This is not true, in the sense that there is no difference between the two, with the exception being that hash is a good deal stronger. The most amazing thing about hashish is the price on the black market. An ounce of hash usually sells for anywhere between $60 and $100, depending on supply and demand. I say the price is amazing because, with one kilo (2.2 lbs.) of grass, a person can easily make seven or eight ounces of hash. The usual price for a kilo of grass is about $150, whereas seven ounces of hash might bring $700.

The process for extracting the essence of marihuana is a simple one, but it requires the utmost care. You need a kilo of grass to begin with, and a screen to sift it through. A kilo of grass usually comes in a block, compressed together, so break down the block and gently put it through the screen. Remove all the dirt and foreign objects, but do not take out the stems. The seeds should also be taken out, as they are much too greasy for good hash. Now that you have separated the kilo and sifted it, place it in a large pot and cover with rubbing alcohol (about one and a half gallons per kilo). Now boil the mixture for about three hours. Be sure to use a hot plate or electric stove rather than gas, as alcohol is highly inflammable, and should never be exposed to a naked flame. After three hours, strain liquids out of the pot and store in a plastic container labeled "solution 1." Now take the mush you have left and repeat the boiling with fresh alcohol for another three hours. After two alcohol extractions, each time using fresh alcohol, follow the same procedure but substitute water for alcohol. The water must be boiled at a higher temperature than the alcohol, but for only one hour. This boiling procedure with water should be performed twice. Once these procedures have been performed, strain off the liquids again and store in another container, and label "solution 2." Now reduce volumes of both solutions by boiling in separate pots, turn down the heat as each solution begins to thicken. When each solution is reasonably thickened, combine them and boil a little more on the hot plate. At this point the solution should have the consistency of modeling clay. Now heat a cupful of turpentine, and add to the mush. Be extra careful with the turpentine, as even the vapors are inflammable. Add 2 ozs. of pine resin and stir pot for ten minutes, under low heat. Now pour mush into a baking tin, two or three inches deep, and heat in the oven for 15 minutes at 350 degrees. After this you should have some really good hash but, if the hash is still greasy after this last step, just leave it in the oven for another ten minutes or so until it dries out. Be careful not to burn the hash.

This last recipe is for the extraction of hashish from marihuana, but in the Middle Eastern countries, where they can afford it, there is another method for the preparation of hash. When the hemp or marihuana plants are drying, they are hung upside down in a room lined with burlap. As the plants dry, the resin and smaller leaves fall onto the burlap. When, after a few weeks, the burlap is taken up, the material covering it is the finest-quality marihuana extraction possible. This substance is taken and boiled, then compressed together to form a hard solid.

Hash can be smoked either in a pipe or by mixing it with tobacco in a cigarette. Traditionally, hashish has been smoked in a hookah or water pipe, which is nothing more than a large pipe that takes the smoke and cools it by running it through water. The hookah is more than just a pipe in many Middle Eastern countries, since it has more than one hose, and more than one smoker can participate at a time. I have heard that substituting wine or flavored brandy for the water is a fantastic way to get there.

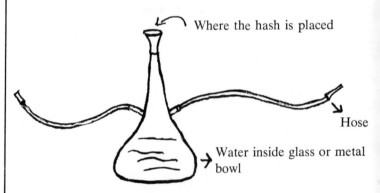

Figure 3. Hookah.

Cooking with hash

Hash is also an excellent way to enhance your cooking. It has had a long history in the kitchen, going all the way back to the early civilizations around the Ganges River. It is also noted that many famous personalities throughout history had experiences with hashish. Marco Polo on his return to Italy mentioned frequently in his diary a strange substance that put a man in a drunkenlike stupor, yet it was unlike anything he had experienced before.

Hash Cookies

4 cups sifted flour	½ teaspoon salt
1 teaspoon baking powder	½ cup butter
	¾ cup honey
4 eggs	

Mix baking powder, salt, and flour together in a bowl, then add to this the eggs and honey. Work the mixture with your hands until it forms a dough. Roll the dough out and cut into three-inch squares. Now put dough aside and work on the filling.

½ cup chopped dates	½ cup honey
½ cup raisins	1 whole grated nutmeg
1 teaspoon ground ginger	⅛ oz. powdered hash
1 teaspoon cinnamon	1 cup chopped figs
½ cup ground almonds	½ cup ground walnuts

Put all the ingredients into a pan and mix with ½ cup water. Heat until fruits are softened and water has evaporated. Pour mixture into a skillet, add three tablespoons butter, and heat for five minutes. The filling is now ready. Place a heaping tablespoon of filling on each piece of pastry. Fold up the edges of the pastry, to keep the filling in, and bake at 350 degrees for about 25 minutes. This recipe usually makes between two and three dozen cookies.

Hash Soup

3 eggs	1 teaspoon powdered hashish
2 oz. sifted flour	
¼ can cooked peas	2 oz. small noodles
½ cup chopped chicken livers	4 tablespoons canned tomato paste
½ chopped onion	½ cup chopped turnip

Take a large pot and grease the bottom with ¼ cup olive oil. Place in the pot the half chopped onions, chicken livers, and turnip. Cook for a half hour over low heat. Now add a pint and a half of water, three tablespoons butter, four tablespoons tomato paste, the peas, and the noodles. Mix flour with a cup of water and make a paste. Stir paste and powdered hash into the pot. Add salt and pepper, and boil for 15 minutes, stirring constantly. As soon as the soup is off the fire, add the eggs and serve immediately.

Hash Brown Bananas

4 bananas	2 slices bacon
2 teaspoons powdered hash	4 tablespoons brown sugar

Cut the bananas into a skillet and fry until slightly brown. Do not overcook. At the same time, fry the bacon in the same pan, for it adds an interesting flavor to the bananas. Mix the powdered hash with the brown sugar. Then wrap each fried banana with a strip of bacon, and serve with hash and brown sugar sprinkled on top.

Hashish Brownies

½ teaspoon salt	½ teaspoon baking powder
¾ cup cake flour	
1 cup sugar	3 eggs
3 oz. unsweetened chocolate	½ cup sweet butter
	5 grams powdered hash

Melt the chocolate and butter together, then add sugar and hash. The mixture must be beaten until it is creamy. Sift flour, baking powder, and salt together, and then add to mixture. Pour the mixture into a cookie tray and bake for thirty minutes at 375 degrees. When cool, cut brownies into small squares and top with chopped nuts.

LSD

I think, of all the drugs on the black market today, LSD is the most interesting and the strangest. It is the most recent major drug to come to life in the psychedelic subculture. Huxley experimented with mescaline many years before psychedelics reached their mass-market proportions, but this experimentation was not with the same frame of mind as these drugs are handled today. Probably the great-granddaddy to the whole psychedelic community was Antonin Artaud, who personally experimented with peyote in Mexico. The difference between Huxley's and Artaud's experimentation was that Huxley managed to keep his experiences under laboratory controls, which he set up himself, whereas Artaud allowed his experiences to become part of his life. Artaud was changed by his encounters with peyote, but is this bad? A dirty shirt is also changed when it is washed. Through this change, Artaud was able to see and understand ideas and concepts on a different level. He was able to tear apart rationalizations, without regard for contemporary methods of organization, or even contemporary versions of truth. Artaud found, in his own way, his own truth and his own structure of values. They locked him up. . . .

I died at Rodez under electroshock.

I died. Legally and medically died.

Electroshock coma lasts fifteen minutes. A half an hour or more and then the patient breathes.

Now one hour after the shock, I still had not awakened and had stopped breathing. Surprised at my abnormal rigidity, an attendant had gone to get the physician in charge, who, after examining me with a stethoscope, found no more signs of life in me.

This passage is taken from *The Artaud Anthology,* published by City Lights Publishers. I find it extremely difficult to throw this off as the ravings of a madman for, if that be true, then there can be no truth, only madness and sanity, logic and illogic. If one then accepts the acceptable, he finds a narrow channel is clear, but the presence of illogic and the so-called insanities will always pry and harp in the distance.

LSD has *never* caused insanity. It does not have that power. Only man can distinguish between sanity and insanity. I have never seen an insane bird. Granted there are some individuals who shouldn't take psychedelics, but this is, and must be, their choice. All LSD does is allow a man to look upon ordinary things, everyday things, and even on himself, many times for the first time, with clarity of vision. He can look and not be hampered by false-propped values and socially limited scope. He can look upon the world and see beauty where it did not exist before. He can perceive the ugliness for the first time. He can roar with laughter at the multitude of absurdities surrounding him. He can look into himself and see truthfully the mildew and the rot.

LSD cannot bring out latent qualities in your personality. It cannot make you into a crazy, just as it cannot make you into a warmer, more beautiful, person. What LSD can do is show you what you as a person are comprised of, and break down truthfully your make-up. LSD is not a religion, and I've never found anything really divine about it at all. The real religion, if you want to put it in those terms, is the being itself. LSD is nothing more than a medium to discover the essence of being.

LSD, or acid, has been illegal for the last few years; therefore it is readily available on the black market. When buying anything on the black market, there are a couple of things to note, but these are especially important with acid.

1. Never buy from a stranger, or on the street.

2. Never front money.

3. If you are holding a large amount of money, do not go anywhere alone with someone you do not trust. Many people who have got into dealing pot and acid are, in reality, junkies.

4. When going to make a deal for dope, do not take a weapon with you. This is provoking violence and legal hassles. If you don't trust the guy, then don't deal with him.

5. Never buy a large quantity of any drug without first sampling it.

6. When making a deal for acid and you are at the dealer's apartment, do not accept food or drink from him; for the real acid may be in the food rather than the cap you sample.

7. Bad acid is usually nothing more than speed, or rat poison.

8. About a year ago there was a substance called L.B.J. going around. If you happen to come across it, *do not* buy it. L.B.J. is a mixture of acid, belladonna, and heroin. It is the freakiest, worst, most fucked-up trip you will ever go on. Belladonna in quantity is a deadly poison.

9. About 99 percent of all of what is claimed to be T.H.C. (synthetic pot) that is for sale on the street is not really T.H.C. at all. The expense of making synthetic pot is said to be about $15 per capsule, and a capsule of alleged T.H.C. usually sells on the street for about $2.50. Obviously the vendors are either philanthropists (not likely) or they are selling you something other than T.H.C.

10. When buying grass, watch out for damp grass or grass sprayed with sugar, as this adds a lot of weight to the dope.

11. Another favorite con game is "in the front, out the back." This usually occurs when your dealer tells you he is going up to an apartment to get your stuff, but you have to front the money, and wait for him on the street. You may be waiting a long time.

12. Do not attempt to smuggle any drugs across the border from Mexico. The federal government has imposed a crackdown and they're busting people left and right.

Making LSD in the laboratory

To make synthetic acid, you need a basic understanding of chemistry and access to a lab. Since I don't quite understand all the chemical hocus-pocus, I'm going to cop out and quote you the patent for it. If you don't understand chemistry, just skip this recipe and go on to the next one for acid, it's much simpler.

Preparation for Lysergic Acid Amides:

United States Patent Office   2,736,728

Patented February 28, 1956

Richard P. Pioch, Indianapolis, Indiana, assignor, to Eli Lilly and Co., Indianapolis, Indiana, a corporation of Indiana.

No drawing. Application December 6, 1954, Serial No. 473,443. 10 Claims. (Cl. 260-285.5)

This invention relates to the preparation of lysergic acid amides and to a novel intermediate compound useful in the preparation of said amides.

Although only a few natural and synthetic amides of lysergic acid are known, they possess a number of different and useful pharmacologic properties. Especially useful is ergonovine, the N-(1(+)-1-hydroxyisopropyl) amide of d-lysergic acid, which is employed commercially as an oxytocic agent.

Attempts to prepare lysergic acid amides by the usual methods of preparing amides, such as reacting an amine with lysergic acid chloride or with an ester of lysergic acid, have been unsuccessful. United States Patents No. 2,090,429 and No. 2,090,430, describe processes of preparing lysergic acid amides and, although these processes are effective to accomplish the desired conversion of lysergic acid to one of its amides, they are not without certain disadvantages.

By my invention I have provided a simple and convenient method of preparing lysergic acid amides, which comprises reacting lysergic acid with trifluoroacetic anhydride to produce a mixed anhydride of lysergic and trifluoroacetic acids, and when reacting the mixed anhydride with a nitrogenous base having at least one hydrogen linked to nitrogen. The resulting amide of lysergic acid is isolated from the reaction mixture by conventional means.

The reaction of the lysergic and the trifluoroacetic anhydride is a low temperature reaction, that is, it must be carried out at a temperature below about 0 degrees C. The presently preferred temperature range is about −15 C. to about −20 C. This range is sufficiently high to permit the reaction to proceed at a desirably fast rate, but yet provides an adequate safeguard against a too rapid reaction which would result in a high reaction temperature and consequent excessive decomposition of the mixed anhydride.

The reaction is carried out in a suitable dispersing agent, that is, one which is inert with respect to the reactants. The lysergic acid is relatively insoluble in dispersants suitable for carrying out the reaction, so it is suspended in the dispersant.

Two gallons of trifluoroacetic anhydride are required per mol. of lysergic acid for the rapid and complete conversion of the lysergic acid into the mixed anhydride. It appears that one molecule of the anhydride associates with or favors an ionic adduct with one molecule of the lysergic which contains a basic nitrogen atom and that it is the adduct which reacts with a second molecule of trifluoroacetic anhydride to form the mixed anhydride along with one molecule of trifluoroacetic acid. The conversion of the lysergic acid to the mixed anhydride occurs within a relatively short time, but to insure a complete conversion the reaction is allowed to proceed for about one to three hours.

The mixed anhydride of lysergic and trifluoroacetic acids is relatively unstable, especially at room temperature and above, and must be stored at a low temperature. This temperature instability of the mixed anhydride makes it desirable that it be converted into a lysergic acid amide without unnecessary delay. The mixed anhydride itself, since it contains a lysergic acid group, also can exist in the reaction mixture in large part as an ionic adduct with trifluoroacetic anhydride or trifluoroacetic acid. It is important for maximum yield of product that the lysergic acid employed in the reaction be dry. It is most convenient to dry the acid by heating it at about 105-110 degrees C. in a vacuum of about 1mm. of mercury or less for a few hours, although any other customary means of drying can be used.

The conversion of the mixed anhydride into an amide by reacting the anhydride with the nitrogenous base, such as an amino compound, can be carried out at room temperature or below. Most conveniently the reaction is carried out by adding the cold solution of the mixed anhydride to the amino compound or a solution thereof which is at about room temperature. Because of the acidic components present in the reaction mixture of the mixed anhydride, about five mols or equivalents of the amino compound are required per mole or equivalent of mixed anhydride for maximal conversion of the mixed anhydride to the amide. Preferably a slight excess over the five mols is employed to insure complete utilization of the mixed anhydride. If desired, a basic substance capable of neutralizing the acid components present in the reaction mixture, but incapable of interfering with the reaction, can be utilized. A strongly basic tertiary amine is an example of such a substance. In such case, about one equivalent of amino compound to be converted to a lysergic acid amide, as well as any unconverted lysergic acid, can be removed from the reaction mixture and can be re-employed in other conversions.

A preferred method for carrying out the process of this invention is as follows:

Dry lysergic acid is suspended in a suitable vehicle as acetonitrile, and the suspension is cooled to about −15 C. or −20 C. To the suspension is then added slowly a solution of about two equivalents of trifluoroacetic anhydride dissolved in acetonitrile and previously cooled to about −20 degrees C. The mixture is maintained in a low temperature for about one to three hours to insure the completion of the formation of the mixed anhydride of lysergic and trifluoroacetic acids.

The solution of the mixed anhydride is then added to about five equivalents of the amino compound which is to be reacted with the mixed anhydride. The amino compound need not be previously dissolved in a solvent, although it is usually convenient to use a solvent. The reaction is carried out with the amino compound or solution of amino compound at or about room temperature or below. The reaction mixture is allowed to stand at room temperature for one or two hours, preferably in the dark, and the solvent is then removed by evaporation in vacuo at a temperature which desirably is not greatly in excess of room temperature. The viscous residue, consisting of the amide together with excess amine and amine salts, is taken up in a mixture of chloroform and water. The water is separated and the chloroform solution which contains the amide is washed several times with water to remove excess amine and the various amine salts formed in the reaction, including that of any unconverted lysergic acid. The chloroform solution is then dried and evaporated, leaving a residue of lysergic acid amide. The amide so obtained can be purified by any conventional procedure.

Dispersants suitable for the purpose of this invention are those which are liquids at the low temperatures employed for the reaction and are of such an inert nature that they will not react preferentially to the lysergic acid with trifluoroacetic anhydride. Among suitable dispersants are acetonitrile, dimethylformamide, propionitrile, and the like. Additional suitable agents will readily be apparent from the foregoing enumeration. Of those listed above, acetonitrile is preferred since it is non-reactive and mobile at the temperature used, and is relatively volatile and hence readily separable from the reaction mixture by evaporation in vacuo.

A wide variety of nitrogenous bases such as amino compounds can be reacted with the mixed anhydride to form a lysergic acid amide. As previously stated, the amino compound must contain a hydrogen atom attached to nitrogen to permit amide formation. Illustrative amino compounds which can be reacted are ammonia, hydrazine, primary amines such as glycine, ethanolamine, diglycylglycine, norephedrine, aminopropanol, butanolamine, diethylamine, ephedrine, and the like.

When an alkanolamine such as ethanolamine or aminopropanol is reacted with the mixed anhydride of lysergic and trifluoroacetic acids, the reaction product contains not only the desired hydroxy amide but also, to a minor extent, some amino ester. These two isometric substances arise because of the bi-functional nature of the reacting alkanolamine. Ordinarily the amino ester amounts to no more than 25-30 percent of the total amount of reaction product, but in cases where the amino group is esterically hindered, the proportion of amino ester will be increased. The amino ester can readily be converted to the desired hydroxy amide, and the over-all yield of the latter increased by treating the amino ester, or the mixture of amide and ester with alcoholic alkali to cause the rearrangement of the amino ester to the desired hydroxy amide. Most conveniently the conversion is carried out by dissolving the amino ester or mixture containing the amino ester in a minimum amount of alcohol and adding to the mixture a twofold amount of 4 N alcoholic potassium hydroxide solution. The mixture is allowed to stand at room temperature for several hours, the alkali is neutralized with acid, and the lysergic acid amide is then isolated and purified.

It should be understood that, as used herein, the term "lysergic acid" is used generically as inclusive of any or all of the four possible stereoisomers having the basic lysergic acid structure. Isomers of the lysergic acid series can be separated or interconverted by means known to the art.

This invention is further illustrated by the following specific examples.

Example One

Preparation of the mixed anhydride of lysergic and trifluoroacetic acids:

5.36 g. of d-lysergic acid are suspended in 125 ml. of acetonitrile and the suspension is cooled to about –20 degrees C. To this suspension is added a cold (–20 degrees C.) solution of 8.82 g. of trifluoroacetic anhydride in 75 ml. of acetonitrile. The mixture is allowed to stand at –20 degrees C. for about 1½ hours during which time the suspended material dissolves, and the d-lysergic acid is converted to the mixed anhydride of lysergic and trifluoroacetic acids. The mixed anhydride can be separated in the form of an oil by evaporating the solvent in vacuo at a temperature below about 0 degrees centigrade.

Example Two

Preparation of d-lysergic acid N,N-diethyl amide:

A solution of the mixed anhydride of lysergic acid and trifluoroacetic acid in 200 ml. of acetonitrile is obtained by reacting 5.36 g. d-lysergic acid and 8.82 g. trifluoroacetic anhydride in accordance with the procedure of example one. The acetonitrile solution containing mixed anhydride is added to 150 ml. of acetonitrile containing 7.6 g. of diethylamine. The mixture is held in the dark at room temperature for about two hours. The acetonitrile is evaporated in vacuo leaving a residue which comprises the "normal" and "iso" forms of d-lysergic acid N,N-diethyl amide together with some lysergic acid,

the diethylamine salt of trifluoroacetic acid and like by-products. The residue is dissolved in a mixture of 150 ml. of chloroform and 20 ml. of ice water. The chloroform layer is separated, and the aqueous layer is extracted with four 50 ml. portions of chloroform. The chloroform extracts are combined and are washed four times with about 50 ml. portions of cold water in order to remove residual amounts of amine salts. The chloroform layer is then dried over anhydrous sodium sulfate, and the chloroform is evaporated in vacuo. A solid residue of 3.45 gm. comprising the "normal" and "iso" forms of d-lysergic acid N,N-diethylamide is obtained This material is dissolved in 160 ml. of a 3-to-1 mixture of benzene and chloroform, and is chromatographed over 240 g. of basic alumina. As the chromatogram is developed with the same solvent, two blue fluorescing zones appear on the alumina column. The more rapidly moving zone is d-lysergic acid N,N-diethylamide which is eluted with about 3000 ml. of the same solvent as above, the course of the elution being followed by watching the downward movement of the more rapidly moving blue fluorescing zone. The eluate is treated with tartaric acid to form the acid tartrate of d-lysergic acid N,N-diethyl amide which is isolated. The acid tartrate of d-lysergic acid N,N-diethyl amide melts with decomposition at about 190-196 degrees Centigrade.

The di-iso-lysergic acid N,N-diethyl amide which remains absorbed on the alumina column as the second fluorescent zone is removed from the column by elution with chloroform. The "iso" form of the amide is recovered by evaporating the chloroform eluate to dryness in vacuo.

Example Three

Preparation of d-lysergic acid N-diethylaminoethyl amide:

A solution of the mixed anhydride of lysergic acid and trifluoroacetic acid is prepared from 2.68 g. of d-lysergic acid and 4.4 g. of trifluoroacetic acid anhydride in 100 ml. of acetonitrile by the method of Example One. This solution is added to 6:03 g. of diethylamino-ethylamine. The reaction mixture is kept in the dark at room temperature for 1½ hours. The acetonitrile is evaporated, and the residue treated with chloroform and water as described in Example Two. The residue treated comprising d-iso-lysergic acid N-diethylaminoethyl amide is dissolved in several ml. of ethyl acetate, and the solution is cooled to about 0 degrees centigrade, whereupon di-iso-lysergic acid N-diethylaminoethyl amide separates in crystalline form. The crystalline material is filtered off, and the filtrate reduced in volume to obtain an additional amount of crystalline amide. Recrystallization from ethyl acetate of the combined fractions of crystalline material yields d-iso-lysergic acid N-diethylaminoethyl amide melting at about 157-158 degrees centigrade. The optical rotation is as follows:

$$[x] \ d^{26} = + 372 \text{ degrees (c.} = 1.3 \text{ in pyridine)}$$

There has been in the last few years a great deal of discussion about the correct treatment for victims of bad LSD trips. When an individual does go into a panic on acid, it is an extremely delicate situation. Although it has been said that tranquilizers, such as thorazine, will help to calm the person down, be very careful, as certain drugs react violently with tranquilizers (STP). My advice in a situation of that sort is just to attempt to create an atmosphere of reassurance and sympathy. In no circumstances, except real uncontrollable panic, should a person on acid be taken to a city hospital. If you want a freaky experience, spend a couple of hours at any city hospital and watch the people die in the halls!

Talk to the person and remind him that he is under the influence of acid. Try to calm him down. Even a change of environment can effectively reverse a bad trip.

Making LSD in the kitchen

For those readers who couldn't make head or tail of the last recipe for acid, there is a much simpler one. It basically extracts the lysergic acid amides either from morning glory seeds or Hawaiian wood rose seeds. It can be prepared in the kitchen.

1. Grind up 150 grams of morning glory seeds or baby Hawaiian wood rose seeds.

2. In 130 cc. of petroleum ether, soak the seeds for two days.

3. Filter the solution through a tight screen.

4. Throw away the liquid, and allow the seed mush to dry.

5. For two days allow the mush to soak in 110 cc. of wood alcohol.

6. Filter the solution again, saving the liquid and labeling it "1."

7. Resoak the mush in 110 cc. of wood alcohol for two days.

8. Filter and throw away the mush.

9. Add the liquid from the second soak to the solution labeled "1."

10. Pour the liquid into a cookie tray and allow it to evaporate.

11. When all the liquid has evaporated, a yellow gum remains. This should be scraped up and put into capsules.

30 grams of morning glory seeds = one trip
15 Hawaiian wood rose seeds = one trip

Many companies, such as Northop-King, have been coating their seeds with a toxic chemical, which is poison. Order seeds from a wholesaler, as it is much safer and cheaper. Hawaiian wood rose seeds can be ordered directly from:

Chong's Nursery and Flowers
P.O. Box 2154
Honolulu, Hawaii

LSD dosages

The basic dosages of acid vary according to what kind of acid is available and what medium of ingestion is used. Chemically the potency of LSD-25 is measured in micrograms, or mics. If you're chemically minded or making your own acid, then computing the number of micrograms is very important. Usually between 300 to 500 mics is plenty for a five- to eight-hour trip, depending on the quality of the acid, of course. I have heard of people taking as much as 1,500 to 2,000 mics. This is not only extremely dangerous, it is also wasteful.

LSD comes packaged in many different forms. The proverbial sugar cube is pretty passé, in the sense that other more feasible methods have taken its place. The most common are listed below.

1. The brown spot, or a piece of paper with a dried drop of LSD on it, is always around. Usually one spot equals one trip.

2. Capsuled acid is extremely tricky, as the cap can be al-

most any color, size, and potency. Always ask what the acid is cut with, as a lot of acid is cut with either speed or strychnine. Also note dosage.

3. Small white or colored tablets have been known to contain acid, but, as with the capsuled acid, it is impossible to tell potency, without asking.

4. I have heard about some characters who attempted to shoot acid. Shooting any drug is a bad scene. Stay away from it. I cannot imagine what their rush was like, but would certainly advise against this form of drug abuse.

Peyote

I remember once when I was in Mexico. It was Juarez or maybe Laredo, I can't remember, but all the border towns are fantastic. There's no crime rate in a border town —at least not in the sense it is reckoned in the United States. How would you measure it? It's just a real pleasure to go where the people aren't all hung up about ethics and moral bullshit. Everyone's been paid off and, if they haven't, they own the town. Every cab driver has a friend who just happens to own a drug store, a friend who just happens to own a farm with a little marihuana on it, and a virgin daughter with three kids.

Well, I remember that my first experience with peyote was there. I'd been drinking, and hadn't quite got two weeks' worth of speed out of my system, when this little kid scared the shit out of me. All of a sudden he starts screaming, "Hey mysta, hey mysta hippee, you vant, you want some good peyote, mama pick herself?" I'm stupid and one of the biggest suckers alive. I would let the devil himself lead me into hell, with my eyes closed, just to see what it was like. I told the kid O.K. He wanted the money first. I'm not quite that stupid. We went together.

We went for a trip together, maybe five or six miles, way out of town. The countryside was really pretty nice, but I couldn't dig it, I was too uptight. Finally he stopped and told me that this was his home. It was five pieces of corrugated iron propped up together with pieces of cloth and wood covering the cracks. Pretty depressing.

Again he wanted to take the money, and have me outside. Again I told him to bring it out to me and I'd pay him. Then he did something that scared the shit out of me. He invited me into his house. I kept wondering how many brothers were waiting for me, but then I guess alcohol and speed tend to inflate the ego, as all I was saying to myself was, "Shit, if they come at me, I swear to God I'll take one of the cocksuckers with me."

He took me around to the back of his home, and held a piece of orange crate open for me. My first impression of the inside was darkness, but then slowly, as my eyes began to get used to the dark, I saw a woman, not a fat mama, as I had expected, but rather a thin, delicate woman, with the lines of the world carved deeply into her face. She was squatting by the glowing remains of a fire, in the center of the room. As she rose to meet her child, I realized she was not as old as I had supposed, and she was strangely exciting in the gloom of the dying embers.

The kid started to scream again. I guess all he could do was scream, since I never heard him talk. He was screaming so fast I couldn't understand a word of it. It was like gibberish, and the faster it came out of his mouth, the faster my head spun. I really began to get the spins. The woman must have realized something was wrong with me, as she took my arm and sat me on the floor. When I sat down I felt better, my senses started to come back to me, and the kid wasn't screaming any more.

I saw his mother rise and walk over to a large earthen pot, where she took something out, and brought it back to me. Then I realized that it must be the peyote, and the peyote was the reason I was there in the first place. I took a handful from her and shoved it into my mouth. It was the most disgusting stuff I've ever eaten. After I had finally managed to swallow it, I handed my entire wallet to the woman. I don't know why I did this, maybe out of relief that the kid didn't have any older brothers, or maybe just because I was incapable of counting. I don't know, but all of a sudden, like a shotgun shell in the gut, my whole stomach was on fire. I could feel all the food and drink inside my stomach churning around and around like a God-damn amusement park. I knew I was going to vomit. I knew there was no stopping it, it was like a rough day at the beach, waves of convulsion.

I got up and ran to the street, wondering vaguely in the back of my mind whether I had not, in fact, been mildly poisoned. As I hit the dirt road, I knew that was it, and let my stomach fly. It seemed the spasms would never end. I felt all my organs being ripped out one after another.

After thoroughly purging myself, I made my way back to town, quite stoned, and missing a wallet.

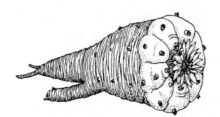

Figure 4. Peyote.

Peyote is a small brown cactus, which in natural growth barely protrudes above the ground. On top of this cactus are small spineless buttons, which resemble mushrooms. It is within these buttons that the mescal is found, and the buttons are usually the only parts eaten, although certain tribes of Indians do eat root and all. Peyote has had a long history that stretches all the way back to the ancient Aztecs, who considered it divine and used it in many of their religious ceremonies.

The use of peyote was rediscovered in a few isolated tribes in Mexico, and its use once again became widespread. The Indians in the Southwest formally organized a church with peyote as one of their sacraments. The Native American Church, which has over two hundred thousand members, is one of the few places in the world where a person can legally get stoned. Their members can legally get stoned and blame all their bad trips on God.

The traditional peyote preparation has always been exactly the same as it is today. The buttons are removed from the cactus, and cut into small round disks. These are then dried in the sun for several days. Then they are crushed and placed in boiling water to make a form of tea. Peyote can be eaten raw, but it tastes like vomit.

And this same one, with a conceit born of this kind of uncouth purgation, started spitting a few moments later. He spat after having drunk the peyote like the rest of us. For the twelve phases of the dance were done, and as dawn was about to break, we were handed the grated peyote, which looked like some kind of slimy chowder; and in front of each of us a fresh hole was dug to receive the sputum and vomit of our mouths, which had been made holy by the peyote's passing through.

Antonin Artaud, *The Artaud Anthology*

The white man goes into his church house and talks about jesus; the indian goes into his teepee and talks to Jesus.

J. S. Syotkin, 1956

The bad taste and foul smell of the peyote can be gotten rid of by a simple process. There are two basic methods which follow, and after them the recipe for preparing synthetic mescaline, which takes a knowledge of chemistry.

Extracting mescaline from peyote in the kitchen
Method One

1. Obtain 50 g. of dried ground peyote and put in a 500 ml. Erlenmeyer flask.

2. Add 250 cc. of wood alcohol, cover the flask tightly, and let cactus powder soak it up for one day, with occasional stirring.

3. Pour off the wood-alcohol solution into a 500 ml. beaker, filter properly, and place in a well-ventilated place to evaporate. *Caution:* Wood alcohol is flammable, keep away from fire.

4. Again soak the plant powder in the flask for two hours, but in 100 cc. of 1-normal hydrochloric acid.

5. Filter, discard the mush, and combine the filtered HCL solution with the residue from the evaporated wood alcohol solution. Filter again.

6. To the solution add enough 2-Normal potassium hydroxide until the solution is neutral (turns ph paper beige).

7. Add 100 cc. of chloroform, stir, and let the mixture stand until it separates into two layers.

8. Separate the two layers, using a separatory funnel and discard the water (top) layer. (See Figure 5.)

9. Add 40 cc. of water to the chloroform, shake, and separate the layers again. Discard top layer.

10. Filter the chloroform, evaporate, and dissolve the gummy residue in 20 cc. of water. Refilter it. Makes about one dose.

Method Two

1. Take fresh peyote buttons, wash, remove skins, and remove all tufts and foreign particles.

2. Take the peyote meat and grind it in a meat grinder or coffee grinder.

3. Allow ground peyote meat to dry, then grind again as before.

Separatory Funnel

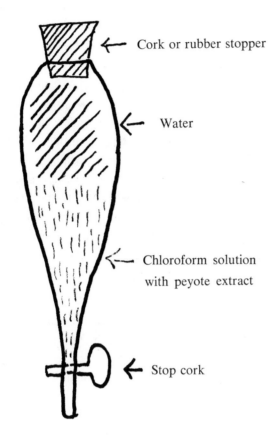

Figure 5. A separatory funnel (used in steps 8 and 9 of the recipe for the extraction of mescaline from peyote).

4. Boil peyote meat for five hours, keeping plenty of water in the pot to prevent burning.

5. Take skin and bark of peyote and break it down by beating on a cutting board. When it is broken down, boil for five hours in a separate pot.

6. Strain liquids from both pots and combine. Throw away the peyote mush.

7. Boil this solution until it becomes dark. Do not allow it to become too thick. Label it solution "A."

8. Now cool solution "A."

9. Take the cool solution "A" and fill half a separatory funnel.

10. Add about an equal volume of ethyl ether, and shake for two minutes.

11. Now allow the liquids to settle and form layers. Draw off the water solution (bottom layer) by turning the stop cork. Do not draw off the ether solution.

12. Now process all of solution "A" in this manner. Label all drawn-off solution "B." Put the leftover ether solution into a container and throw away.

13. Boil down solution "B" to cut down volume, but do not allow it to become too thick.

14. Add a phenophthalein indicator to solution "B," until the solution turns red.

15. Mix in small amounts of a diluted sulfuric acid solution, until the red color disappears. Do not add any more acid than required.

16. Add one teaspoon of baking powder (to neutralize the acid) for each gallon of solution. Boil again to reduce volume.

17. Place solution "B" in the refrigerator for several hours, but do not freeze it.

18. While it is still cold, pour off as much of the liquid as possible, leaving the crystal in the container. Rinse the crystals with near-freezing water.

19. Add rinse water with water poured off crystals. Boil this solution to reduce volume and then cool in refrigerator. Repeat procedure for formation of the crystals. These crystals are nearly pure mescaline sulphate. Allow crystals to dry and then capsule.

This usually makes between 30-80 mg. per button.

Making synthetic mescaline in the laboratory

The next recipe is for making synthetic mescaline, and, as I do not understand it, I have copped out again and quoted straight from the book. If you do not understand chemistry talk, skip this one. It will give you more headaches than it's worth. It is taken directly from the *Journal of the American Chemical Society,* a trade publication, which for the layman is as screwy as Greek.

The process of making a new synthesis of mescaline: Makepeace U. Tsao, "A New Synthesis of Mescaline," *Journal of the American Chemical Society,* Vol. 73, pp. 5495-96 (November, 1951)

The cactus alkaloid, mescaline, B-(3, 4, 5 Trimethoxy-phenylethylamine, has been studied for some years, because of its most interesting effects on the psychic states of human subjects. Since the elucidation of the chemical structure of the alkaloid through the synthesis of Spath 2[1]-7 a few other methods of preparation have been published. A simple synthesis utilizing lithium aluminum hydride is presented in this report. The synthesis may be outlined as follows: gallic acid—3, 4, 5-Trimethoxybenzoic acid, -methyl ester of 3, 4, 5-Trimethoxybenzyl alcohol—3, 4, 5-Trimethoxybenzyl chloride-3, 4, 5-Trimethoxyphenylacetonitrile-Mescaline.

Experimental:

Methyl Ester of 3, 4, 5-Trimethoxybenzoic acid: To a solution prepared from 100 g. of 3, 4, 5-Trimethoxybenzoic acid (0.47 Mole), 20 g. of sodium hydroxide, 55 g. of sodium carbonate and 300 ml. of water is added, with stirring, 94 ml. of methyl sulfate (0.94 Mole) during the course of 20 minutes. The reaction mixture is refluxed for one-half hour. The crude ester (65 g., 61%) precipitates from the cold mixture. From the filtrate, 38 g. of starting material is recovered upon acidification with diluted HCL. The ester is further purified by solution in the minimum amount of methanol and treatment with norite. Usually it is necessary to repeat this treatment to obtain a colorless crystalline product that melts at 80-82 degrees. Semmler, [9] who employed a different process, reported m.p. 83-84 degrees.

3, 4, 5-Trimethoxybenyl alcohol: To suspension of 4.6 g. (0.12 Mole) of lithium aluminum hydride in 200 ml. of anhydrous ether is added, in the course of 30 minutes, a solution of 22.6 g. (0.1 Mole) of the methyl ester of 3, 4, 5-Trimethoxybenzoic acid in 300 ml. of ether. The solid which forms is carefully decomposed first with 50 ml. of ice-water. After decantation of the ether, 250 ml. of ice-cold 10% sulfuric acid is added. The product is extracted with 150 ml. of ether. The combined extracts, after drying over sodium sulfate, are freed of ether and the residue distilled; b.p. 135-137 degrees (0.25 mm); yield 14.7 g. (73%). This compound was obtained by a different method by Marx;[10] b.p. 228 degrees (25 mm).

3, 4, 5-Trimethoxybenzyl chloride: A mixture of 25 g. of 3, 4, 5-Trimethoxybenzyl alcohol and 125 ml. of ice-cold concentrated HCl is shaken vigorously until a homogeneous solution is obtained. In a few minutes a turbidity develops, followed by a heavy precipitation of gum-

my product. After 4 hours and dilution with 100 ml. of ice-water, the aqueous layer is decanted and extracted with three 50 ml. portions of benzene. Then the gummy organic residue is dissolved in the combined benzene extracts. The benzene solution is washed with water and dried over sodium sulfate.

The benzene solution is transferred to a distilling flask, and the benzene is removed under diminished pressure. The red semi-solid residue is suspended in a small amount of ice-cold ether and filtered through a chilled funnel. The crystalline product, after washing with small portions of cold ether, weighs 9.7 g. The combined filtrates on standing in refrigerator yield more crystals. The total yield is 13.0 g. (48%). After four recrystallizations from benzene, colorless needles are obtained; m.p. 60-62 degrees.

Anal. Calcd. for $C_{10}H_{13}O_3CI$: C, 55.42; H, 6.05. Found: C, 55.55; H, 6.13.

This compound is extremely soluble in ether, alcohol and acetone, but slightly soluble in petroleum ether. Standing at room temperature for a few weeks causes the crystals to turn into a red semi-solid. An alcoholic solution of pure material gives an instantaneous precipitation with alcoholic silver nitrate.

3, 4, 5-Trimethoxyphenylacetonitrile—A mixture of 9 g. of potassium cyanide in 35 ml. of water and 60 ml. of methanol and 9.7 g. of 3, 4, 5-Trimethoxybenzyl chloride is heated for 10 min. at 90 degrees. The solvents are partially removed under diminished pressure. The residue is then extracted with 90 ml. of ether in three portions. The combined extracts are washed with water and dried over sodium sulfate. After the removal of the drying agent, the ether solution is warmed on a steam-bath and the ether is removed with a stream of air. On chilling, the residue yields scalelike crystals. Recrystallization from ether gives rectangular prism: Yield 2.5 g. (27%): m.p. 76-77 degrees. Baker and Robinson[12] reported a melting point of 77 degrees for this compound.

Mescaline—In 150 ml. of anhydrous ether is suspended 0.85 g. of lithium aluminum hydride powder. With stirring, 2.0 g. of 3, 4, 5-Trimethoxyphenylacetonitrile in 150 ml. of anhydrous ether was added during the course of 15 minutes. After 25 min. stirring, 10 ml. of ice-water is dropped in carefully. Then a mixture of

10 g. of sulfuric acid in 40 ml. of water is added at a moderate rate. The aqueous layer is separated and treated with concentrated sodium hydroxide. The brown oil is extracted with three portions of 30 ml. each of ether. The combined extracts are washed once with water and dried over stick potassium hydroxide. To the decanted ether solution is added a mixture of 1 g. of sulfuric acid and 25 ml. of ether. The white precipitate is washed several times with ether; yield 1.2 g. (40%). After two re-crystallizations form 95% ethanol, the colorless long thin plates soften at 172 degrees and melt at 183 degrees.

A sample of mescaline acid sulfate prepared from the natural source and kindly furnished by Dr. Seevers of the Department of Pharmacology softens at 170 degrees and melts at 180 degrees. The picrate, prepared from the acid sulfate, melts at 217 degrees (dec.), after three recrystallizations from ethanol. The chloroplatinate prepared from free base melts at 184-185 degrees. Spath gave the following melting points: sulfate, 183-186 degrees; picrate, 216-218 degrees; chloroptinate, 187-188 degrees.

1. E. Spath, *Monatsh.,* 40, 129 (1919).

2. K. H. Slotta and H. Heller, Ber. 63B, 3029 (1930).

3. H. Frisch and E. Waldman, German Patent 545, 853, July 3, 1930, *C.A.* 26, 3521° (1932).

4. K. Kindler and W. Peschke, *Arch. Pharm.,* 270, 410 (1932).

5. K. H. Slotta and G. Szuzker, *J. prakt chem.,* 137, 339 (1933).

6. G. Hahn and H. Wassmuth, *Ber.,* 67, 711 (1934).

7. G. Hahn and F. Rumpf, *ibid.,* 71b, 2141 (1939).

8. A. H. Blatt, "Organic Synthesis," Coll. Vol 1. 2nd ed., John Wiley and Sons, Inc., N.Y., N.Y. 1946, p. 537.

9. F. W. Semmler, *Ber.,* 41, 1774 (1908).

10. M. Marx, Ann. 263, 254 (1891).

11. All M.P.'s are uncorrected.

12. Baker and R. Robinson, *J. Chem Soc.,* 160 (1929).

Editor's note: The next to the last step, 3, 4, 5-Trimethoxyphenylacetonitrile, can be ordered directly from Aldrich Chemical Co., 2371 N. 30th St., Milwaukee, Wisconsin.

Mescaline is very similar to LSD and psilocybin, in that the effects tend to disorder the senses. It may create anxiety and slight nausea about two hours after ingestion, but as the experience proceeds all the impressions and observations of the subject are intensified. Time and space are distorted, or completely ignored. A definite change in perception takes place. Objects may seem as if they are suspended in a liquid, or a general flowing movement may be present. The subject may be very conscious of his ego, and a sense of threat and fear may accompany the intensification of colors.

Mescaline, as with all psychedelics, is a very personal experience. It affects every person differently so, in that sense, it is impossible for me to try to describe the experience. The normal dosage of mescaline is about 500 micrograms, and it may have toxic reactions with an overdose of 1000 mics or more.

Mescaline is a hallucinogenic alkaloid, which is extracted from peyote cactus, or can be synthesized in the laboratory, as in the previous recipe. The chemical structure of mescaline closely resembles STP, which is a much stronger psychedelic. The reason black-market distribution and sale of mescaline are not more widespread than at present is that LSD is considered five thousand times more powerful with almost the same effects. Mescaline is also slightly more expensive than acid; a cap of mescaline usually goes for between $5 and $7, whereas you should have no trouble finding a good cap of acid for $3 or $4.

My ideas of space were very unusual [under the influence of mescaline]. I could see myself from head to foot as well as the sofa on which I was lying. All else was nothing, absolutely empty space. I was on a solitary island floating in ether. No part of my body was subject to the laws of gravitation. On the other side of the vacuum, the room seemed to be unlimited in space—extremely fantastic figures appeared before my eyes. I was very excited, perspired and shivered, and was kept in a state of ceaseless wonder. I saw endless passages with beautiful pointed arches, delightfully colored arabesques, grotesque decorations, divine, sublime and enchanting in their fantastic splendor. These visions changed in waves and billows, were built, destroyed and appeared again in endless variations, first on one plane and then in three dimensions, at last disappearing in infinity. The sofa-island disappeared; I did not feel my self; an ever-increasing feeling of dissolution set in. I was seized with passionate curiosity, great things were about to be unveiled before me. I would perceive the essence of all things, the problems of creation would be unravelled. I was dematerialized.

Louis Lewin (1964)

Psilocybin

Psilocybin, like mescaline, is extracted from a plant. Psilocybin is extracted from *Psilocybe mexicana,* a small mushroom that grows in wet or marshy pastures. Other species of mushrooms which have psychedelic qualities are: *Conocybe siliginoides, Psilocybe aztecorum, P. zapotecorum, P. caerulescens,* and *Stropharia cubenis.*

Psilocybin, like peyote, was and is still used to a small degree in the religious rites of the Mexican Indians. It was referred to as teonanactl, or in English as God's flesh. The Indians usually eat between 10 and 15 mushrooms, which, like peyote, have a very unpleasant acrid smell. Usually nausea follows ingestion. The effects of psilocybin last for about five to seven hours.

When you take the actual raw mushrooms, the dosage is about 10 to 20 medium-sized buttons. A faster method of ingestion is to prepare a soup, using any regular mushroom soup recipe. Although this tends to increase the speed in which the psilocybin enters the blood stream, it also increases the unpleasant taste and smell. When taking synthesized psilocybin, usually a capsule of between 20 and 60 milligrams will produce a four- to six-hour trip.

Figure 6. *Stropharia cubensis* and *Psilocybe mexicana.*

How to grow psilocybe mushrooms in the kitchen

The recipe for growing these mushrooms follows on the next page. It is simple enough that anyone should be able to perform it in his kitchen.

Recipe for growing psilocybe mushrooms:

It is important, in working with fungi, to use "pure-culture" technique to prevent the fungi one is working with from becoming contaminated with unwanted air-borne fungi. This pure-culture technique is easily acquired by reading the chapters devoted to it in any introductory bacteriology laboratory manual. Better yet, anyone who has had a course in bacteriology can easily demonstrate the technique of transferring the fungi and making the necessary "inoculating loop," which is used to transfer the fungi from one tube or bottle to another without getting the material contaminated.

The careful handling of the fungi psilocybe is most important, as the psilocybe are easily overgrown and ruined by other molds present in the normal environment. The material on which the fungi is grown is called the "medium" or "media." Preparation of the medium varies somewhat according to the kind used, but in general the procedure is the same. Briefly the ingredients are weighed (great accuracy is not generally required), dissolved in the required amount of water (distilled), and distributed into containers for sterilizing. The use of pint or quart fruit jars, with the jar mouth covered with a heavy gauze aluminum foil, is adequate.

Inasmuch as media are prepared to grow the fungi in pure culture, all microorganisms, other than the one to be grown, must be excluded. This makes it necessary to sterilize the medium before using it, to kill any bacteria or fungus spores which are present in the medium or on the glassware. Sterilization is accomplished by placing the containers with the medium into a pressure cooker, preferably the canning type with a pressure gauge, and sterilizing, (called "autoclaving") for 15 to 20 minutes at 250 degrees. Allow the pressure cooker to come down in pressure very slowly or the medium will boil over.

Quart fruit jars should not be filled with more than two cups of any medium used; the pint jars with not over three-fourths of a cup.

Media which contain sugar (glucose, sucrose, maltose, etc.) may caramelize somewhat if heating is continued beyond 20 minutes at 250 degrees F. This caramelization may be toxic to the fungi and they will fail to grow, or will grow but little, or no psilocybin will be produced.

After preparation and sterilization, it is well to leave media at room temperature for about three days without opening them, as a check to see if the medium is really sterile. If any growth of fungi occurs, or a film of bacteria forms across the medium (usually seen or smelled), the sterilization process is faulty. In the latter case, discard the medium. No medium can be satisfactorily resterilized for culturing psilocybe.

In order to have a medium on which to maintain the fungi over long periods of time, it is well to prepare some tubes of medium which contain agar as a solidifying agent. The most satisfactory tubes are those about six inches long and a half inch in diameter with screw caps having rubber liners (obtainable from any lab supply source). Fill the tubes one-third full of agar medium (after melting the agar —see formulae), sterilize, and cool to room temperature to solidify the agar. Inoculate the fungi into the water with sterilized inoculating loop, as required by pure-culture technique. These tubes are held at room temperature for a few days—even a week—or until there is a growth of the fungi over the surface. The caps are screwed down tight and the cultures are stored at refrigerator temperature. This constitutes your "stock cultures" and is the source for inoculating larger quantities of the medium. The use of stock cultures insures a constant supply of viable, uncontaminated culture material. The psilocybe will keep up to a year at refrigerator temperature without being transferred to a new medium.

The larger bottles of medium are inoculated with a small amount of the whitish thread of the fungi (the threads are called "mycelium"), using careful pure-culture technique. Leave the culture at room temperature—about 70 to 75 degrees. This is easily maintained if one has a cellar; or one may have a refrigerator man put a thermostat in an ordinary refrigerator so as to maintain the needed temperature range. The psilocybe fungi will grow at a higher temperature, but the psilocybin production will be low or none.

It is not necessary to obtain the mushroom form of the fungi (called fruiting bodies, or carpophores) in order to have psilocybin production carried out. The mycelium contains as much as the fruiting bodies. When the mushroom threads have grown in the medium for about 10 to 12 days, they should be harvested. (This time is the most variable factor in obtaining the maximum yield of psilocybin. Trial and error under individual conditions of growth is necessary to standardize the yield. Keeping careful records of the medium used, how prepared, and temperature and time will allow one to improve the yield with practice.) Scientifically, harvesting is done just about four days after the last of the sugar has been used by the fungi. Harvesting is done by removing the medium: liquid medium by filtering through flannel and keeping the mycelium mat; solid medium by simply removing the mycelium mat. The mycelium, which may be a gooey mess, is dried at very low heat (not over 200 degrees F. in an oven with the door slightly ajar). Powder the dried material. The powder may be extracted by soaking in methanol, filtering, and evaporating the liquid with a low heat. Do this in a ventilated room, and be sure all the methanol is gone.

There will be psilocybin in the medium also, but it is generally in small amounts and not worth the effort to extract it.

The above procedure may seem complicated, but after a few tries it is rather straightforward. Psilocybin production is dependent upon a lot of factors which are not yet all known. There is no way but trial and error in developing media and methods. This recipe is taken directly from *The Turn-On Book,* BarNel Enterprises.

Psilocybe cubensis grows and fruits readily on potato dextrose, yeast, or rye grain medium; however *Psilocybe mexicana* will grow and fruit on potato dextrose but not on the rye grain medium.

Recipe for potato dextrose yeast agar:

1. Wash 250 grams potatoes (do not peel).
2. Slice ⅛ inch thick.
3. Wash with tap water until water is clear.
4. Drain, rinse with distilled water.
5. Cover with distilled water and cook until tender.
6. Drain liquid through flannel cloth or several thicknesses of cheesecloth into a flask or jar.
7. Rinse potatoes once or twice with a little distilled water.
8. Keep liquid and throw potatoes away—add enough distilled water to make up one liter of liquid.
9. Bring liquid to a boil, and add 15 grams agar and stir until dissolved (watch carefully or it will boil over—best to use a stainless steel pan), 10 grams dextrose, and 1.5 grams yeast extract.
10. While liquid is hot, distribute into desired containers.
11. Autoclave for 15 minutes at 250 degrees F. (about 15 lbs. pressure).
12. PDY broth is made the same way but without the sugar.

Recipe for rye grain medium:

For half-pint jars:

50 grams rye grain (whole)

80 ml. water

1 gram chalk (calcium carbonate)

For pint jars:

100 grams rye grain (whole)

160 ml. water

2 grams of chalk (calcium carbonate)

For quart jars:

225 grams rye grain (whole)

275 ml. water

4 grams chalk (calcium carbonate)

Note: If rye grain medium seems dry, add small amounts of distilled water.

How to make synthetic psilocybin in the laboratory

The next recipe is for the synthesis of psilocybin. It is the last technical recipe in the book, since this book is not directed at chemistry majors. To understand and perform this recipe, you need a basic understanding of chemistry and access to a laboratory.

Synthesis of Psilocin and Psilocybin

translated by Rolf Von Eckartsburg

Hofman, Heim, Brack, Kobel, Frey, Ott, Petrzilka, and Troxler, "Psilocybin and Psilocin, zwei psychotrope Wirkstoffe aus mexikanischen Rauschpilzen," *Hevetica Chemica Acta,* Vol. 42, pp. 1570-71, 1959.

(4-Benzyloxy-indolyl-(3)))-gloxylsaure-dimethylamid (V)

To a solution of 50 grams 4-Benzyl-oxy-indol (IV) in 1.2 liters dry ether one lets drop while stirring it well and at a temperature of 1 to 5 degrees C., 40 ml. Oxalylchlorid and keeps stirring after the mixture has been accomplished for an additional one hour at temperature of 5 to 10 degrees C. this orange-red solution. Following this it was cooled further with a mixture of ice and table salt and slowly a solution of 100 g. Dimethylamin in 100 ml. of ether was added by slow dripping. After continuing for an additional one-half hour, the stirring at room temperature, the ppt. was filtered off by suction using washing with ether and then with much water. The raw product which was obtained dry in a vacuum was dissolved in a mixture of benzol and Methanol and was brought to crystallization through an addition in portions of Petrol-ether. Prisms from smp. 146-150 degrees C. Yield 52.6 gram (73%). The color reaction according to Keller is bluish-green.

C_{19} H_{18} O_3 N_2 Ber. C 70.8 H 5.6 O 14.9 N 8.7%
(322.4)   Gef. 70.6   5.7   14.6   8.7

4-Benzyloxy-W-N,N-dimethyltrytamin (VI)

A solution of 52.5 grams (V) in one liter abs. Dioxan

was dripped under lively stirring into a boiling (seething) solution of 66g LiAlH$_4$ into one liter of the same solvent and continued stirring for 17 hours at the same temperature. Following this, the complex was decomposed as well as the superfluous reduction-substance under good cooling with ice using Methanol, then 500 ml. of saturated sodium sulfate solution was added, the precipitation sucked off and thoroughly washed with Methanol and Dioxan. The filtrate is put "wine-sour" and side-products are removed through shaking with ether. Following this the basal-alkaline reaction product was withdrawn (drawn out) after alkalization with NaOH by means of chloroform. Out of this chloroform extract, dried through potash and concentrated to a small volume, (V1) crystallized following addition in portions of Petrol-ether in fine needles of smp. 125-126 degrees C. yield of crystallization 33 grams. From the "mother-lye" after a chromatographic cleaning with 300 g. Al$_2$O$_3$ through which (VI) was distilled by means of benzol which contained 0.2% alcohol, an additional 7.7 grams of pure amalgamate was gained. Total yield 85% of Th.

C$_{19}$H$_{22}$ON$_2$ Ber. C77.5 H7.5 05.4 N9.5%
(294.4) Gef. 77.6 7.4 5.5 9.8

4-Hydroxy-W-N,N-dimethyltrptamin (Psilocin) (11)

A solution of 37.5 grams (VI) in 1.2 liters of Methanol was "shaken" on an Aluminum-oxide-carrier under addition of 20 grams of 5% Palladium catalyst with Hydrogen, in which process during 12 hours the theoretically computed quantity of 3.2 liters were absorbed. Out of the concentrated solution which was filtered from the catalyst and reduced to a small volume there crystallized (11) in hexagonal plates of smp. 173-176. Yield 21 g. (81%). Color reaction of Keller blue-green.

C$_{12}$H$_{16}$ON$_2$ Ber. C70.6 H7.9 N13.7%
(204.3) Gef. 70.4 8.3 14.1

The synthetic substance agrees in all properties, particularly also in the I.R. spectrum with natural psilocin.

4-Dibenzyl-phosphoryloxy-W-N,N-dimethyltryptamin (VII)

6.3 grams (11) were dissolved in 30.5 ml. 1N methanolic NaOH, the solution under nitrogen dried and vaporized and the residue dried for 3 hours in a high vacuum at 40 degrees C. The residue was dissolved in 100 ml. t-Amylalcohol, added to this was a solution of Dibenzylphosphoryl-clorid in 30 ml. CC1$_4$ which was made fresh from 8.3 grams Dibenzyl phosphit. This was shaken for two hours at room temperature. Then it was boiled down, the residue absorbed in Chloroform-alcohol 9:1, filtered from NaCl and the filtrate chromatographed at a column of 750 grams of Al$_2$O$_3$. With the same solution-mixture 6.8 grams (VII) were "eluired." From Chloroform-Alcohol crystals of smp. 238-240 degrees C.

C$_{26}$H$_{29}$O$_4$N$_2$P Ber. C67.2 H6.3 N6.0 P6.7%
(465.5) Gef. 67.1 6.7 6.2 6.4

O-Phosphoryl-4-hydroxy-W-N,N-dimethyltryptamin (Psilocybin) (I)

A solution of 6.8 grams (VII) in 100 ml. Methanol was shaken on an Al$_2$O$_3$ carrier with Hydrogen until saturation after 5 grams of 5% Palladium catalyst had been added. The boiled-down residue of the solution which had been cleaned from the catalyst was let into 200 ml. water and the undissolved side-products were filtered out. The watery solution was steamed dry and the residue was absorbed in a little Methanol from which (I) separated itself in fine prisms. When the change-in-crystallization from water was made, we obtained soft needles from smp. 220-228 degrees C. Yield 3.0 grams (42%). Color reaction of Keller, violet.

C$_{12}$H$_{17}$O$_4$N$_2$P Ber. C50.7 H6.0 N9.9 P10.9%
(284.3) Gef. 50.5 6.1 9.5 10.8

The synthetic product agrees in all properties, particularly also in the I.R. spectrum with the psilocybin isolated from the mushroom.

The only laws I respect are the ones which make old men and women warmer in the winter, children happier in the summer, and beer stronger.

—Brendan Behan, *Borstal Boy*

DMT

How to make DMT in the kitchen

DMT stands for N,N-dimethyltryptamine. DMT is a semisynthetic compound similar to psilocin in structure. (Psilocin is the hallucinogenic substance based in psilocybin.) DMT is extremely fast-acting. Within several minutes of ingestion, the effects can be felt, but it doesn't last as long as other psychedelics. The intensity, on the other hand, is as strong; for about 30 to 45 minutes you are completely under the influence of this drug. The most common method of ingestion is smoking, but I have heard that there were some capsules around for about two years. Whether they were good or not, I have no idea. Carefully soaked parsley leaves are the usual medium for smoking, although some persons have dipped marihuana in it and said the experience was fantastic. Other compounds similar to DMT are both DET and DPT.

The next recipe is for DMT. It is very simple and can easily be performed in the kitchen. All the chemicals and equipment are available from any chemical supply house or hobby shop.

Recipe for DMT:

1. Mix thoroughly and dissolve 25 grams of indole with a pound of dry ethyl ether in a 2,000-ml. flask (two-quart jar).

2. Take ice tray and fill with chipped or shaved ice. Now cool solution for about 35 minutes until it reaches the temperature of 0 degrees C. At the same time cool 50 ml. of dry oxalychloride to about 5 degrees below 0 degrees C. in the same ice tray.

3. *Very slowly* add the oxalychloride solution to the indole solution.

Warning: When these two chemicals are mixed together, there is an extremely violent reaction. Avoid boiling over, avoid contact with skin, and avoid fumes.

4. Wait until all the bubbling has died down, then add a few handfuls of common table salt to the ice tray, to cool the solution further. Put this solution aside and label it "solution 1."

5. Cool 100 ml. of dry ethyl ether, in a 500-ml. flask, to 0 degrees C. in a salted ice tray. At the same time cool an unopened 100-gram bottle of dimethylamine to 0 degrees C. in the same ice bath.

6. Open the seal of the dimethylamine bottle and slowly pour a steady stream into the ether. Label "solution 2."

7. Very slowly and carefully add solution "1" and "2" together.

8. Now take the mixed solutions from the ice tray and bring up to room temperature, stirring the solution all the time. You should be left with a solution which is almost clear. If it is still murky, continue stirring until it becomes as clear as possible.

9. Now filter the solution to separate the precipitate by suction, as shown in Figure 7.

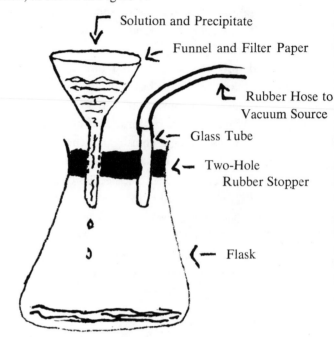

Figure 7. Primary filtering of homemade DMT.

10. Refilter with suction after pouring technical ether over the precipitate.

11. Repeat filtering once more with ether and then twice with water.

12. Let this substance dry on a plastic or china plate. (Do not use metal.) After drying, a solid material will be formed. Take these particles and place them in a 800-ml. beaker.

13. Mix 100 ml. benzene with 100 ml. methyl alcohol. After the mixture has been stirred, cover solid particles from step 12 with about a half inch of the solution and heat the beaker in water until all solid material has dissolved. Add more solvent if necessary. See Figure 8 below.

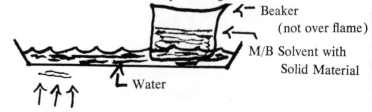

Heat Source   Figure 8. Heating DMT solution in water bath.

14. After all the solid material has dissolved, remove beaker from the heat, and allow it to cool. As it cools, small needle-shaped crystals will appear. When this happens, try to pour off as much of the solvent as possible without disturbing the crystals.

15. Place crystals in a 1,000-ml. flask and dissolve in tetrahydrofurane. (Use only as much as absolutely necessary.) Label this solution "A."

16. Slowly mix 200 ml. tetrahydrofurane and 20 grams lithium aluminum hydride in a 500-ml. flask, and label it solution "B."

Warning: Lithium aluminum hydride ignites on contact with moisture. *Do not* use on humid days. Protect eyes and wear rubber gloves.

17. Mix solutions "A" and "B" slowly, stirring constantly.

18. Prepare a water bath and heat solution in water bath for three hours, stirring for four minutes every half hour. When not stirring, use aspirator tube as shown in Figure 9.

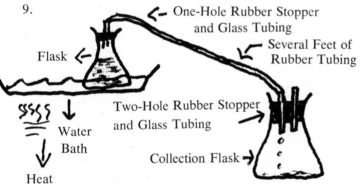

Figure 9. Final collection of DMT.

19. When this is completed, allow the flask to remain at room temperature for about 20 minutes. Then place in salted ice bath and cool to 0 degrees C. Add a small amount of chilled methanol, stirring gently until solution appears murky.

20. Filter this murky solution through a paper filter in a funnel, and collect the filtered liquid in a flask.

21. Add 100 ml. of tetrahydrofuran through the filter and collect in the same flask. Now heat this solution in a water bath until most of the tetrahydrofuran is evaporated and a gooey substance remains.

22. Place little piles of this substance on a cookie tray and, with a heat lamp, dry for three or four hours. Now

you have D.M.T. To ingest, crumble a small quantity with parsley or mint, and smoke. Do not inject. Do not smoke with tobacco. DMT is a powerful psychedelic and should not be *abused*.

Author's note: All chemicals in the last recipe can be ordered by mail from any of the large chemical manufacturers. Lithium aluminum hydride may be ordered from Metal Hydrides Inc., Beverly, Massachusetts (it costs about $20 per 100 grams). All other chemicals can be ordered from Van Water-Rogers.

Bananas

Believe it or not, bananas do contain a small quantity of *Musa Sapientum bananadine,* which is a mild, short-lasting psychedelic. There are much easier ways of getting high, but the great advantage to this method is that bananas are legal.

1. Obtain 15 lbs. of ripe yellow bananas.

2. Peel all 15 lbs. and eat the fruit. Save the peels.

3. With a sharp knife, scrape off the insides of the peels and save the scraped material.

4. Put all scraped material in a large pot and add water. Boil for three to four hours until it has attained a solid paste consistency.

5. Spread this paste on cookie sheets, and dry in an oven for about 20 minutes to a half hour. This will result in a fine black powder. Makes about one pound of bananadine powder. Usually one will feel the effects of bananadine after smoking three or four cigarettes.

Figure 10. Table of weights.

Pounds	Ounces	Grams	Kilos
1	16	453.6	0.4536
0.0625	1	28.35	0.0283
	0.0352	1	0.001
2.205	35.27	1,000	1

Amphetamines

Amphetamines act as a stimulant on the central nervous system. They do not produce energy as food does, but rather put into action energy that is already present in the body. Amphetamines are broken down chemically into three types: salts of racemic amphetamines, dextroamphetamines, and methamphetamines, which only differ in potencies. Amphetamine, or speed, is used medically to combat chronic depression, as it does give the user a feeling of euphoria, while controlling his appetite.

On the black market, amphetamine is usually sold in one of two ways, either in a pill form (benzedrine, dexedrine, desbutal, desoxyn, or dexamyl) or as a crystalline powder (methedrine). Methedrine is usually injected, although it can be snorted (sniffed) or eaten in small quantities. Speed usually sells for about 10 to 25 cents a pill depending on potency, or in nickel bags and spoons of methedrine which comes in a tiny wax paper envelope.

Amphetamine does not cause addiction; but it is habit-forming, and a definite tolerance is built up to it, causing one to increase dosages. After a long period of time, usage will cause paranoia and real mental disorientation; this is especially true with methedrine. A heavy amphetamine scene, whether it be with pills or crystal is just as bad as, if not worse than, a heroin scene.

There are several methods of obtaining pills or ups. The first and easiest is to find a friend who is overweight and get him to go to a doctor for diet pills, as most diet pills are amphetamines. The best place in the world to buy benzedrine, or any of the rest of the amphetamines, is a Mexican border town, where every cab driver has his own stash, but this does entail bringing the stuff across the border, which can be a bad scene.

Any person can go to a doctor and claim he sleeps all the time—that he just can't stay awake. There is a great probability that the doctor will prescribe amphetamines. If you manage to get hold of prescription blanks, be very careful in filling them out, as pharmacists are watchful for mistakes and often go into the back and call the doctor on the phone if they feel suspicious. Another excellent way to obtain pills is to become friendly with a nurse or intern at a large hospital. Although they wouldn't be able to get you quantities, this method is probably the safest.

Description of amphetamines:

Benzedrine: A flat, pink, heart-shaped tablet, and in 10-milligram white tablets with a groove down the center. There are some time-release 15-milligram capsules.

Biphetamine: These are sold in 12-milligram capsules with a black top and a white bottom. The 20-milligram capsule is all black, and the 7-milligram capsule is all white. They are all inscribed with either "RJD or RJS." The manufacturer's recommended dose is one capsule daily.

Desbutal: These are sold in 5-milligram green capsules, 10-milligram pink and blue tablets, 15-milligram yellow and blue tablets. The manufacturer's recommended dosage is one 5-milligram capsule two or three times daily, or one of the 10- or 15-milligram tablets once in the morning.

Dexamyl: Dexamyl combines an amphetamine stimulant with a barbiturate depressant, to counteract the amphetamine side effects (i.e., nervousness). Dexamyl is sold in spansules, which have a green cap and a clear body showing green and white pellets. They are also sold in 5-milligram green heart-shaped tablets, with a groove down the center. In Great Britain they are sold as Drinamyl (purple hearts).

Methedrine: Methedrine is sold in 5-milligram white tablets with a center groove, or in ampules for injections containing 20 milligrams. Most common, on the black market, is crystal meth, which is powdered methedrine, usually cut with something else (powdered sugar or baking soda).

Amyl Nitrate

Amyl nitrate is sold in small glass capsules, and is only effective when inhaled. It is used medically for the treatment of heart attack victims. When the glass is broken, the user quickly inhales the fumes. It takes only a second to take effect, but it only lasts for two to three minutes. It is a very strong drug, and has the quality of prolonging sexual orgasms. It is sold in most states without a prescription. Overindulgence may lead to a headache or nausea, but poisoning is very rare.

Cough Syrup

Now this is a really strange scene. With all the pot and other dope going around, some people still insist on drinking cough syrup to get high. Robitussin A-C can be purchased without a prescription, but you may have to sign for it in New York. It contains a small quantity of codeine, pheniramine, maleate, and glyceryl guaiacolate (a muscle relaxant). The effects are sedation and euphoria. The most common method of ingestion is to mix Robitussin A-C with an equal amount of ginger ale and drink. Never underestimate the potency of any drug. You can have an overdose of cough syrup.

Barbiturates

Barbiturates are basically the opposite of amphetamines: that is, they act to depress the central nervous system. In small doses they act as tranquilizers, but in larger doses they are sleeping pills. The sleep induced by barbiturates is not a normal sleep, in the sense that it seriously cuts down on the normal dream activity. Prolonged use of sleeping pills can lead to complete psychological crack-ups, as the mind has no way to release itself. Barbiturates are often a means of comitting suicide. Therefore, as with all drugs, know what you are doing.

> The barbiturate addict presents a shocking spectacle. He cannot coordinate, he staggers, falls off bar stools, goes to sleep in the middle of sentences, food drops out of his mouth. He is confused, quarrelsome and stupid.
> William Burroughs, *Naked Lunch*

Types of Barbiturates:

Luminal: Fatal dosage is about 800 to 1,000 milligrams. Luminal is considered a strong long-acting barbiturate. It is usually sold in purple (16-milligram), white (32-milligram), or green (100-milligram) grooved tablets.

Amytal: This is also considered a strong long-acting barbiturate. A heavy dose is between 100 and 250 milligrams. Amytal is sold in light green (15-milligram), yellow (30-milligram), orange (50-milligram), and pink (100-milligram) capsule-shaped scored tablets, with "Lilly" inscribed in the different colors listed above.

Amytal Sodium: Very similar to the above amytal, but is sold in light blue capsules with a darker band of blue where the upper and lower parts meet. Same dosage as above.

Butisol Sodium: Butisol is sold in flat green, orange, pink, or lavender tablets inscribed with "McNeil." A heavy dose is 150 milligrams.

Nembutal: Nembutal is a short-acting barbiturate with sedative and hypnotic effects. A heavy dose of nembutal or "yellow jackets" is about 200 milligrams. This, as with all barbiturates, is extremely dangerous when taken, if the liver is infected or impaired. Nembutal is sold in 30-milligram all-yellow capsules, with an "a" on the bottom part; 50-milligram capsules with yellow caps and white bottoms with an "a" on the bottom part; and 100-milligram all-yellow capsules with the word "Abbott" inscribed.

Seconal: Seconal is probably the most popular black-market barbiturate, as it is very popular with doctors. It is referred to as "red devils, red birds, or reds," because of the color of the capsules. It is sold in 32-milligram red capsules, and a heavy dose is about 150 milligrams.

Librium: Librium is a minor tranquilizer, and the usual recommended dosage is from 5 to 15 milligrams three or four times a day. This is one of the easiest depressants to obtain, as doctors tend to prescribe it for anything from sleeplessness to acute nervousness. It is sold in 5-milligram green and yellow capsules inscribed "Roche 5," 10-milligram brown and green capsules inscribed "Roche 10," and 25-milligram green and white capsules inscribed "Roche 25."

Valium: This is also a minor tranquilizer, with the recommended dosage being about 5 to 10 milligrams, two to three times a day. It is sold in white 2-milligram and yellow 5-milligram tablets inscribed with the word "Roche."

Thorazine: This is a very strong drug. It is classified as a major tranquilizer and should be used with the utmost care. Thorazine is used at such hellholes as Bellevue to keep mental patients quiet. The usual recommended dosage is about 25 milligrams. It has been used in the treatment of bad acid trips. However, as I stated earlier, I feel that thorazine will quiet a person down, but has no regard for when he wakes up. I would not recommend its use.

I've never tried this one, but a close friend of mine from Texas swears by it. Apparently he learned it while he was going to school near the Rio Grande and there was an overabundance of desert toads. In the skins of toads there is a substance called "bufotenine," which is a hallucinogen.

Procedure for isolating bufotenine from toad skins

1. Collect five to ten toads. Make sure they're toads, as frogs will not work. The best kind are tree toads.

2. Kill them as painlessly as possible, and skin immediately.

3. Allow the skins to dry in a refrigerator for four to five days, or until the skins are brittle.

4. Now crush into a powder and smoke. (Due to its bad taste, it should be mixed with mint or some other fragrant smoking medium.)

5. Enjoy yourself, it's legal, but pray there's not reincarnation.

Glue

I don't understand how anyone would want to sniff glue, when just as legally they could smoke toad skins. Glue sniffing is really a bad scene, as it causes headaches, confusion, depression, lack of appetite, nausea, and in larger doses coma and death. It has also been attributed to much irreparable brain damage.

The method in which it is "normally" sniffed is as follows: Place half a tube of airplane glue (do not use library paste) or any carbon tetrachloride-based liquid in a plastic bag. Then stick your head inside and inhale. The effects only last between 45 minutes and an hour, but during that time the individual can undergo disordering of his coordination, double vision, and even some not so "groovy" hallucinations. The person usually falls into a drunken-like stupor, but some people have been known to react violently.

Nalline

This is a freak—a drug someone forgot to make illegal. It is used mostly to combat the overdose effects of a stronger narcotic, but it can, in small doses of five to ten milligrams, produce a relaxed feeling, similar to marihuana. In large doses it can have adverse effects, and may produce anxiety, hallucinations, and nausea. It is available without a prescription in most states, but it should be treated carefully, as it is still a powerful drug.

Cocaine

Cocaine is, in a pure form, a crystal white powder, which is usually sniffed or injected, as much of its potency is lost when taken by mouth. Since shooting or injecting any drug is one of the worst scenes imaginable, I will not get into it at all. Sniffing coke or cocaine is a unique experience. It works on the central nervous system as a stimulant in order to produce euphoric excitement and in some cases hallucinations.

Heroin

This is about the worst scene available. Junkies are like trapped animals—desperate, wounded wild animals—who will do or perform any act to get bread for some shit.

If you are really interested in this shit, and think it's cool, take a trip to 70th Street and Broadway in New York City and wander around a little bit. If you're not turned off to it right away, there's something basically wrong with you to begin with.

It is possible to shoot heroin several times before one feels the actual addiction, but the withdrawal is pretty terrible, and usually the place is pretty bad where it takes place—that is, the Tombs or Riker's Island.

Nutmeg

Nutmeg can be used for a psychedelic experience, since it does contain the ingredient elemicin, which has hallucinatory properties. This recipe cannot be compared to the one for rotten peppers published in the *East Village Other,* as nutmeg does work mildly, whereas rotten peppers only smell bad.

Method for the preparation of nutmeg:

1. Take several whole nutmegs and grind them up in a coffee grinder. You will never again be able to use the grinder without smelling nutmeg, so use an old one.

2. After the nutmegs are completely ground, place in a mortar and pulverize with a pestle.

3. The usual dosage is about 10 or 15 grams, ⅓ to ½ an ounce. A larger dose than this may produce excessive thirst, anxiety, and rapid heartbeat, but hallucinations are rare.

Paregoric

Paregoric is tincture of opium and camphor in a combined solution, medically used in controlling diarrhea. It is not used today as much as it was in the 1920's and 30's, but it is still available in many states without a prescription. It can be drunk—usually about a pint—or cigarettes can be dipped in it and left to dry, then smoked. It does act as a constipator, and this should be taken into account before use.

Peanuts

This is another recipe that I have never tried. It was given to me by the same friend who gave me the one using toad skins. It may work, it may not, but it's worth a try, since it's legal.

1. Take one pound of raw peanuts (not roasted).

2. Shell them, saving the skins and discarding the shells.

3. Eat the nuts.

4. Grind up the skins and roll them into a cigarette, and smoke.

Hydrangea leaves

There has been much talk about hydrangea leaves and their psychedelic qualities. You can get high from smoking hydrangea leaves, but they are a deadly poison and have been known to kill people. Do not smoke or ingest in any other fashion.

Treat drugs with respect, moderation, and common sense

One last word on drugs, because I feel that I may have created some confusion as to the actual use of drugs. They should be used as an experience in life, rather than making the experience itself outside the bounds of being. Treat drugs the same way a normal person treats alcohol—with respect, with moderation, and with basic common sense. Make it a rule not to take any capsules without first looking them up in a reference book to confirm exactly what they are. An excellent book on this is *The Drug Takers,* published by Time-Life, which includes pictures of all the common pills and capsules.

Avoid shooting or injecting any drug into yourself, and, for God's sake, have the common sense not to allow anyone else to do it. More cases of young people with hepatitis are brought into Bellevue every day just because of a lack of common sense.

Mixing barbiturates and amphetamines usually results in an insane, unpleasant experience, although there are some freaks who swear by it. Mixing barbiturates with alcohol can also be a bad scene. Most importantly, check all the facts before taking any drug.

Avoid unpleasant company when high on drugs, especially acid or mescaline, as sometimes bad company can throw an individual into a panic just as easily as he can himself. This is also true to a smaller degree with pot. Smoke with friends. Some sadistic cocksuckers have been known to play incredibly cruel games with an individual's mind while he is stoned.

If you are in the company of someone who has been given an overdose of heroin, do not panic. Walk him, keep him active, until you can get him to a doctor or hospital. In no circumstances allow him to drift off into a coma. I have heard of home remedies, such as injecting a salt solution into the person, but I have no medical verification for this, and do not recommend it.

Treat any and all drugs with respect, for most of the time they are stronger than you are.

chapter two: Electronics, Sabotage, and Surveillance

Figure 11. Eavesdropper.

This country, with its institutions, belongs to the people who inhabit it. Whenever they shall grow weary of the existing Government, they can exercise their constitutional right of amending it, or their revolutionary right to dismember or overthrow it.

Abraham Lincoln

This chapter is designed to explain and discuss an aspect of revolution that for the most part everyone has forgotten —that being its constructive elements, rather than the blind "window-smashing" nihilism that everyone is accustomed to. This chapter deals with strategy and tactics. A revolution, to be successful, must be a balance between passion and practicality. Revolution must employ the maximum amount of planning and the minimum amount of violence and destruction. Riots, street violence, and demonstrations have little place in a real insurrection. It is much harder to create than to destroy, and a revolution must be created.

This chapter does not in any way deal with symbolic protest. I detest symbolic protest, as it is an outcry of weak, middle-of-the-road, liberal eunuchs. If an individual feels strongly enough about something to do something about it, then he shouldn't prostitute himself by doing something symbolic. He should get out and do something real. The age of demonstrations is over, or at least I hope it's over. It lasted much too long as it was. Three years ago the Provos in Holland realized this and completely changed their tactics. They moved from the realm of peaceful demonstrations to that of guerrilla theater, which included rolling ball bearings at mounted police; letting several thousand mice, with hammers and sickles painted on their backs, loose at the Queen's birthday party; and threatening to pollute Amsterdam's water supply with LSD, which happened to be legal at the time. Such measures are not revolutionary in themselves, but the reaction of the military and police to these actions causes a growth of revolutionary feeling.

In Prague, during the Russian takeover, there were a multitude of underground stations ready to broadcast, there was a completely organized revolutionary press, and many a cellar was converted into a factory to manufacture Molotov cocktails and other weapons. Now the question comes up: Why is the United States so far behind these countries? Or, to phrase it another way: Why are American anarchists and revolutionaries more intent on burning flags and draft cards, than on employing constructive nonsymbolic tactics, which are directed at positive change. I guess one of the answers, or maybe part of the answer, is the myth of the difficulties in running a government. This idea that running a representative government is difficult is bullshit. I agree it becomes difficult when conflicts of interest appear on the scene, but otherwise it's as simple as running anything else. American youth is frightened of the responsibility of building a new government, frightened of themselves, and frightened most of all by their own potential actions.

A friend of mine has often said that, when the youth in the South feels threatened by the government, then the revolution will really be under way. I have come to believe him, because in the South there is a great deal more feeling toward the community. In other words, the union of the rural community has not broken down, as it has in the North. In the North the young so-called revolutionaries are fighting for ideals, rather than realistic goals. A revolution was never fought, throughout history, for ideals. Revolutions were fought for much more concrete things: food, clothes, housing, and to relieve intolerable oppression. The real duty of a revolutionary is to create and expose intolerable oppression. The rural South, when it feels that these things are in peril, will react quickly and violently, as they will be fighting for their communities, just like the Black Panthers and Young Lords are fighting for their communities. The so-called "revolutionary" students in the colleges and universities are fighting for abstract ideals. I know of no one, outside of Patrick Henry, willing to die for an abstraction.

The way inflation is rising, and the manner in which the president and congress are handling it, can all but insure a major depression in the near future. This economic disaster will act as a unifying factor, in the sense that those same longshoremen and union personnel who are so alienated from the youth of today will find themselves fighting right next to youth for their very survival. The Black Plague in London was ended by the Fire of London.

Several groups are already attempting to cultivate bonds with unions, by supporting strikes and marching on picket lines. The only problem with these groups is that they don't understand that they will never get the support of the working class while they are shouting Marxist dogma and rhetoric.

In the last few months the newspapers have been full of news about the army and G.I.s' civil liberties. It never occurred to the newspapers that some of these men went into the army with a single purpose: to create an atmosphere which would invite mutiny and rebellion. The Bolsheviks did exactly the same thing in 1914 and 1915, for the easiest way to form a liberation army is to use someone else's, especially if it belongs to your enemy. Many bases have created underground newspapers and broadsides which show a relatively large degree of freedom of speech.

Many violent and nonviolent outside groups have already formed underground railroads to help resisters and deserters into safe countries. Because of an ingrained fear of standing up by oneself, it is obvious that, as the movement grows, so will the desirability of joining the movement, and its chances for success.

The government, with the army's help, of course, has fertilized the development of one of the largest undergrounds, in Viet Nam, simply by its oppressive laws regarding the use of marihuana. This oppressive act in itself has unified more servicemen than probably all the other acts of oppression put together. A government creates its own revolution. There can be no revolt without it.

Freedom is not a commodity which is "given" to the enslaved upon demand. It is a precious reward, the shining trophy of struggle and sacrifice.

Kwame Nkrumah, *I speak of Freedom*

Electronic bugging devices

One of the largest problems with any name that sounds the least bit technical is that it frightens people to death, and they steer completely clear of what they do not understand. The field of electronic eavesdropping is the simplest and one of the cheapest methods of espionage available to the movement at this point.

Any underground movement or truly revolutionary group must keep up with the technology of the times. It is useless to fight a battle with sticks and stones. There have been claims that World War III will not be fought with atomic weapons, but rather by computers millions of miles apart: The machine that blows its fuse first, loses. Electronics play a huge role in the American life style today and will play a tremendous part in any type of insurrection that is to take place.

It seems strange that private industry and practically all the governmental agencies (not only the FBI and CIA) have been employing these tiny devices for years with fantastic success, without the individuals in the underground getting hip to the fact that they could also be used against these corporations and agencies with the same degree of success. Information is a large part of any movement, as without it groups are literally stumbling around in the dark, and whatever is accomplished is pure luck.

When the time comes that the movement needs equip-

ment and the urban struggle really takes shape, then the most obvious place to get this equipment is from the enemy. An electronic bug planted today will deliver the necessary information, when the time arrives. The location of the enemy is an extremely important thing to know, as the time will come when an entire army regiment will sweep through a community, and remove many so-called suspects for "questioning and detainment." Just as with Auschwitz, the army will provide liberal lawyers, who will become safely indignant, and scream, "I'll get this situation straightened out, just as soon as I can find out who's in charge."

Any kind of sabotage or ambush activity will be absolutely pointless without some sort of information as to the enemy's action and movement. This cannot be seen today as clearly as it will be seen in the future, as the newspapers are still allowed a token degree of freedom.

Much to our surprise, we found that a large number of Federal agencies used wiretapping despite Federal laws, State laws, and agency regulations.

. . . There are miniature microphones, some smaller than a thin dime. They can be hidden in any variety of ways. There are microphones that can be attached to a spike, and driven through the wall of one apartment to the plaster wall of the next. There are tube mikes which are built into the walls of a building when it is constructed. These gadgets are widely used by private detectives and industrial and labor spies. Surprising as it may seem, *they are in no way illegal under federal law.*

. . . Bugging conference rooms where taxpayers are interviewed, often with their attorneys, is another trick employed by the Internal Revenue Service to catch suspected tax cheats.

Senator Edward V. Long, February 2, 1966

There are several types of electronic eavesdropping or bugging devices, and I will handle each in turn. The most common form of bug is wiretapping or the monitoring of phone conversations. This is the simplest thing for any governmental agency to do, as in most cases it only takes one phone call and the officials receive complete cooperation from the phone company itself. This is a warning to all those who rap a lot over the phone; *no one is so small as not to be noticed.* If what you have to say over the phone cannot be said to a cop, better keep it to yourself.

On June 17, 1966, State Senator Mario Umana of Massachusetts, Chairman of the Massachusetts Commission on Electronic Eavesdropping Devices, told a committee on eavesdropping that the New England Telephone and Telegraph Company was running a system with which it monitored *every* telephone line in Boston over a period of more than a year.

All this may seem very complicated and technical, but in reality bugging a telephone is so simple that many schoolboys do it illegally as a joke on their parents or friends. There are many recipes for homemade phone taps, but most of these are not really effective, and store-bought products are much more efficient and very cheap.

The easiest way to install a tap is to connect a second extension to an already-present phone. This is a very primitive and outdated method today, as when you pick up the receiver there will be a click, and the phone company will register an overload on that account. A simple way to get around this is to buy a "byphone," which will allow you to listen to the phone conversation without picking up the receiver and overloading the phone line. Byphones are sold at Continental Telephone Supply for about $10. This device is installed by placing it in the slot behind any standard desk phone, and listening to the conversation by use of the earphone. It is not necessary to lift the arm of the extension phone. (See Figure 12.)

Figure 12. The byphone.

Maybe even simpler than the last tap is the induction-pickup method for monitoring phone conversations. An inductive pickup is nothing more than a household nail wrapped with tightly coiled wire and placed alongside the telephone lines. This homemade method can be effective, but, as with the first method, I strongly recommend a store-bought device. They usually run about $3 to $5. Most are simply connected to the bottom of the phone, with the wire leading from the pickup to your headset well concealed, either in the woodwork or some equally unobtrusive place.

In this same class of induction-pickup probes is what is called the "sucker." This is nothing more than an induction-pickup probe in the form of a suction cup, which can be attached to any spot on the phone. The sucker is ideal for recording messages, as it can be hooked up directly with a tape recorder. The "suckers" sell for as little as 88 cents through certain mail-order firms listed at the end of the chapter.

The actual wiretapping, that is in the news so much, is really as simple as the bugs just mentioned, but it is a little more expensive. The "black box" is a line locator which enables a person to clip the lines he is interested in and, through a transformer, listen to or record the desired conversation. The best location for use of "black boxes" is at the telephone junction itself, but they can also be used anywhere along the phone line. Most individuals who employ these boxes usually make their own, as often they are nothing more than a transformer, alligator clips, and a set of headphones, but you can purchase them from R & S Research, Inc., Houston, Texas, for about $35.

The next form of telephone bug is the line transmitter, which transmits, by way of radio waves, the phone conversation you wish to listen to. The great advantage to this is that the person doing the tapping never has to enter the premises or tamper with the phone. Also, with its tiny size, it can be concealed almost anywhere along the phone line without too much difficulty. Most of these devices work on standard FM bands, and they broadcast anywhere from 200 feet to a quarter of a mile. I can think of few things as funny or irritating to the police department as finding out that their own phones were tapped and all their conversations were being broadcast over an entire community. These little telephone radio line transmitters can be bought from several mail order houses for $45 to $60, or the plans can be purchased for $2.98 from Tri-Tron, Dallas, Texas.

These are basically the cheapest and most efficient bugs, although there are many more sophisticated devices that do all sorts of incredible things. If you're rich and have a little knowledge of electronics, then the whole field of bugging is wide open for you, as all the major electronics companies are selling ready-made bugs that can be installed in seconds. One of the most popular of these ready-made bugs looks exactly like the transmitter in a regular phone. It can be installed in less than ten seconds, as the device simply replaces the phone company's transmitter. These little mechanisms are so good that, in a lot of instances, they have even fooled the phone company. They run about $200 and are available from either Tri-Tron of Texas or from Continental Telephone in New York.

For the real dodos, pre-bugged telephones are available. The installation is nothing more than unplugging the old phone and replacing it with the new pre-bugged one. (Many professional phone tappers pose as telephone repair men.) These pre-bugged phones are sold mainly through mail order houses and run about $250.

The most sophisticated bug I have found available to the general public—and who the hell knows what the government has?—is what is called "The Infinity Transmitter." This is a device that allows the individual to dial any number, regardless of distance, and, through an electronic tone oscillator, deactivate the ring, thereby allowing the tapper to hear anything within earshot of the phone without the instrument being taken off the hook. These little wonders of our age sell for about $1,000, but I think some companies offer a discount.

What is really ironic is that people are only slowly realizing that telephone tapping is actually going on. I have spoken to some people who have just recently been busted for drugs, and they are genuinely confused. They just seem unable to understand why the cops chose their apartment to raid. If you deal dope on the phone and live in an area like Harlem or the Lower East Side, you're a fool and you deserve to get busted.

When I was living on St. Mark's Place with a friend, we had a feeling our phone was tapped, but had no proof until one day when my friend went to make a phone call. Somehow those mechanical geniuses had screwed up the tap, and we had a direct line to the desk sergeant at the 9th precinct. Needless to say, it caused many hours of amusement.

In the same class as telephone taps, and probably more dangerous, are the undercover cops and FBI men who infiltrate activist groups. It's really getting to the point where you don't know whom to trust. One point about an undercover cop in New York City, which does not apply to FBI men, is that most of them have beards but short hair. This is because the plain-clothes man is often transferred around the city and, if he managed to grow long hair, how would it look in Queens? On the other hand, FBI men are usually on the job for much longer periods of time and are able more fully to don their disguises. If you think you know a plain-clothes cop, do yourself a favor and stay clear of him and warn your friends about him. If you've got the guts, you can have a great deal of fun, since you know he's a pig, but he doesn't know that you know. The *East Village Other, The Rat,* and *The Berkeley Tribe* have all been very good over a period of time, in publishing pictures of undercover cops.

During the revolution in Ireland, the British used a very brutal and cruel form of terrorism to subdue the population. Although the idea of terrorism revolted the Irish Republican Army, they resorted to it as a last measure against the British, and it worked. There was an understanding in the Irish Republican Army that for every farmer who was killed by the British, two English civilians would die. For every farmhouse burned to the ground by the British, two Loyalists' houses would be burned. The British decided to stop their terrorist tactics.

The same type of terrorism is being practiced in every ghetto of this country today, and it is my firm belief that the only way to stop it is to show everyone what terrorism is all about, and that two can play at the same game.

Microphones

The choice of microphones for eavesdropping is an interesting one, as many different types are made, and certain ones will not be as effective as others. The microphone must be small enough to be hidden easily, and at the same time powerful enough to pick up whispers at 20 feet. These microphones can then be rigged up to voice-activated tape recorders, basic audio amplifiers, or any radio frequency transmitter.

There are several basic types of microphones, and all have disadvantages. Try to stay away from listening devices that depend on batteries for their power supply, as nearly always the batteries will die out at the important moment in the conversation. Probably the most important rule for bugging or telephone tapping is not to try to retrieve the bug after it is placed, as more buggers get caught this way than any other. Many professional tappers and buggers have learned that using two microphones instead of one is a good safeguard against one failing, but at the same time it increases the chances of someone discovering it.

The first and probably most common type of microphone is what is called the "carbon" button. These contain fine granules of carbon between thin plates of the diaphragm; as the sound strikes the diaphragm, this in turn compresses and decompresses the carbon, thus regulating the amounts of electricity passing through it (See Figure 13). These carbon buttons are used in telephones and in many microphones for cheaper tape recorders. There are a few disadvantages to this type of microphone; carbon buttons are not sensitive enough to pick up sounds over 15 feet away. They also require large amounts of power.

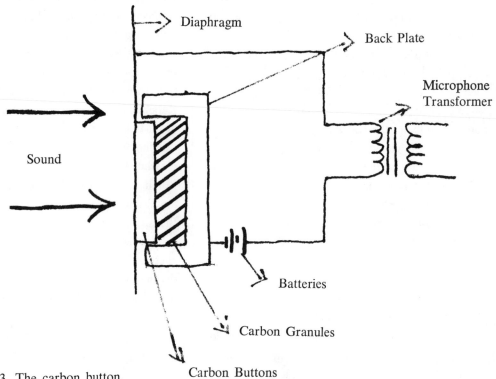

Figure 13. The carbon button.

The second type of microphone device is called the Crystal Microphone, because it employs the use of certain crystals. This is a good type of microphone because it does not need external voltage, as the crystal when subjected to pressure creates its own voltage. They are also pretty sensitive, but should be hooked up to an amplifier. The only real disadvantage in this type is that they are relatively unstable when used out of doors, and even indoor temperature changes can render them useless. They can, on the other hand, be bought for as little as 50 cents through certain mail order firms.

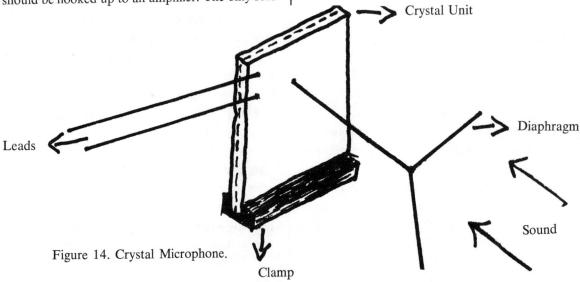

Figure 14. Crystal Microphone.

The third type of microphone is the "dynamic microphone," which is probably the most efficient and stable. It is nothing more than a loudspeaker operating in reverse. It is a rugged microphone and is sensitive, but it usually needs additional amplification.

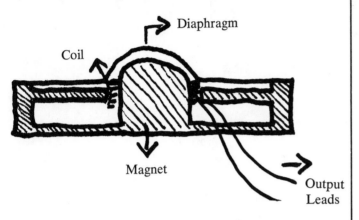

Figure 15. Dynamic Microphone.

There are too many different types of mikes manufactured to go into all of them, but the ones most suitable for bugging and espionage work will be discussed here. Some of the most popular ones are listed and pictured in the Continental catalogue. There is the sugar cube mike, which looks like a sugar cube. There are mikes that resemble ball-point pens. There are buttonhole mikes, which appear to be nothing more than a button. There are mikes manufactured within the mechanisms of watches. There are even entire units, consisting of microphone, amplifier, and recorder that are small enough to fit in a cigarette pack. The best bet is to shop around the catalogues with your various needs in mind. Undoubtedly you will find something that will meet your requirements.

There are two other snooping devices which I feel must be mentioned—mainly because they remind me of the "media myth" of the cloak-and-dagger and round-bomb-type anarchist. The first is the notorious "Snake," which is

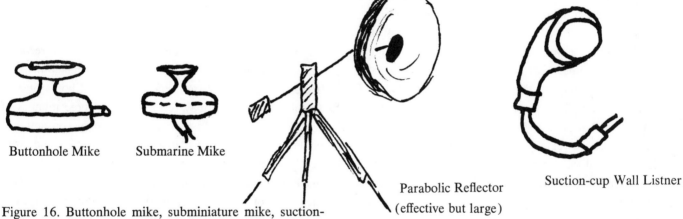

Buttonhole Mike   Submarine Mike

Parabolic Reflector
(effective but large)

Suction-cup Wall Listner

Figure 16. Buttonhole mike, subminiature mike, suction-cup wall listener, and the parabolic reflector.

the latest electronic device for keyhole listening. It is equipped with a long nose which can be easily put into any crack or keyhole, or even unreeled out a window. It can be obtained from Tri-Tron in Texas for about $40.

The other cloak-and-dagger listening device is what is called the "electronic stethoscope." This is probably the

most popular of all room-to-room listening devices. It hears and penetrates through thick walls, carpets, floors, and can record entire conversations by plugging it into any tape recorder. There is virtually no way of detecting this type of gismo. They can be purchased from Consolidated Acoustics for as little as $13.00.

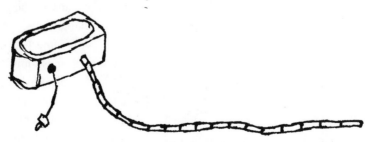

Figure 17. The snake.

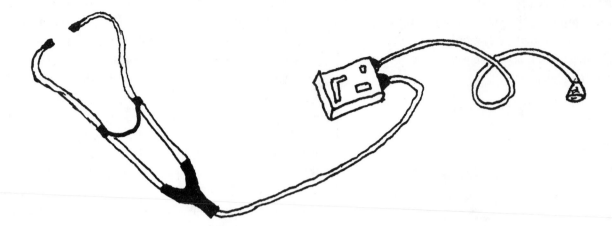

Figure 18. The electronic stethoscope.

Bumper beepers

Ever since the movie *Goldfinger,* where superspy James Bond follows supercriminal Goldfinger around Europe, everyone has been talking about "bumper beepers." These bumper beepers are ordinary bugging transmitters which, instead of sending out voices, send out beeps. Trailing automobiles becomes very easy, since the trailer can stay out of sight and rely on the beeping device to lead him. Most beepers are placed on the underside of cars, attached by either metal straps or strong magnets. The trailing car has a built-in receiver and is able to gauge the direction in which the subject car is going, the speed at which it is traveling, and the distance between the subject car and the trailer. The major difference in all these devices is the distance they cover. A medium-priced unit ($150) can usually transmit detectable beeps up to three or four miles. Continental Telephone (New York) puts out two models, both selling for $375. One is installed under the dashboard and transmits through the radio antenna, whereas the other one contains its own power source and is equipped with a powerful magnet so that it can quickly be attached to any part of the underneath of an auto. There are less expensive beepers from Fudalla & Associates (tail-A-beep for $75) and Miles Wireless Intercom, Ltd. (Car-Beeper for $150).

These beeper devices do have disadvantages, in that, however well they are hidden, a small wire must be left exposed to act as an antenna, unless you are able to use an already existing radio antenna. Also the time needed to install one of these devices is great and offers a real hazard. The best way to get one of these installed is to pay off a garage mechanic.

Voice-activated tape recorders

The most popular method of electronic espionage is telephone wiretapping. In the past this had some overwhelming disadvantages, which the voice-activated tape recorder has done away with. Any method of surveillance involves a great amount of wasted time. For several hours of continual listening, one may receive two or three minutes of useful conversation. In the past, this type of constant surveillance required that a man sit for hours on end, with headphones and a tape recorder, starting and stopping the machine. Now, this is no longer necessary, as "Vox" (the nickname of the fully automatic voice-activated tape recorder) will upon hearing a voice turn itself on, and at the termination of the conversation turn itself off. There are a few voice-activated machines on the market today. Probably the best of all is the Kinematrix's Voice-Matic, which incorporates an auto-timing device that allows the machine to distinguish between real silence and momentary lapses in conversation. This Voice-Matic sells for about $35 and should be obtainable through most of the mail order electronic supply companies listed in the back of this chapter.

To bring almost any bugging or listening device to life, the eavesdropper must employ the use of an AM or FM band receiver. This is nothing more than a normal radio tuned to one particular band. It is impossible for me to list here all the different types of receivers, as none of them is manufactured with the art of bugging in mind. Choose the type of device that best suits the individual needs of the type of surveillance work you will be involved with.

After purchasing the type of unit that best meets your requirements, keeping in mind versatility, portability, and durability, take the receiver to a local radio or TV repair shop, and have them retune it for you. By retuning it, you will have less of a problem with other, more powerful, transmitters interfering with your desired frequency. Prices vary greatly—anywhere from about $40 for a do-it-yourself kit, to $300 for a pretty sophisticated receiver. It is not necessary to purchase the transmitter and the receiver at the same time, or even at the same outlet. In fact, I would recommend that it be done separately, as many governmental agencies are extremely interested in persons purchasing this type of equipment. One doesn't have to be paranoid, just very careful, and employ common sense in whatever operation is being performed.

Electronic bug detection

Electronic bug detection will probably be the most difficult aspect of this entire field, as you will be working on your own, without the aid of much useful information that can be gathered from the telephone company or other agencies. (Most telephone bugs, except the most sophisticated ones, can be detected by an overload on the phone line itself.) A good tool for bugging detection is a normal AM-FM radio receiver, portable, with a telescopic antenna. For application, extend the antenna in the room suspected of being bugged, and tune the receiver carefully from the bottom to the top, covering all the FM frequencies, at the same time talking to yourself continually. At one point, if a bug is present, you will be able to hear your voice through the receiver, although the voice may be indistinguishable, because of top-volume feedback. This feedback will always be a deafening continuous howl, scream, or high-pitched whistle. To learn the exact location of the bug, cut the volume of the receiver, and slowly move around the room. The feedback will increase in volume as you get closer to the bug. When a bug is discovered, there is a moment of confusion and fear in regard to its elimination. In one sense, destroying a bug is an admission of guilt, and can do nothing more than provoke the enemy to rebug in a more sophisticated manner. For that reason I would hesitate to remove a bug. Instead I would attempt to use it against the bugger himself, by feeding him false and misleading information.

In some cases, the bugger may have taken precautions against this type of detection and, by readjustment of his oscillating capacitor, he may be transmitting on a range below the sensitivity of your radio. In this case, employ your television set in the same manner as you did with your radio, using the ultrahigh frequency knob. As you move across the range of frequencies, keep your eyes on the picture, until you have found a pattern of dark wavy lines that move in relation to your own voice, coupled with top-volume feedback. The actual location of the bug is a little more difficult, unless your TV set is battery operated, but by use of several extension cords and slow movement this can be accomplished.

This feedback technique can also be used when the bugging involves CB (citizen band) walkie-talkie. One of the simplest methods of bugging is to tape down the transmitter button on a cheap walkie-talkie, and plant it where the conversation is to be held. The process of detection is exactly the same as above, except that, instead of using a radio or TV set, one uses a tunable citizen band receiver to check for feedback.

Although the previous "feedback technique" can be effective, it is time-consuming and not 100 percent efficient. For these reasons, electronic experts have invented and marketed a small meter, which detects transmitters. The interesting problem that these experts had to overcome was, with all the high-powered radio and TV stations transmitting, how would it be possible for an individual to detect a low-powered transmitter, such as a microphone? This was overcome by simply reversing the gauge. In other words, when the meter was "wide open," no signal was present. However, the closer the meter is taken to the transmitting device, the less of a reading the meter registers. These field-strength meters are available from most large electronic companies and range in price from about $10 to $200, depending on quality and strength.

A device similar to the "strength meter," which a Texas company has marketed, utilizes a small bulb, which blinks only in the presence of a bug. The true value of this device is that it is capable of separating normal radio waves (which do not affect it) from the dangerous radio signals emitted from a bug. It is available from Dee Company, Houston, Texas, for about $200.

If you're not electronically minded, or just not equipped to find the tap on your phone, Continental Telephone has a device that allows you, through the use of its meter, to determine if the wire is tapped, and, if so, where it is located. Unfortunately this device (called "the Private Sentry") costs $250.

Electronic jamming

Most of the devices written about so far in this chapter are legal, with regulations placed on their application, but the very possession of certain jamming devices is illegal. These jamming devices basically destroy the effectiveness of a bug rather than locate it. The reason the Federal Communications Commission has put strict regulations on these is the effect they have on other means of communications, such as completely destroying AM radio reception, rendering TV sets useless, making communications on police band radios impossible, and even to some degree interfering with aircraft communications. To be truly effective as anti-bugging devices they must cover the whole spectrum of radio frequencies, which in turn will cause interference to other outside receivers and transmitters. For this reason control is of the essence. When determining what exactly you wish to jam, you must also determine the frequency to be used, so as not to interfere with other signals. If you decide to use a jamming device for an illegal purpose, you must at all costs maintain mobility. (Jamming from the back of a moving truck has been proven effective.) Mobility is necessary, because the FCC also employs detecting and locating devices for use against underground radio stations and unregulated jamming devices.

There are basically two types of jamming devices, the first of which is not manufactured commercially and would have to be built by the individual. This type is called "spark-gap device," and is more powerful than the other, covering a much greater distance. The second type is referred to as "the white noise device," and is manufactured by Continental Telephone, Dectron Industries, Inc., and Telsec, with a price range from about $150 to $350, depending on strength.

Electronic scramblers

Electronic scramblers are devices that simply act as anti-bug mechanisms by transforming normal speech patterns into unintelligible sounds. The most primitive method, outdated today, is recording a message on a tape recorder, and then transmitting it, either by playing it backward or at a different speed. Although this method may momentarily frustrate the bugger, if he has half a brain, it won't take him long to decode your message. The basic principle of scramblers, or any coding device, is to render the message useless to anyone except the desired recipient in control of the decoding device.

There are several types of electronic scramblers, all effective but all sharing the same disadvantage—price. The most inexpensive one I found in any catalogue ran about $500, but then anyone with a slight knowledge of burglary will not be put off by this obstacle. This most popular type is manufactured by Dectron, and is used as an extension to the telephone. The speech is garbled before it enters the mouthpiece of the phone, and decoded after it has left the receiver. A pair of these run just over $500, but the real disadvantage to these devices is that the individual code your devices are working with is retained in a vault by the company, so that anyone with access to that vault can break down your security.

The second device used for scrambling is manufactured by an English company, and it works on the principle of inverting the normal speech patterns. In other words, it makes low notes high, and high notes low. This offers the individual a little bit more security, as each person's speech frequency is as different as his fingerprints. Their major disadvantage is price. It sells for between $1,000 and $1,500.

The third type of scrambler is used only for radio transmission. This device can also be purchased through Dectron, for about the same price as mentioned before. The radio scrambler works on basically the same principle as all other scrambling devices, in that it inverts or disorders the frequency and pitch of the speech pattern while it is being transmitted, and then reverses the garble to render it understandable to the receiver.

Mail order and retail electronics outlets

I have listed below some of the major electronic mail order and retail outlets. Many companies that sell this type of equipment do so only to police officers, and require the purchaser to prove his relationship with some law enforcement agency. For that reason they have not been included. The companies listed are all involved in the manufacturing and/or sale of eavesdropping and surveillance equipment.

S.A.C. Electronics, 4818 West Jefferson Blvd., Los Angeles 18, California

Baker Electronics Co., R.R. 3, Greencastle, Indiana (mail-order plans and kits only)

Dehart Electronics, P.O. Box 5232, Sarasota, Florida

Continental Telephone Supply Co., 17 W. 46th St., New York, N.Y. (fantastic catalogue)

Martel Electronics Sales, Inc., 2356 S. Cotner Ave., Los Angeles, California

R & S Research, Inc., 2049 Richmond Ave., Houston, Texas

Mittleman Manny, 136 Liberty St., New York, N.Y. (only custom devices—$400 and up)

Clifton, 11500 N.W. 7th Ave., Miami, Florida

Consolidated Acoustics, 1302 Washington St., Hoboken, N.J. (only listening devices)

Ekkottonics Co., P.O. Box 5334, Milwaukee, Wisconsin (cheap)

Dectron Industries, Inc., 13901 Saticoy St., Van Nuys, California (only anti-bugging equipment)

Dee Co., Box 7263, Houston, Texas 77008

Tri-Tron of Dallas, 330 Casa Linda Plaza, Dallas, Texas (discount bugging equipment)

Security Electronics, 11 East 43rd St., New York, N.Y.

Telephone Dynamics Corp., 1333 Newbridge Road, North Bellmore, N.Y. (only miniature microphones)

Simlar Electronics, Inc., 3476 N.W. 7th St., Miami, Florida

Tracer Systems, 256 Worth Ave., Palm Beach, Florida

The Federal Communications Commission and the Supreme Court have been uptight about wiretapping and eavesdropping for some time. They have both passed laws and made regulations concerning electronic surveillance. For these reasons, I would emphasize the utmost care and knowledge in the application of these devices. What is interesting is the actual wording of the law, where any interstate wiretap (interstate does not mean interstate, it applies to all tapping through some strange logic) except in a matter of security is against the FCC's regulations and is punishable by a fine of no more than $10,000 or five years in jail. The neat little exception made for security gives all of the government agencies, particularly the FBI and CIA, and all local police departments, free license to practice all and any forms of surveillance without any restrictions. Although certain cases have been dismissed in court cases because of "tainted" methods of collecting evidence, in reality if the government feels an individual is a security risk (for any reason) it can produce tapes in court that have been gathered by wiretapping, supposedly not as evidence, but the defendant goes to jail anyway.

America, at this point, is operating on a life-size Monopoly Board. Everyone who isn't in jail or going directly to jail is buying and selling thousands of pieces of paper, with absolute seriousness of purpose, unable to realize that there will be only one winner, and when he gets out of jail, he's going to kick all their asses.

Broadcasting free radio

In any underground, throughout history, a prime concern has been communications or propaganda. Propaganda, as a word, has ugly connotations, but in reality it means nothing more than the distribution of information. This country has begun to develop an underground network of communications, in the many small newspapers which have cropped up all over the country. Although there is a spark, there is also a monstrous lack of communications, once you get outside any of the large metropolitan areas. In preparation for writing this book, I had to do a great deal of reference work. In this reading I encompassed almost all extremities of the political spectrum, from far left to far right. These extremities are so alike, and could be so powerful if they ever got over their preconceived impressions of each other and started to communicate. This is the reason I feel the underground has to take propaganda one step further, from the printed page, to the radio broadcast.

> The radio is a factor of extraordinary importance. At moments when war fever is more or less palpitating in every one region or a country, the inspiring, burning word increases this fever and communicates it to every one of the future combatants. It explains, teaches, fires, and fixes the future positions of both friends and enemies. However, the radio should be ruled by the fundamental principle of popular propaganda, which is truth; it is preferable to tell the truth, small in its dimensions, than a large lie artfully embellished.
>
> Che Guevara, *Guerrilla Warfare*

Kwame Nkrumah, in his *Handbook of Revolutionary Warfare,* also stresses the use of radio propaganda. He breaks it down into two basic forms: The first and most important is the same as Che was writing about in the above quotation, this being to communicate truth to people of the country about the struggle. Nkrumah takes this idea one step further, and says that really to communicate the underground must speak on many different levels, and this is a key point. How can an anarchist who has a right-wing background understand or relate to a left-wing anarchist, who uses Marxist terminology? This forces the underground to communicate with many different frames of reference. This hasn't happened in this country: Everyone from far left to the far right is hung up with dogmatic ideals, overused terminology, and is absolutely blind to practicality.

Nkrumah's second concept of propaganda is for the purpose of subverting the enemy.

An indispensable preliminary to battle is to attack the mind of the enemy, to undermine the will to fight so that the result of the battle is decided before the fighting begins. The revolutionary army attacks an irresolute and demoralized army.

—Nkrumah, *Handbook of Revolutionary Warfare*

This use of propaganda to discourage the enemy has also a great place in the struggle that is going on in this country today. It has been used to a small degree, with fantastic success, around military bases. There was a regiment of the National Guard that refused to go to Chicago during the National Democratic Convention. Underground newspapers and handbills have encouraged G.I.s to dissent and desert, and have shown them that it is possible. The effectiveness demonstrated by this demoralizing form of propaganda depicts nothing more than the real turmoil that exists. The successful effect of this communication has resulted from one aspect of its nature—that being its passionate regard for truth.

Printing a revolutionary newspaper is a great deal easier than forming an underground radio station. Although the government has strict restrictions on printed material, it is nothing like the regulations it places on radio and television broadcasting. The FCC runs the radio networks with an iron hand, with the ever present threat of revoking a license. For this reason, any radio station which is striving to be absolutely free must make the ultimate break with the FCC. This can be accomplished in two ways. The first and most dangerous, but at the same time the most effective, is by using high power equipment, jamming out other stations, from a mobile base of operations. The FCC has incredibly sophisticated equipment, and can locate any pirate radio station in a matter of minutes. For this reason, mobility is essential. Transmitting from the back of a disguised truck has been used successfully, although the movement of the truck while broadcasting must be constant, never repeating the same pattern, but at the same time keeping within the broadcast power area. This means of transmission is especially effective at gatherings, such as demonstrations and riots, to keep people informed as to the movement of the enemy. The best method of obtaining equipment is building your own, as to buy a large transmitter requires the individual to be licensed. Not only that, it's expensive. You can build your own from plans and equipment purchased through mail order, from most of the companies listed earlier in this chapter.

The second method for getting around the strict FCC regulations is legal. Under the FCC's low-power-transmission regulations, one can legally broadcast below 100 milowatts at any empty space on the AM or FM dial, without registering or being licensed. The disadvantages are obvious: One can only broadcast up to one mile. Even within that mile, interference from the high-powered commercial stations is present. And if enough people get into this form of broadcasting the FCC is going to make some sort of regulation against it. This method is not just theoretical, it has been implemented on the Lower East Side, by John Giorno and his Guerrilla Radio. He broadcast from the top of St. Mark's-in-the-Bowerie's bell tower at 1400 on the AM dial, and claims he did everything the FCC said he couldn't. I am sorry to say I did not hear the broadcast, as I was out of the one-mile area at the time.

Telephone and communications sabotage

Telephone sabotage can be applied on many levels. First I will explain what I am not going to write about. I feel there is no need for me to explain how to make free phone calls by telling the operator that you dialed the wrong number, just as I am not going to get into explaining how to use a number 14 washer with Scotch tape in a pay phone, or cheating on credit card calls, or spitting on a penny. These are all explained in *Fuck the System,* a pamphlet on living freely in New York City. The interest I have in telephone sabotage is purely communicational and commercial.

Commercial in the sense, that over the past few years my absolute hatred of vending machines and pay phones has led me to break into almost every kind I could find. Parking meters are the easiest by far: All you need is a hammer and chisel or a large monkey wrench. Soda machines are almost as easy, but real delight comes from ripping a Kotex machine off the wall of a women's rest room, or sticking a small explosive charge in the coin slot of a pay toilet. I have never been able to break into a pay telephone—smash them, yes, put them out of order, but never able to open them up and remove the coins. This is for several reasons: One is the time element, as most public phones are easily seen, and the other is that all public phones are installed with amazing locks, which have completely baffled me.

To get back to the purpose of this section, I must emphasize the importance of breaking down the enemy's communications. This in turn results in confusion and chaos. Imagine, for a moment, a squad car without a means of communicating with its precinct, or an enemy aircraft with its radio jammed. This act of breaking down the enemy's lines of communications is not an end in itself, rather it is a tactic—a small, but extremely important, part of a total operation.

When considering communications, it is best to start from a primitive base and work up to more sophisticated tactics. The first and simplest method for rendering a telephone inoperative is only temporary. It entails calling the phone company and asking that a certain number be disconnected. This will work for individuals, but not for agencies or law enforcement organizations. An important factor in any form of telephone sabotage is the time aspect of verification—in other words, the amount of time it takes the phone company to trace a call. The phone company can tell right away if you are calling from a pay phone, so this should be avoided. Call from a private phone which you cannot be connected with, and limit your conversation to under ninety seconds. *Important:* Most law enforcement organizations, companies, corporations, and businesses have more than one phone line, and in most cases one or more will be unlisted.

A common misconception is that a person can render a phone useless by dialing a number and, before the party answers, leave the phone off the hook. This is not true, and doesn't work. Even if the caller doesn't hang up his phone, the receiver can get a dial tone by hanging up himself and holding the hook down for a little over thirty seconds. Although this method does not work in the city (I know be-

cause I have experimented with it), I have heard reports that it has been used in rural areas with varying degrees of success. I would suggest trying it out with a friend, to see if it is effective in your area.

The other truly effective method is the most dangerous. It entails the actual cutting of phone wires. This is much easier in a rural area where the phone lines are above the ground, and there are not so many of them. It should be noted that complete telephone communication with a small town or village can be broken in less than ten minutes. Probably the most important thing here is having a complete understanding of what you are doing, and using the correct tools. Phone lines do carry electrical charges and, without complete knowledge of what you are doing and without the correct tools, it would be very easy to electrocute yourself. In rural areas, the basic tools should be: rubber-soled shoes (sneakers); pliers with rubber grips; large heavy-duty wire or tin cutters, also with rubber grips; a pair of surgical rubber gloves; a small flashlight (operate at night); and a body strap to allow you free movement of your hands once at the top of the pole. *Important,* before attempting any telephone wire cutting, get hold of a copy of the telephone repairman's manual, and read it.

This same operation can be performed in urban areas, although the process is much more involved. In most urban areas the phone lines run beneath the street level, and they are usually incorporated into tunnels dug for the sewers. At this point it may seem simple but, in addition to the phone lines in the sewers, there are also all the high-voltage electric lines. If you cut into one of these, I don't care how well insulated you are, you'll fry. An urban saboteur should either be in possession of a detailed map of the phone lines, available at any municipal library, or carry a small electric line locator, so that he can find the right line to cut. The urban guerrilla, on this sort of mission, should carry all the tools the rural guerrilla would have, except he should exchange the body strap for a rubber-insulated hack saw, also add a crowbar. The hack saw is for the metal encasement that surrounds all phone and electric wires in the sewers. Access to the sewers is pretty easy, as most manholes will take you into an amazing complex of all different-sized tunnels, where you can get thoroughly lost, unless you have had the foresight to study a map of the sewers, also available from any municipal library. Know exactly where you are going, know all the obstacles that you may come in contact with, and have several routes of escape planned, in case of an emergency. Needless to say, if you decide to go into the sewers, dress accordingly. It's cold, damp, infested with rodents, and dark, and many tunnels are partially full of water.

A word of caution about using explosives to sever phone lines: In the sewers, don't. In Paris in 1945, the French resistance decided that to aid the oncoming Allied troops, they would cut all lines of communication from the Nazi Headquarters and Berlin. This proved unsuccessful, for many reasons, but the important fact was that they did attempt to use explosives in the sewer system. A small charge was placed right on the phone lines, and detonated from a good distance away. The phone line was cut but, unknown to the resistance, so was a gas main, right next to lines. The result: phone lines cut, a large number of civilians dead, and a block and a half completely leveled. Not only was the area totally destroyed, it was flooded by the bursting of water mains which also shared the sewers with the phone wires.

One can use small explosive charges in rural areas, as the lines are above the ground.

I despise you.
I despise your order, your false-propped authority.
Hang me for it ! ! !

—Louis Lingg, 1898

Other forms of sabotage

A great deal of sabotage employs the use of explosive charges, but these methods will be discussed in a later chapter; here I will attempt to discuss nonexplosive sabotage operations. Sabotage plays a very important role in any form of warfare, especially in the guerrilla struggle. The urban areas are extremely conducive to the type of sabotage I will be dealing with in this section, as the distances are short between targets, and it is easier to create chaos and havoc when dealing with large numbers of people, in a relatively small area. This havoc and chaos that I have been talking about needs a definition, since I am using the terms in a different context than what they mean traditionally. Havoc and chaos are and should be the smallest part of the revolution. They take the smallest amount of time, and the maximum amount of planning. This time will be governed by a mob, driven not by fear, but by anger, and the passionate belief that they do what they do because they are the people, and more importantly they believe they have impunity. I do not speak of the tactics of nihilism, breaking windows and setting garbage cans on fire, for they accomplish nothing.

A few of the more active individuals in New York City placed a strong form of epoxy glue in all the keyholes of the stock market, on Wall Street. When this substance dried, it hardened into a material as tough as steel. The Stock Exchange opened three hours late, after locksmiths had been called in to remove the useless mechanisms. Epoxy glue is fantastic, and its uses are unlimited.

Since machines run the society we live in, it's only fair that an equal degree of destructive creativity be leveled against them. Computers, because of their very nature, are extremely easy to render inoperative. When paying bills by computer, always remember that you have the ultimate advantage of an open mind, and the ability to rationalize, whereas the machine is programmed to do one thing. A good method of sabotage is simply to punch a few extra holes in the IBM card. Most of the time the card will be rejected, and it will cost the company a few dollars to rectify the mistake. I have heard of people who have performed this operation, and have been issued several hundred dollars' worth of credit. This can be performed with impunity.

When I was working for a large New York corporation, I had to deal with a bank, every day. I realized, after a period of time, that the people who were working at the bank had lost their identities, and were nothing more than machines themselves. Well, this sort of psychological sur-realistic science fiction really got me interested. I viewed myself as a saver of identities, as the Messiah of the Spirit of Individualism. I was brought to earth quickly. These people didn't want to be saved. I was going to turn them all on to acid, but then I decided that a better tactic would be to screw up the object of their emulation, the computer. On my daily deposit I placed a large quantity of Scotch tape. This resulted in the deposit slips, themselves, getting stuck in the bowels of the computer. It took the bank three or four hours to take the machine apart, and unjam the mechanism. In unjamming the machine they somehow altered the program, and it didn't work right for weeks. I never had the guts to return to the bank, but I hope the clerks lost their reverence for the divine, infallible machine.

Another form of sabotage is shoplifting. There is a big

difference between a common thief and a revolutionary: The revolutionary will steal from large corporations, and the common thief will steal from anyone. If you can ever get over the Protestant ethic, you will be able to see what I mean. Every revolutionary has his own method of stealing, and there are too many for me to get into, but I will try to state some basic common-sense tactics.

1. Operate in pairs with one person holding the employee's attention, the other stealing him blind.

2. As a revolutionary, your job is to rally popular support, not to alienate people. For this reason, do not steal from small stores.

3. Get into and out of the store as fast as possible. Do not spend a long time trying to hide the merchandise, or making sure no one's looking at you.

4. If you are caught, play along. In other words, be humble, and pretend to be nervous. Always apologize profusely, and even cry if you can. The chances are good the store won't have you arrested.

5. If you are caught and let go with a warning, never return to the same store.

6. Usually large department stores do not arrest shoplifters the first time, unless they are violent, or the merchandise is over a certain dollar value. Be careful all the same.

7. Circular mirrors are very popular with large stores, where blind corners are present. These can effectively be used against the employees by simply reversing their purpose. *Watch out for two-way mirrors.*

8. If you're going to get into shoplifting in a big way, check out all its aspects. A large store located near a big subway stop, (Times Square, Grand Central, or Penn Station) offers a great means of escape, especially in the rush hour, if a chase develops.

9. Never carry identification with you. Work out a system with a friend (see the last chapter) whereby he will be able to verify your false name and address.

10. Needless to say, never carry dope, weapons, or anything else illegal with you.

11. If caught for shoplifting or robbery never admit to being part of the movement. It will get you more time in jail.

Another extremely easy method of sabotage can be employed against motor vehicles. Law enforcement cars, jeeps, weapons carriers, all the way up to tanks, can be rendered useless by several simple operations. The first of these is the simplest, but it is only temporary. It entails removing an important part of the vehicle's mechanism, such as the distributor cap or battery. There is no doubt that this will work, and can be accomplished in a matter of seconds, but the vehicle can also be repaired in a matter of seconds, if the parts are available.

The second method, which is equally effective, and by no means temporary, can also be performed in a matter of seconds. It is accomplished by pouring several pounds of either sand or sugar into the vehicle's gas tank. This results in these foreign particles jamming and virtually destroying the motor. The sugar will crystallize in the fuel line and carburetor and effectively block the operation of the engine. The sand, on the other hand, will rip the inside of the engine to shreds. Both of these ingredients will stop the operation of a vehicle permanently, as repair would require a complete overhaul of the engine, which is usually impossible in combat situations.

The third method is total destruction of the vehicle, by burning or exploding. An important thing to keep in mind, before destroying anything, is the use it might have to the movement. To burn a car, just siphon some of the gasoline out of its tank, by means of a section of hollow tube, and pour it over the car. If the car is locked, smash the windows and soak the inside with gas also, then ignite.

A very important thing to remember in any form of subversive activity is to allow an escape route. Things are bound to go wrong, I don't care how many precautions a person takes there will be something he hasn't thought of. Cars are an excellent method of escape. Of course it helps a great deal when stealing a car, if the person has left his keys in the ignition, but, if not, there are other ways. Any auto repair manual can tell you how to jump the ignition, or "hot wire" a car. Volkswagens are extremely easy. Another trick which can be used with old Chevrolets (before 1964) is to catch a car with the ignition switch on "OFF." The keys can be extracted from the ignition of an old Chevie without locking it. The car's engine will be off, but it can be started by simply turning the receptacle for the key, and stepping on the gas pedal. I drove a car from New York to Florida without a key.

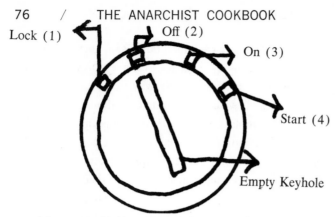

Lock (1)   Off (2)   On (3)   Start (4)   Empty Keyhole

Figure 19. Keyhole for typical pre-1964 Chevie.

The car may be started without a key when it is left in any of the positions (2, 3, 4).

There are a few basic rules for sabotage and guerrilla activity in general:

1. Make sure the operation will be effective. Never waste time with either a violent or nonviolent operation which is ineffective.

2. Hit the enemy where they least expect it, and where it will hurt them the most.

3. Most sabotage should be carried out at night.

4. Timing must be perfect, as the longer the operation takes the greater the chances are of something going wrong.

5. Work only with people you trust. Many spies and informers will suggest plans that could only get you busted. Work in small groups, or cells, consisting of no more than four people.

6. All operations should be simple and fast, and several means of escape should be planned.

7. All weapons should be concealed, all explosives should be treated with the respect they deserve. (Check the chapter on explosives for correct handling.)

8. All groups must have a leader. He should be picked for his leadership qualities. He will make all major decisions.

9. The need for secrecy is obvious. Security and secrecy must be maintained without reservation.

10. Any member who breaks the code of the group must be executed, in full view of the other members.

The time has passed for demonstrators and pseudo-revolutionaries and students to occupy the political scene. The time is here for a mass uprising, incorporating all these elements, armed with single-minded deadly intolerance.

There is no justice in bureaucracy for the individual, for bureaucracy caters only to itself. The writers, artists, and poets of the revolution will have a job that has never before

in history been so great, for they must create a value structure for the New World, for The New American. I stated in the introduction that this would not be in a contemporary sense a political book, and I feel that it is not, inasmuch as I have tried to avoid using the dogma that is so prevalent now. It seems acceptable today to scream for revolution, without any concept of what will follow it. This is just what the forces at large want, for who will follow a man who doesn't know where he's going?

To be successful, man must change himself, the individual must have a revolution within himself, for then and only then will he be able to change the world. There is no room for narrow-mindedness in the coming insurrection. Each man must break, with passionate understanding, the chains which chain him to himself. For if one man dies in indifference, the entire revolution dies with him. One cannot practice the same bureaucracy one is fighting against; the revolution is secondary, the system is secondary, politics is secondary, to the individual.

Effective sabotage, like the practical joke, must employ a grain of truth in a solution of deadly irony. This means that sabotage serves two basic purposes: first of all to weaken the enemy, and second of all to build the morale of the liberation army. Although revolution and sabotage are deadly serious, one should always retain his sense of humor and apply it if possible to the operations used. An example, which can be employed today with the draft system, is to use the weaknesses of the bureaucracy against itself.

When a young man is forced to go down to his local board and register for the draft, he is required to give only a small amount of information. To use this fact effectively against the Selective Service System, a large group of young men must go to a local board and register twice or three times under false names, in addition to their real registration. This will cause the bureaucracy of the Selective Service System to go berserk. They're already so uptight about people attempting to avoid the draft that they would really flip out if all of a sudden their records showed that several hundreds or thousands of people just didn't show up, and couldn't be traced. It would never enter their heads to think it might have been a put-on. An interesting theatrical twist to this same idea is to have everyone do his false registrations on the same day, so that many, many pre-induction physicals are due on the same day. Thus the full impact of the missing persons will hit the induction center at one time.

chapter three: Natural, Nonlethal, and Lethal Weapons

**The right to keep
and bear arms**

It is not a matter of being compelled to break eggs before an omelet can be made, but the eggs doing their own breaking in order to be able to aspire to omelethood.

—Sufi

It is criminal to teach a man not to defend himself when he is the constant victim of brutal attacks.

—Malcolm X

As I have stressed before, men, not weapons or equipment, make up a revolution. A revolution is made up of ideas that cannot be implemented without struggle. But struggle is no goal unto itself, nihilism is a childish answer to adult problems. When thinking about weapons, one must bear several things in mind: the availability of these weapons and ammunition, the effectiveness of the weapons, and the portability of the weapons. When struggling with an enemy that is more powerful than the guerrilla army, an excellent tactic is using the enemy's weapons, since there is a virtually unlimited supply of parts and ammunition. All weapons that are not stolen from the enemy should be paid for in full, as a revolutionary's purpose is to rally popular support, rather than alienate the people he is supposedly fighting for.

By weapons, I do not mean to say just firearms. In this chapter I will try to cover most of the weapons a revolutionary or guerrilla would need. These needs will differ somewhat from rural and urban locations. I will attempt to cover not only the weapons that are available to the individual, but also weapons employed by the army and the police force. This will be for two purposes: first to acquaint the freedom fighter with what he will be up against, and secondly to inform him on the use of these weapons once captured.

This chapter could be quite large. For that reason, I have broken it down into several basic sections, with demolitions following in the next chapter. The first section will cover hand-to-hand combat, one's natural weapons, and a few hand weapons—both police and civilian. These devices will encompass equipment available from suppliers, equipment that can be stolen, and equipment that can be made at home. The next section will cover lethal weapons (handguns, rifles, shotguns, and larger machine guns).

The last section will discuss the use of chemical agents and gas, both defensively and offensively. An important factor to bear in mind at this point in the revolution is the legality of these weapons. Most of the weapons that are described in the following chapter are illegal and possession, whether concealed or not, can lead to long jail terms. For that reason I strongly re-emphasize security, secrecy, and the fact that the application of these weapons must be careful, deliberate, and extremely well planned.

I have no patience with individuals who claim that everything will be beautiful if guns and other weapons are outlawed. These people do not have the foresight to realize that, if weapons are made illegal, they will only be possessed by enemies of the people (i.e., the army, the police, outlaws, and madmen). I feel very strongly that every person should be armed and that he or she should be prepared for the worst. There is no justice left in the system. The only real justice is that which the individual creates for himself, and the individual is helpless without a gun. This may sound like the dogma expounded by radical right-wing groups, like the Minute Men. It is.

Unity is the only way in which the people of this country can overthrow the fascists, communists, capitalists, and all the other assholes who claim running a representative government is so difficult. The emphasis has been taken from the Bill of Rights and placed on the type of interpretation of the Constitution that best suits the people in power.

Natural weapons

A chapter on weapons should begin with the basics—those being the primitive, but effective, maneuvers of the body, for the purpose of killing a man. I will not try to get into judo, karate, or any other form of sporting combat, for that would take a book in itself. What I will try to do with this section is describe the basic methods of killing another man with one's own hands. If this turns your stomach, just remember that your enemy does know what he's doing, and, if you don't, he then has the obvious advantage. Two good reference works on this subject are *The Special Forces Combatant Manual* and *The Marine Corps Field Manual on Physical Security*. This training is of great use to any person interested in revolution in a serious sense. It will build confidence in the individual and take away false security and reliance on a firearm. It is also useful for night patrols, and for sabotage missions where silence is of the essence. There are five basic fundamentals of hand-to-hand combat:

1. Make full use of any and all available weapons.

2. Attack aggressively, if possible by surprise, using maximum strength against your enemy's weakest point.

3. Maintain your balance at all times and destroy your enemy's.

4. Maneuver your enemy in such a way as to use his momentum to his disadvantage.

5. Learn each phase of the training before trying to attain speed. Precision is, at the beginning, more important.

Hand-to-hand combat

When engaged in hand-to-hand combat, your life is always at stake, and you should recognize that fact. Using any available weapon is just common sense. Throwing sand in the enemy's eyes can result in temporary blindness and confusion; this should be taken advantage of immediately. There is only one purpose in hand-to-hand combat, and that is to kill. Never face an enemy with the idea of knocking him out. The chances are extremely good that he will kill you.

When a weapon is not available, one must resort to the full use of his natural weapons. The natural weapons are: the knife edge of your hands, fingers folded at the second joint or knuckle; the protruding knuckle of your second finger; the heel of your hand; the little finger edge of your hand; your boot; elbow; knees; and teeth.

Attacking is a primary factor. A fight was never won by defensive action, and this is not a high school brawl, this is a matter of life and death. Attack with all your strength. At any point or in any situation some vulnerable point on your enemy's body will be open for attack. Do so screaming, as a scream has two purposes: first, to frighten and confuse your enemy; second, to allow you to take a deep breath, which in turn will put more oxygen in your blood stream, and afford you more strength than you would normally have. Your balance and the balance of your opponent are very important factors; since, if you succeed in making your enemy lose his balance, the chances are nine to one you can kill him in the next move. The best overall stance for hand-to-hand combat is where your feet are spread about a shoulder's width apart, with your right foot about a foot ahead of the left. Both arms should be bent at the elbows parallel to each other, either side of the face and throat. Stand on the balls of your feet, and bend slightly at the waist, somewhat like a boxer's crouch. Employing a yell or scream, or sudden movement with either hand, can throw your enemy off-balance.

There are many vulnerable points to the body, and the next several pages will cover each briefly, with explanations of direct attack.

Eyes: Temporary or permanent blindness can be induced by several means, first by forming a "V" shape with your index and middle fingers and driving them into your opponent's eyes, keeping a stiff wrist and fingers. Done with force this can be permanent. The thumb or middle knuckle can be used in gouging the eyes.

Nose: The nose is an extremely vulnerable point of attack. It can be struck with the knife edge of the hand, across the bridge. This will cause breakage, sharp pain, temporary blindness, and, if the blow is hard enough, death, as the nose bone with force can be driven up into the brain. Another method of attacking the nose is to deliver an upward blow with the heel of your hand. This will have the same effect as the blow on the bridge.

Adam's apple: The Adam's apple is usually pretty hard to get at, because anyone who values his life has learned to keep his chin down, but if you find you do have an opening, strike a hard blow with the knife edge of your hand. This can either be a forearm or backarm blow. The chances are, if you connect with a hard blow, your enemy will die, with a severed windpipe, but if the blow was only partially effective you may still find your enemy in severe pain or gagging. Another method of attack on a man's Adam's apple is squeezing it between your forefinger and thumb.

Temple: An enemy can easily be killed by a sharp blow to the temple, as there are a large nerve and an artery close to the skin. A heavy blow delivered with the knife edge of your hand will kill instantly. A moderate blow to the temple will cause severe pain and concussion. If you succeed in knocking your enemy down, kick him hard in the temple, with the toe or heel of your boot. It will insure that he will never get up again.

Nape of the neck: A rabbit punch, or blow delivered with the knife edge of the hand to the base of the neck, can easily kill a man by breaking his neck, but to be safe it is better to use another weapon, such as the butt of a gun, or a hammer. If you can knock your opponent to the ground, apply a kick to the back of his neck with either a knee drop or the heel of your boot. Generally speaking, the side or heel of the boot is a better weapon than the toe, as it tends to slide off the object it is attacking.

Upper lip: The point where the nose cartilage joins the upper section of the jaw is where a large network of nerves is located. This network of nerves is extremely close to the skin, and a sharp upward blow, with the knife edge of your hand, will cause extreme pain and unconsciousness.

Ears: Coming up behind the enemy and cupping the hands in a clapping motion over the victim's ears can kill him also immediately. The vibrations caused from the clapping motion will burst the victim's eardrums, and cause internal bleeding in the brain.

Chin: Ever since the cowboy movies got a firm hold on the American people, every other punch has been directed at the chin. The chin isn't that vulnerable. An effective blow can be delivered with the heel of the hand, but stay away from swinging with a closed fist. More fingers are broken and wrists sprained by people swinging with a closed fist.

Groin: This is the one spot that everyone who has ever been in a fight is conscious of, and tries to defend. If it is left open, attack viciously with your knee in an upward motion. A person can also use his fist or heel, especially if he has managed to floor his opponent.

Solar plexus: The solar plexus is a large network of nerves located at the bottom of the rib cage. A blow should be struck slightly upward with the protruding knuckle of the middle finger. A sharp blow can cause severe pain and unconsciousness.

Spine: The spinal column houses the spinal nerves, and a well-directed blow to this region can easily kill or paralyze an enemy. The only really effective means of delivery for a blow of this sort is after you succeed in knocking your enemy to the ground. The blow can be made by either the knee, elbow, heel, or toe. It should be directed about two inches above the belt line, as this is where the spine is least protected.

Kidneys: A large nerve that branches off the spinal cord comes very close to the skin at the kidneys, and a direct blow to the kidneys can cause death. To attack this area, you can either use the knife edge of your hand or a fist that is folded at the second knuckle. If you have knocked your opponent to the ground, a blow may be delivered with the toe or heel.

Collar bone: A sharp blow delivered with either your elbow or the knife edge of your hand can break the collar bone and bring an enemy to his knees.

Floating ribs: The floating ribs are sensitive parts of the body and can either be attacked from the front or back. It is best to attack and deliver a blow to the enemy's right side, since this is where his liver is located. A stunning blow can effectively be delivered by using the knife edge of your hand or, if you have managed to down your opponent, you can kill your enemy with a kick from your

heel, elbow, knee, or toe. Remember always that you are not engaged in a high school brawl, you are fighting for your life, and therefore should use full force at all times.

Stomach: There are many combinations of blows which can form a basic attack pattern, but one of the most basic is a blow to the stomach. Excepting the solar plexus, the stomach is an area which cannot be treated as an end in itself, rather as a starting point for a series of blows. The best way to strike the stomach and get maximum penetration is to go at it with a fist formed by folding the fingers at the second knuckle, and striking deeply with a slightly upswing. A blow to the stomach will cause the enemy to bend deeply forward. When this occurs, either strike your enemy full force with your knee in his face, or employ a well-directed rabbit punch to the base of his neck.

Armpit: A large network of nerves is very close to the skin in the armpits. The great problem with a direct strike to this area is its lack of accessibility. For that reason, it is more likely that you would attack this area after you have managed to bring your opponent to the ground, and are in control of his arm. An attack should be led by a toe or heel kick. A sharp blow to this area will cause severe pain and temporary partial paralysis.

Instep: The bones in the instep are very small and weak, and can be broken quite easily. A stomp, using the edge of your right boot to your enemy's right instep, is effective and at the same time protects your groin area. The instep is an area to remember, as it is almost never defended or protected, and, if directly attacked, can render an enemy immobile and in severe pain. This attack area is also useful for breaking an opponent's grip, especially if he is holding you from the back (i.e., a full nelson).

Knee: Kick your enemy's kneecap by delivering a blow with the edge of your boot (not with the toe, as it is liable to slip off, and leave your enemy unharmed). The blow should come on an upward swing there to catch the underneath of the kneecap and rip the cartilage and ligaments. This will cause severe pain and affect mobility. If you manage to get behind your enemy, a blow to the knee can just as easily and effectively be delivered.

Shoulder: If you manage to get hold of an opponent's arm, it takes very little strength to twist it, thus causing dislocation. This operation should be performed quickly. It is not the job of a guerrilla fighter to torture his enemy. He should dispose of him as fast as possible. The twisting action involved in this operation might remind one of a half nelson or hammer lock performed quickly with the object in mind to create disability rather than pain. The type of action can also be performed well if you have managed to bring your opponent to the ground. It can be followed by a knee drop to the spinal cord, which will result in paralysis or death.

Elbow: The joint in the elbow is one of the weakest points in the body, and can be dislocated or broken with a relatively forceful blow. Grasp your enemy's wrist or forearm and pull it behind him. This will cause his arm to stiffen. As you are doing this, strike a sharp blow with the heel of your hand to the backside of his stiffened elbow. This will result, depending on the strength of the blow, in either dislocation or breakage.

Wrist: A wristlock is useful for several reasons. Most importantly, an enemy can be controlled in this position. A wristlock is nothing more than placing both thumbs on the back of an opponent's hand and bending it at a right angle to the forearm. This will produce extreme pain and loss of balance.

Fingers: The fingers are an important consideration, because more than half the blows your enemy is capable of delivering entail the use of the fingers, in one form or another. The fingers can be broken in several ways. One of the most effective is by using the left hand as a lever: Grasp the wrist and pry it down, while at the same time bend, with the right hand, the middle and index fingers back. This will cause breakage. This operation can be used to break many grips.

A word of caution should be noted at this point. These operations should be practiced before used. As with almost everything else, just reading about techniques is not good enough. One must practice and become skillful, fast, and precise. In training yourself, you should never forget that only a small amount of pressure is capable of killing or maiming an individual. Therefore, take it easy on your training partner.

Application of hand weapons

If a weapon is available, only a fool will choose to use his hands and feet, but what is more important is the application of these weapons. I would rather fight a man with a knife, without a knife myself, if the person did not know how to use it—meaning that I had two hands free where he had the hindrance of a weapon he was not skilled in using. When considering a type of makeshift weapon, always take into account what it is going to be used for, and how well you will be able to use it.

Hand weapons

A bayonet hilt, tent peg, or any blunt object can be extremely effective in silencing a sentry. A sharp blow with any of these objects, directly to the back of the neck, will in most cases break the enemy's neck and kill him instantly.

A blackjack can easily be made from wet sand and an old sock. You fill the sock about a quarter full of sand, tying a knot just above the sand. When attacking an enemy, you should strike hard at the nape of the neck. This will result in the same injuries as described in the above paragraph.

If you have a rifle, but no ammunition, use the gun as a weapon itself. By striking the butt of the rifle deeply into the hollows of a man's back you will be able to stun him. By striking the same hollow with the toe of the rifle, you'll likely kill the man.

Knives

Probably the most commonly used weapon outside of a firearm is a knife, and at the same time it is perhaps the most misused weapon of all. More freedom fighters have died through stupidity and lack of training than all the other causes put together. Of course your enemy is going to kick a knife from your hands if you extend it out in front of you. Exactly the same situation with a handgun; a pistol should always be kept at the hip and out of the possible grasp of the enemy. An important factor in employing a knife as a weapon is the grip which you will use. The best over-all grip is as follows: Lay the knife handle diagonally across the palm of your outstretched hand. Now, with your thumb and forefinger grip each side of the handle, just beneath the guard, but do not encircle it. With the rest of your fingers grasp the remaining portion of the handle and encircle it.

Figure 20. The correct grip for holding a knife.

This type of grip allows you to maneuver the knife in most directions easily and quickly. The stance for a knife fight is just as important as the grip on the knife itself. You should get into a half crouch, feet spread shoulder width apart, putting all your weight on the balls of your feet. If you are right-handed, then your right foot should be just behind the left. The knife should be held close to the hip and out of the reach of the enemy.

When attacking with a knife, there are certain vulnerable spots you should try for. These will result in death or severe injury.

Throat: The throat is one of the most vulnerable spots in the body and should be treated as such. Any person who has the smallest idea of what's going on will defend his throat well. If you see an opening, or are able to manufacture one with your free hand, then there are two basic forms of attack. If the enemy is overprotective about his throat, do not pursue the issue, look for another point of attack. In no circumstances risk your own balance for an attack you may not be able to complete. The first type of attack to the throat area is a straight upward thrust to the hollow at the base of the neck, about an inch below the Adam's apple. This will cause immediate death, since the thrust will sever the jugular vein. The second type of attack is a slash movement to either side of the throat. This will result in cutting the carotid artery, which carries blood to the brain. A slash of this type will cause death in a few seconds. Since the throat is so vulnerable, it will in most cases be well defended. It is sometimes better to wound an enemy in another spot first, so as to cause him confusion and the dropping of his throat defenses.

Stomach: The stomach should be considered more of a diversionary tactic, than a fatal end in itself. Although a deep stomach wound will result in death if left unattended, a great tactic is to employ a combined thrust and slash to the stomach. This will result in confusion and fear. His confusion may cause him to drop his throat defense and try to protect the already-inflicted stomach wound.

Heart: The heart is another fatal spot to be considered in your attack, but it should be noted that the heart is well protected by the rib cage, and is pretty hard to hit. A sharp thrust will usually slip off the rib cage and penetrate the heart. This will result in death instantly. This type of thrust should incorporate an upward swing.

Wrist: This is an excellent place to consider, especially if your enemy tries to grab for the knife, your arm, or a piece of clothing. A slash to the inside of the wrist will cut the radial artery, which is only a quarter inch below the skin surface. With a severed radial artery, a man will lose consciousness in about thirty seconds and die within two minutes.

Upper arm: The upper arm is as vulnerable as the wrist, in that a well-placed slash will sever the brachial artery and cause death in about two minutes. A slash should be used on the upper inside arm regions, since a thrust would give you less of a chance of making the desired contact. If a thrust is unsuccessful, it will tend to throw you off balance, and leave you open to attack.

Inside upper leg: A slash combined with a thrust movement directed to the inside of the leg just below the groin will result in severing some very large arteries, and will render the limb useless.

Kidneys: This type of attack can only be launched from the rear of the enemy, and is especially effective for missions that require absolute silence. One should launch the attack when he is about five feet from the back of the victim. Then, with one movement, he must simultaneously thrust the knife deep into the kidneys and cover the victim's mouth with his free hand. After a few seconds, he should remove the knife, slashing as it is being retracted, and then cut the victim's throat. By the time his throat is being cut, the victim should already be dead, but everything must be insured.

Collar thrust: The subclavian artery is located about three inches below the surface of the skin, between the collar bone and the shoulder blade. When attacking this point, you must come up from the enemy's rear, holding the knife as if it were an ice pick. You must thrust straight down into the indentation by the side of the neck. A good policy to follow when employing this form of attack is to cover the victim's mouth and nose, to avoid any unnecessary noise. This artery is difficult to hit, so when withdrawing the knife use a slashing motion, to make the wound larger and insure that you have severed the artery. Once it is severed, the enemy will die almost instantly.

There is nothing funny about killing a man, and these methods are not a joke. They work, and are being used today by the Army, Marines, and Special Forces, in Southeast Asia. When attacking or being attacked, remain as calm as possible. Do not lose your head, through anger or fear. A freedom fighter's worst enemies are his emotions. Watch your opponent's actions, try to guess what his next move will be, and prevent him from making it. I have no patience with a man who agrees that he is threatened, but refuses to protect himself, because he is disgusted with, or afraid of, violence. Everyone feels fear, and the brave are only those who can think logically and calmly about their fear, placing it in its proper relation to the matter on hand. The phrases "Dirty Fighter," or "no hitting below the belt," are for children or sportsmen. Violence is a deadly serious adult operation, with no room for second thoughts.

The act of silencing sentries is especially important when involving oneself in a guerrilla struggle. This type of attack will be used many times in ambushes or sabotage attempts. The primary key to this type of attack is speed and silence. Any of the above attacks, which are based on approaching the enemy from the rear, can be employed to silence a sentry or guard by simply covering his nose and mouth with your free hand, while thrusting the knife into one of the fatal spots with the other. An interesting and effective method is to use the enemy's weapon against himself. You approach the guard from behind, and simultaneously deliver a rabbit punch to the nape of his neck, and grab the front of his helmet and pull sharply back. Now, if his helmet is strapped on, this will cause his neck to break, with instant unconsciousness, followed by death. If his helmet is not strapped on, the chances are good that your rabbit punch will render him unconscious, but, to make sure, follow through with the free helmet and crack his skull open with it. This operation can be performed fast enough so that the guard will not have a chance to cry for help.

Impromptu weapons

The main point in any hand-to-hand combat situation is for the individual to assess the problem at hand and use the operation he believes will result in the type of effect desired. The training of any guerrilla should incorporate a real balance between self-confidence and fear. Always remember that your enemy will know what he is doing, and most of the time better than you do. For this reason it is better to have an advantage to begin with, whether it be a weapon, or just the element of surprise. A guerrilla fighter has to be the most ferocious fighter in the world; because in the established legal terms, he has committed high treason, and will not be taken prisoner. If a guerrilla is caught,

he must expect torture and death. This is one of the real advantages in the liberation struggle.

In this section I have included several recipes for hand weapons, which tend to be both semilethal and lethal. There are also a couple of recipes for sabotage, which didn't fit into any other chapters.

One of the simplest and most effective weapons in this class is the old-fashioned hatpin. It is about three to four inches in length with a plastic knob on one end. It can be purchased from almost any five-and-ten-cent store. This can be used as a lethal silent weapon, as illustrated by the following true story. A revolutionary group in Ireland was being threatened by an informer, who had gone over to the enemy. They knew that he had to be exterminated, for the safety and morale of the entire band. He was heavily guarded, but, through some surveillance work, they managed to find out where he ate, the times of his meals, and the number of guards. One day, while the informer was eating, a member of the guerrilla force unknown to the informer entered the dining room and sat down next to him. He ordered food so as to place the guards at ease, and then ran a four-inch hatpin into the informer's ear. The pin went directly into his brain. He died instantaneously, soundlessly, and with what would appear to be a heart attack. The assassin left the eating place, with impunity, as he had propped the dead man up, and wandered back to his base camp.

Figure 21. Common hatpin.

Old-fashioned hatpins are among the easiest weapons to conceal.

When martial law is declared, all weapons, except those that are well hidden, will be confiscated. Therefore, impromptu weapons must be created. This is a good recipe for a hand-to-hand combat weapon which has proven effective at several demonstrations. All you need to make one of these weapons is an empty beer or soda can and a can opener. With the can opener fray the two ends of the can outward, into a maze of jagged points. To put into operation, tape the center section with electrical tape, to form a good grip, and swing the can back and forth in front of your adversary.

Figure 22. Beer-can hand weapon.

Knives are an essential tool as well as weapon for any person aspiring to be a guerrilla. There are many types of knives, and all have different purposes and uses. The knives I am going to discuss will be those that can be employed both as tools and weapons, with the maximum amount of efficiency. The sheath or hunting knife is a primary tool for any rural or urban guerrilla. The best types are the ones designed for use by the military themselves. The knife illustrated in Figure 23 is the Marine Corps combat knife, which has a sturdy seven-inch blade, and a leather, grooved handle for sure grip. The blade is covered with a water-resistant substance, which prevents rusting or corrosion, but doesn't interfere with the use of the blade. This is one of the best knives on the market.

Figure 23. Marine Corps combat knife.

Another extremely dependable knife is the Air Force survival kit. This is more than just a knife, it is a kit, which includes a five-inch blade with sawteeth on the back. It has a heavy hexagon butt which can be used for a hammer, and a grooved leather handle for sure grip. It comes with a leather pouch which houses a sharpening stone. It is pictured in Figure 24.

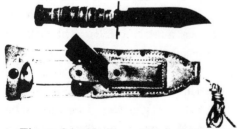

Figure 24. Air Force survival kit.

Another type of sheath knife is the throwing knife. This is a great weapon, *only* if the person is trained with it. Do

not take the chance of using one of these without the skill acquired by much practice. Another important disadvantage to the throwing knife is that it is just a throwing knife and cannot be used for any other purposes because its edges are generally pretty dull. If you have the skill and know-how to throw knives, this can be a silent and deadly weapon. These are relatively inexpensive, but need to be sharpened often.

Figure 25. Throwing knife.

Figure 25 depicts a typical inexpensive throwing knife; it is ten inches long and perfectly balanced. It has a leather handle, which insures a good grip in almost any situation. Watch out for wooden handles for just that reason.

The three types of knives illustrated are about the best for combat in either rural or urban environments. Bayonets and machetes can and should be employed in rural areas, but they are much too large for combat or tool use in the cities. The knives discussed on the previous page are available from almost any Army-Navy store without restrictions, except that in some areas they will ask you your age.

Switchblades (spring-operated pocket knives) and stilettos (also spring-operated pocket knives, except the blade shoots straight out the handle) are effective in the sense that they can be employed with great speed, but in my mind their disadvantages override any effectiveness. First of all there is no way to open them if the spring breaks, and it seems that in a real emergency little things like springs always break. The second disadvantage is in their size. They are usually pretty small, but there are larger ones which tend to be slower and much more prone to breakage. Third, they are illegal, and who wants to go to jail for carrying an ineffective weapon? There is a general rule which applies to most tools and weapons; the fewer moving parts the better the weapon.

An important factor with any weapon is the psychological effect it will have on the enemy. Therefore any type of odd-shaped knife is a good weapon; the more brutal looking the better. A curved carpet cutter is a good example of this. Although a straight razor falls into this classification, it is one of the worst weapons in the world. A straight razor has no lock, and the blade can flip back and cut off the holder's fingers. Also stay away from garbage like icepicks, car antennas, bicycle chains, and all the rest of the street-gang bullshit. None of these weapons is effective, and the chances are very good that your enemy knows it.

Brass knuckles and clubs

There are several other weapons which are extremely effective in hand-to-hand combat. The weapons I will discuss on the next couple of pages are in the club family. Most of the ones illustrated and described are police weapons, since the police have the most effective ones. There is a very common misconception that clubs are not lethal weapons. They are lethal in the sense that, if you whack someone over the head with a club, the chances are

50-50 that his head will either crack or smush.

Brass knuckles are an extremely effective semilethal weapon, for use in hand-to-hand combat. They are easy to make, although they are also inexpensive, if you can find them. They are illegal in most states. There are several types of brass knuckles. The first and most common is illustrated in Figure 26.

Figure 26. Brass knuckles.

It is nothing more than a metal bar, that can fit onto the hand, connected with four ringlike holes for the fingers. The other types include the Kelly Come Along (Figure 27)

Figure 27. Kelly Come-Along.

Figure 28. Sap gloves.

and sap gloves (Figure 28), which are nothing more than a pair of leather gloves with a metal bar sewed into them, either over the knuckles or palms.

In Figure 29, all the billies on the left are legal, in the sense that a civilian may possess them. The flat slappers, brass knuckles, sap gloves, and Kelly Come-Alongs are illegal to all but police officers. The billies can be bought without restriction at almost any Army-Navy store.

Cattle prod

Another great weapon against horse guards is what the farmers call a cattle prod, and the police call a "mob-control stick." These are devices that look very similar to a billie club, except at one end they have two rather long prongs, which transmit a relatively low voltage shock. Although the shock is low voltage, it's enough to throw a rider from his horse, or completely confuse an attacker, to the point that he is helpless. These are available from Continental Telephone Supply Co., 17 W. 46th St., New

York, New York, for under ten dollars. The police version is illustrated in Figure 30.

Figure 30. Mob-control stick.

Garrote

A weapon which is definitely considered lethal is the garrote. This is an ultra-effective device for beheading people. It incorporates all the facets which make up a great weapon: speed, silence, simplicity, and deadliness. It is constructed from two pieces of wood with a section of piano wire attached.

Upon approach, the hands are raised, crossed as the wire is brought forward, down, and over the head of the enemy. Thus at the back of the head the wires are crossed over and the left hand pulls to the left, and the right hand to the right. This is an extremely deadly weapon.

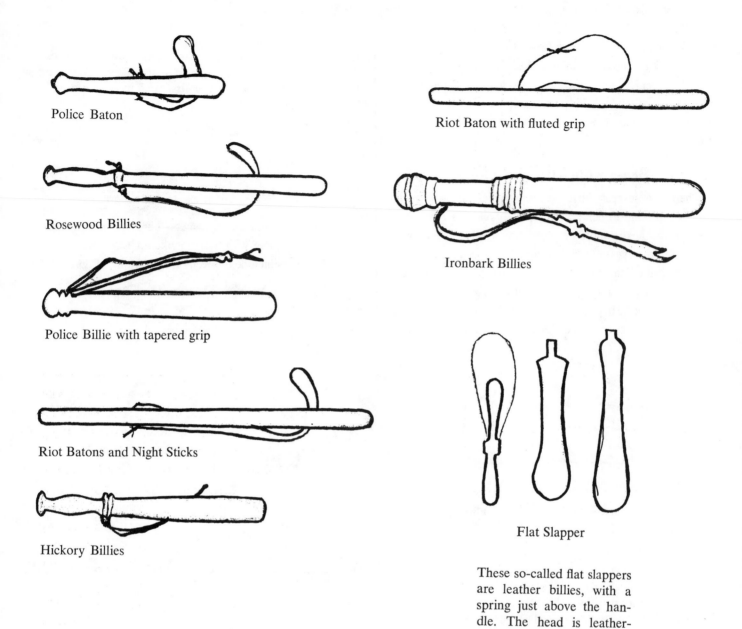

Police Baton

Riot Baton with fluted grip

Rosewood Billies

Ironbark Billies

Police Billie with tapered grip

Riot Batons and Night Sticks

Flat Slapper

These so-called flat slappers are leather billies, with a spring just above the handle. The head is leather-covered lead.

Hickory Billies

Figure 29. Different types of billies and blackjacks.

Figure 31. Garrote.

Guerrilla training

When discussing any type of weapon, the most important factor is not the acquisition of that weapon, but rather its application. An example of this is present everyday in any slum neighborhood. The gangs of young kids that run around with their makeshift weapons could be one of the most potentially dangerous forces in America, if they only learned how to make full use of the weapons available to them. Every great political leader and powerful tyrant has realized the wealth of energy, courage, and blind cruelty in the age group between 12 and 16 years old. These kids aren't scared, they have no concept of death, they love excitement, and with training could make the best commandos. Hitler used the young people of Germany in "Hitler Youth," a young terrorist organization that was probably one of the most effective the world has even seen. Mao also employs 13- and 14-year-olds in his Red Guard, because they have not yet developed a conscience for their actions. The development of this age group has begun in the United States with political involvement on a high school and junior high school level, but, at the same time, the energy present must not be drowned in dogma. It must be channeled through education into specialized fields, which will be necessary to the great change in store for them.

Any moron can obtain weapons, but what he does with these weapons is the factor which will determine the success or failure of a particular operation. This is the major cause of the failure of the Minute-Men. They have the weapons, but not the training or the technical know-how, to be effective with them. Nkrumah, in his book on revolutionary warfare, basically outlines the types of training a guerrilla fighter should have. He says that, before any actual weapons or physical training begins, the recruit must be educated in the justness and the reality of his cause. This type of mental training, indoctrination, is very important, but at the same time is not easily accomplished. The untrained recruit knows nothing of guerrilla warfare. All he understands is the oppression, the lies, and the bullshit that have been fed to him for so long. This is what the revolutionary force cannot resort to. They must create for the new recruits, as well as the older combat veterans, a brotherhood of truth, without dogma, relying on human passions, feelings, and the basic moral fiber of the individuals. It is impossible to explain Mao's principles to a 14-year-old. For that reason, the educators of the revolution must get rid of the archaic terminology, and speak to the people, rather than down to them.

Untrained individuals must be trained in shooting rifles, pistols, and some small machine guns. This type of ballistics training includes not only shooting accuracy and marksmanship, but also safety measures, care and cleaning, and actual combat application. While the physical and technical training is going on, the educators must instill in the trainees a discipline. This discipline must be an internal self-discipline for the survival of the group, in contrast to the external mechanical type of discipline that they are fighting against. The best type of training is actual combat with a guerrilla band, so, as soon as an individual has progressed far enough, he should be taken into combat, as an equal member of the band. In the training of a fighter, an attempt must be made to understand the common problems of the men. The most common of these will be fear. This should be talked about, and real attempts should be made at all levels to understand it, although cowardliness must never be tolerated.

There is an extremely effective method for sabotaging trucks and other military vehicles. Two guerrillas stretch a heavy duty cable across a highway diagonally. They must pick a highway which is frequently used by the enemy. The cable can be attached to trees or poles placed there, for that purpose. Once the cable is pulled taut, the guerrillas must paint it black so it won't show up in the vehicle's headlights. Now the guerrillas leave, insuring their safety. As the vehicle hits the taut cable, it will slide down the cable rather than breaking it, into a tree or well-placed mine.

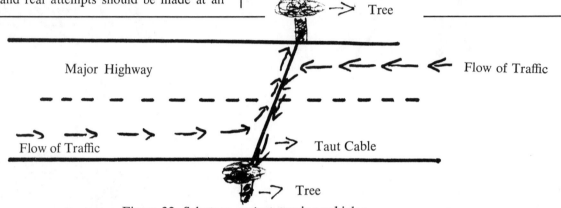

Figure 32. Sabotage against moving vehicles.

There are five basic methods of obtaining weapons (firearms). One can always purchase them. Although mail order gun selling is now illegal, many states are very lenient on sale of weapons. Raiding arms depots is also very effective, but should only be considered when the guerrilla band already has enough weapons to sustain an attack of this size. Disarming police or military personnel is a good method. It also boosts the morale of the guerrilla troops. One can attempt to make firearms himself, but this should only be done if the individual has had prior training and knows exactly what he's doing. A faulty weapon endangers the entire band. The cleverest and safest method of obtaining weapons is to post a guerrilla as a worker in a munitions factory, and steal what is needed and leave the other weapons so damaged that they are useless.

When discussing firearms, as with almost everything else in this book, I feel obligated to caution the reader against his own ignorance and carelessness. A gun is not a toy. A gun is not a plaything. Treat your weapon with respect, because the time may come when its proper use can save your life. This will probably sound corny, if you have not had experience with a gun. If you have had experience, you know it's true. A few rules for the use of a weapon:

1. Treat your weapon as your most prized possession.

2. Clean it regularly.

3. Do not jokingly point a gun at anyone, including your enemy.

4. Do not allow anyone but yourself to shoot your weapon.

5. Understand your gun, to the point where it becomes an extension of yourself.

6. Take pride in your abilities in regard to shooting, but in no circumstances boast about them.

7. The guerrilla organization has no use for cowboys or hotshots.

8. In most situations, shoot to kill, but there are circumstances where a wounded man can cause more trouble for your enemy than a dead man.

Pistols and revolvers

Every man in a guerrilla band should have as part of his basic equipment a handgun. The pistol or handgun, as with all firearms, should be of a type for which ammunition and parts are readily available. Obsolete weapons should not be used. For this reason, using the same type as your enemy has great advantages. Do not get hung up with strange weapons. Stick with the simple regulation-type pistols and rifles. Do not use antiques.

There are basically three types of pistols, the difference being primarily in loading, and rapid fire. The type you won't have to worry about is the muzzle loaders. The other two are the revolvers and automatic and semi-automatic magazine-type pistols. Both have advantages and disadvantages.

The pistols listed below are there for several reasons: They are used to a great degree by either the police or the military, they are powerful enough to have fairly good stopping power, their prices are not too outrageous, and spare parts and ammunition are pretty easy to come by.

Figure 33. Browning high-power automatic pistol.

This is a sturdy 32-oz. gun, with a 13-shot magazine. It includes both thumb and magazine safeties; therefore, a shot cannot be fired without the magazine in place. $108.50

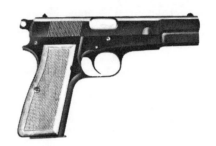

Figure 34. Smith & Wesson 9-mm. automatic pistol.

This is a smaller weapon weighing only 26 ozs., without the magazine. It comes with an 8-shot magazine and features hammer-release safety, short-recoil double action, locked breech. And the slide locks open on the last shot. $100.00

Figure 35. Colt Commander automatic pistol.
This is a .45 automatic that uses a 7-shot magazine, weighs about 26 oz. It has good fire power and packs plenty of punch. It has both a grip and thumb safety. Priced about $115.00. Also available in Super automatic .38.

Figure 36. Smith & Wesson combat masterpiece revolver.

This is an inexpensive .38-caliber special. It uses a 6-shot cylinder and, loaded, weighs about 36 ozs. This is an attractive weapon because of its efficiency and price. $89.00. All prices quoted new, cut in half for used prices.

Figure 37. Charter Arms undercover .38 special.

This is a small (6¼″), light (16 oz.), revolver, with a 5-shot cylinder. It is available in 2″ or 3″ barrels, and is a powerful little gun. It is excellent for undercover work, where a weapon would have to be concealed. The most attractive aspect about this little weapon is the price, $75.00 new.

Figure 38. Colt official police revolver.

This is a heavy-duty (35-oz.), .38 special police weapon, which has obvious advantages. The cylinder packs six power punches, with good stopping power. If you are unable to get one without paying for it, they usually run about $110 new.

Figure 39. Llama Model VIII automatic pistol.

This pistol (either .38 or .45) has been manufactured for law-enforcement officers and defense only. These are not hunting guns. They are heavy-duty, hard-hitting, accurate handguns. The .38 uses a 9-shot magazine, whereas the .45 uses a 7-shot clip. These weapons have been popular in the past because of their many safety features. I rate this weapon very well, and feel that it is in a class with the Browning 9-mm. automatic. Priced $75.00 for .38, and $78.95 for .45.

Smith & Wesson as a company has manufactured as many military and police weapons as any other. Before you purchase a weapon, I would advise sending away for their catalogue. Smith & Wesson's list of military and police weapons is basically as follows: .38 Chief's Special M-36 priced $76.50, .38 Bodyguard M-37 priced $79.00, .38 Military and Police M-10 (either round or square butt) priced $76.50, Military and Police .38 Special Airweight M-12 priced $79.00, .38 Combat Masterpiece M-15 (either 2- or 4-inch barrel) priced $89.00, and the Highway Patrolman, a .357 magnum M-28 priced $98.00.

It is a good policy to stay away from .22- and .25-caliber weapons, as they do not have the stopping power necessary for most military operations. A .22 magnum pistol can effectively be employed at close range, for assassinations, but is not generally advisable.

When purchasing any weapon second-hand, be very careful and inspect the weapon thoroughly, since if it does explode, it will be your face or hands that it blows to pieces. Also place equal importance on the security of the individual selling the weapon, as many states have strict laws governing firearms, especially handguns.

Although some of the easiest handguns to come by are foreign military weapons, I would suggest the same care in picking out a foreign weapon as you would employ when purchasing a used weapon. There was a motorcycle band in California which beat the gun laws in an interesting manner, for a while. They wore side arms in a holster at the hip when they rode. By wearing them in plain sight, they conformed to the concealed weapons regulations. Needless to say, this scared the shit out of the cops, and not many of the cyclists received speeding tickets until the law was changed.

Small-arms (hand-guns) ammunition should be no problem if you have been reading this chapter straight through, and have picked out a weapon that has its bullets readily available. The principles behind bullet projection are different and should be noted. There are basically two priming methods for all small arms ballistics. The first I will not discuss, as it is not used in the United States, and is generally considered not as safe as the boxer method. The boxer primer is used for the most part throughout the United States. It is manufactured in two parts, the primer separately from the cartridge case and then inserted into it as a unit.

The boxer primer consists of a small anvil and the igniting charge. When the primer cup is struck, it is indented and the igniting charge is compressed between the cup and the anvil. The flame that results passes through the anvil and through the vent which leads to the interior of the case, and ignites the main powder charge.

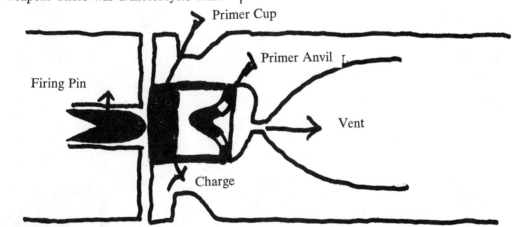

Figure 40. Boxer primer.

There are several different types of slugs for each caliber weapon. The primary difference is in the shape of the nose of the slug (i.e., round nose, flat point, spire point, soft point, etc.). The dum-dum bullet is illegal, but many companies have attempted to incorporate some of the dum-dum's characteristics without going to the point of becoming illegal themselves. The dum-dum is nothing more than a slug with a groove or cross filed on its nose. This is done so that the bullet will literally explode within the body of the victim. An interesting experiment with a dum-dum is to fire one at relatively close range at an old phone book. The front of the book will show a hole about the size of a quarter, whereas the back will be blown completely off and shredded into thousands of pieces. If the texture of a phone book is comparable to the texture of the human body, then you are able to project the impact of this type of bullet.

It is easy to pick up a weapon and in a short while become a reasonably good shot. This makes it extremely easy for the virtually untrained individual to come to believe that he is an expert in ballistics. False confidence is as great a fault as no confidence at all. In the training of any freedom fighters there must be a merger of fearlessness and intelligent caution. A dead man has no use for confidence or courage.

Holsters

There are many types of holsters for these handguns. Each is designed with an individual purpose in mind. A good holster has to have three basic considerations: safety of the gun within the holster, security against loss of the gun, and speed in which the gun can be drawn into action. The holsters pictured below try to incorporate these three facets. I would warn against holsters with devices for quick draw. Devices always fail when you need them most.

Figure 41. Snap holster.

This is an excellent type of fast-draw holster. Many police and military installations have started using them. They have a small screw which places tension on the gun, making it impossible to fall out. $5.50

Figure 42. Spring holster.

This type has a leather strap which goes over the gun itself to insure the security of the weapon. At the same time it slows down the act of drawing out the weapon, but not to the degree that it makes much of a difference. Priced at about $5.00

Figure 43. Spring shoulder holster.

This works basically on the same principle of a tension screw as did the holster before. This holster is designed to hang straight down, without interfering with arm movement. It will be invisible under a coat. Priced at about $15.00

Figure 44. Closed-end quick-draw holster.

This is probably the fastest type, which offers a metal plate that keeps the butt of the gun away from the body, and within quick grasp. A sturdy holster that usually runs about $16.00

Rifles

Rifles should be acquired by the same five methods as those recommended for hand weapons. Most of the safety principles that apply to pistols also apply to rifles, with the exception that rifles are much more important to the success of any guerrilla operation, because of their powerful nature. Although pistols are extremely handy at close range and for self-defense, they become almost useless over longer distances, or when applied to almost any military operation. Every person, whether in wartime or not, should keep a pistol and a rifle in his house at all times. If a person is not going to protect himself, and wishes the government to do it for him, how can he complain when the government decides to protect itself against him, and executes him? As perverted as man's senses are, he must refer back to the basic laws of nature, and animal survival. This in itself should show cause enough for every family to own a weapon with which it can protect itself. One of the greatest myths of all time is that so-called civilized man is no longer an animal, and for that reason can strive to disarm himself and grow fat with false concepts. He has used some sort of warped logic and agreed to hand over his security to a bunch of power-hungry individuals, who will use this security and the helpless individual to any extent they wish. A true man, in the real sense of the word, is like a wild animal, in that his freedom, and the freedom of his family, is based on one factor: his ability to protect himself and his family from outside restrictions. It has got to the point in this country where men believe they are men, just because of their birthright. If that is true, then, by the same logic, an animal held captive in a zoo is still a wild free beast. A male must make himself a man, he must enable himself to stand up on two legs, unafraid because he has confidence in his own security and in his own power. There is no place for emotionally or politically cuckolded people in the society I speak of. Survival of the fittest. If we must have violence, then let it be real violence, let it be for survival, and not halfway around the world for "ideals."

Emasculation, if allowed to take place, can lower a man or woman to the state of a domesticated, well-trained animal: performing tricks, begging for food, and relying totally on an outside force for his right to survive. If a man doesn't understand weapons and is frightened of them, his friends should teach him about them. They should not be condescending, but rather understanding; for the fault is not his, it is just a lie he has been made to believe.

A revolution, peaceful or violent, or any form of change, is a gamble, and should be treated as such. I have never heard of a real gambler placing a bet if he didn't feel that the odds were in his favor. How can a man face life without any odds in his favor? Governments have created popular lies to break the spirit of real men, to render them helpless, useless little creatures, to be manipulated like chess pieces. The government has cleverly perverted the individual's concept of human dignity to its own use. Whereas once true human dignity stemmed from self-sufficiency and the sanctity of the human spirit, it is now measured in materials—how much a man makes, what he can afford, how much credit can he get, where he lives, and who he knows. If a man is to be a man, a free spirit unto himself, he must arm himself not only with weapons but with ideals and concepts he is willing to fight and die for. An animal will risk its life to preserve the life of its young. Human beings have been so warped that they will think twice about this primary reaction.

The rifles described below are good in the same senses as the pistols were: availability of ammunition and parts, power, and ability to be transported over long distances.

Lee-Enfield No. 1 and No. 4 .303-caliber bolt-action rifle: This is one of the best low-priced rifles. It features safety devices and other advantages that few bolt-action rifles can match. It is fast, simple, and very reliable. It was used by the military in both World War I and II. For the rifle (used) and about 1,000 rounds of ammo you will pay about $75.00.

Figure 45. Browning high-power rifle. This bolt-action rifle has standard mauser action and comes in 222, 243, 270, 284, 30-06, and 308 calibers. The 30-06 is a powerful lightweight weapon, has 6-shot clip, and sells for $300.00.

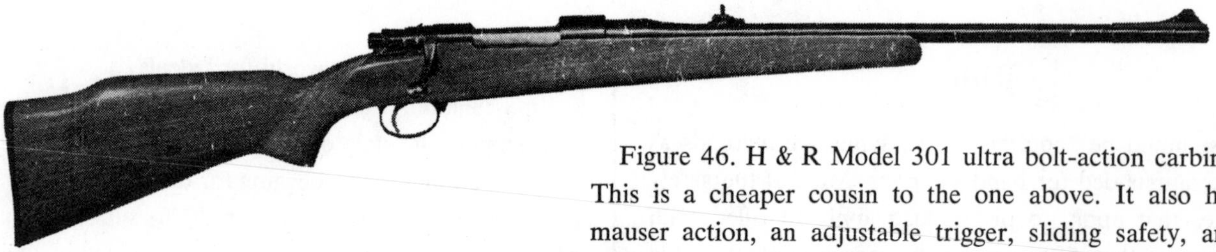

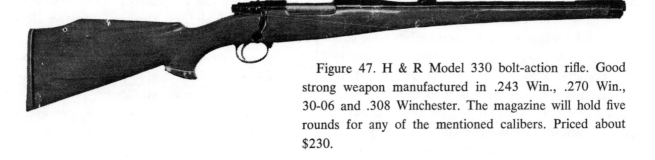

Figure 46. H & R Model 301 ultra bolt-action carbine. This is a cheaper cousin to the one above. It also has mauser action, an adjustable trigger, sliding safety, and comes in .243 Win., .270 Win., 30-06 and .308 Winchester. Magazine capacity is about five rounds for all calibers, and price runs about $145.00 new.

Figure 47. H & R Model 330 bolt-action rifle. Good strong weapon manufactured in .243 Win., .270 Win., 30-06 and .308 Winchester. The magazine will hold five rounds for any of the mentioned calibers. Priced about $230.

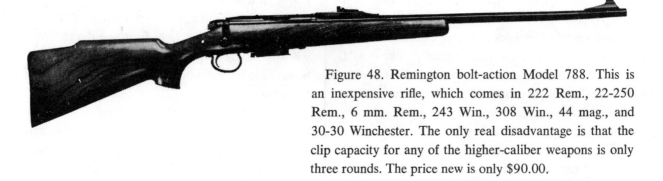

Figure 48. Remington bolt-action Model 788. This is an inexpensive rifle, which comes in 222 Rem., 22-250 Rem., 6 mm. Rem., 243 Win., 308 Win., 44 mag., and 30-30 Winchester. The only real disadvantage is that the clip capacity for any of the higher-caliber weapons is only three rounds. The price new is only $90.00.

A bolt-action rifle requires less maintenance and makes a better sniping weapon than do most other types. About $100 should buy you a weapon (used) and 1,000 rounds of ammo. The bolt-action weapons listed below are military and can be picked up second-hand with considerable savings, but, as with purchasing anything second-hand, extreme caution should be taken.

1903 Springfield bolt-action 30-06 or mauser 98 bolt action: These are extremely accurate with excellent ballistics. With 1,000 rounds cost should be no more than $100.

Mossberg Model 800 (nonmilitary) bolt-action rifle: Comes in three calibers, .308 Win., .243 Win., and .22-250 Rem., each having a five-shot magazine capacity. New, this rifle costs about $105.50.

Savage 110 E Bolt-Action Rifle (nonmilitary): Standard 30-06, 243, and 308-caliber rifles, with 5-shot magazines (4 shot clip with one shot in chamber). A good heavy-duty weapon costs $110.00 new. (Savage have a good line of medium-priced bolt-action weapons. Send for catalogue.)

Smith & Wesson Bolt-Action Rifles: Smith & Wesson have five bolt-action models; all models are available in standard calibers (270, 30-06, 308, and 243). They all have 5-shot magazines and run from $200 upward.

Sears 53 B A R: Available in same standard calibers as above with 5-shot magazine (nonmilitary). New runs about $119.99.

Although bolt-action rifles require less maintenance than most others, I have listed here a few types of lever-action weapons. All of these are pretty sturdy and inexpensive, and might be used interchangeably with a bolt-action weapon. I still recommend bolt action for over-all general use.

Marlin Lever Action (Model-366-T) Carbine: Straight from the Old West, this is a fast 7-shot repeater. It is only available in 30/30 Winchester. The price is about $100 new.

Figure 49. Marlin 62 Levermatic Rifle: This is a cheap but effective lever-action weapon which comes in either of two calibers: .30 U.S. Carbine or 256 Magnum. It has a 4-shot clip, open sights, and a positive safety. Priced new at $75.00.

The Savage Model 99 lever-action rifle: Savage offers a pretty good line of lever-action high-powered rifles. This model is an inexpensive one featuring all the standard calibers, and a 5-shot clip. Priced new at about $50.00.

Winchester also offers a pretty good line of lever-action rifles, but it seems that they may be hung up with trying to create replicas of Wild West guns, rather than effective weapons. The model-94 is an effective, fast-action, 30/30 Win., which holds 6 cartridges and sells for $100.

Semi-automatic and automatic weapons

Listed and pictured below are some effective U.S.-made military and civilian semi-automatic and automatic weapons. These are important to any successful guerrilla movement and should not be overlooked, even though there are restrictions on them in various locations.

Figure 50. Universal Enforcer automatic carbine.
Universal Enforcer Automatic Carbine (handgun): Well, this is a strange one, but it looks pretty good. It is a 30 M1 carbine, which can be used with either a 5-, 15-, or 30-shot mag. It weighs around 5 pounds and is priced at about $130.00.

Armalite Ar-180 Carbine: This is a semi-automatic carbine. It is gas-operated and is .223 cal. It uses 5-round magazines, and is designed with good safety features. It sells for about $237.00 including two magazines.

Figure 51. Armalite Ar-180 carbine.

Browning High-Power Automatic Rifle: This is a semi-automatic, gas-operated rifle, which comes in .270, .308, .243 Winchester, and 30.06 calibers. It has a detachable five-shot trap door magazine, and adjustable rear sights. It sells new for about $175.00.

Figure 52. Browning high-power automatic rifle.

Eagle "Apache" Carbine: This is a semi-automatic recoil rifle, that uses 45 ACP cartridges in a 30-shot magazine. Lightweight (9 lbs.) rifle with only four moving parts. Sells for about $130.

Figure 53. Eagle "Apache" carbine.

Harrington and Richardson 360 Ultra-automatic: This is a four-shot, gas-operated semi-automatic rifle available in 243 and 308 calibers. This rifle is equipped with a sliding trigger guard safety and a recoil pad, and sells for about $190.00.

Figure 54. Harrington and Richardson 360 ultra-automatic.

J & R 68 Semi-Automatic Carbine: This recoil-operated carbine fires from a closed bolt. It is 9 mm. parabellum, which operates from a 30-shot staggered box magazine. Ultra lightweight (7 lbs.) carbine sells new for $150.00. Disadvantage—Plastic stock.

Figure 55. J & R 68 semi-automatic carbine.

Remington 742 Woodmaster: Gas-operated rifle, 243 Win., 6 mm. Rem., 280 Rem., 308 Win., and 30-06, with a 4-shot magazine, fully automatic. Gas operation reduces recoil in the lightweight weapon (7½ lbs.). Sells new for about $160.

Figure 56. Remington 742 Woodmaster.

Plainfield Machine Co. Carbine: This is a newly manufactured, low-priced, lightweight, automatic rifle, which gives the appearance of the popular G.I. model. It is a 30 cal. M1 carbine which is a great buy at $105.00 new.

Figure 57. Plainfield Machine Co. carbine.

Universal 1000 Auto-loading Carbine: This is a 30-caliber M1 carbine which is gas-operated and uses a five-shot magazine. It weighs only five and a half pounds, and sells for about $117.00 (uses 5-, 15-, 30-shot magazines).

Figure 58. Universal 1000 auto-loading carbine.

Winchester 100 Auto-loading Carbine: This gas-operated carbine with cam-rotating bolt, is available in 243, 284, and 308 calibers. It features a solid frame, side ejection, and a crossbolt safety. Sells for about $150.00.

Figure 59. Winchester 100 auto-loading carbine.

Figure 60. Ruger .44 magnum carbine.

Ruger .44 Magnum Carbine: This is an automatic carbine with a rotary 5- or 10-shot magazine. It features a crossbolt safety and a hammer safety. It weighs only five and three-quarter pounds and breaks down to 24". It sells for $118.00.

Although I stated previously that foreign weapons could bring on problems, in such areas as ammunition and repairs, I have listed below a few extremely good foreign semi-automatic and automatic weapons. Most of these weapons can be bought secondhand, and in most cases I have listed the average secondhand price.

G-3 Assault rifle: This is a West German weapon, semi-automatic, with a 20-shot clip. The rifle and about 1,000 rounds of ammo should not cost more than $300.

The Colt AR-15: This is a rapid-fire close-range weapon, holding 20 rounds of 5.56 mm. (223 Rem.). This is a lightweight, very handy rifle. The rifle and 1,000 rounds of ammo should not cost more than $275.00. The Colt AR-15 and the G-3 are a great team together.

BM-59 Assault Rifle: This is a 7.26 NATO weapon, based on the M1 Garand action. It has a 20-shot magazine. The rifle and 1,000 rounds of ammo should not run more than $250.00.

M-1 Garand Rifle: This is a standard military weapon, used in both World Wars and in Korea. It has semi-automatic action and uses 30-06 ammo. Beware of all but original M-1's. The rifle and 1,500 rounds of ammo in clips should cost around $200.

M-1 Carbine: This is also a military weapon, built for strength and endurance. The rifle, 1,500 rounds of ammo, plus 12 magazines of 15 rounds, plus 5 clips of 30 shots, should not run over $150.00.

A M-1 Garand rifle and a M-1 Carbine make a good team together.

Shotguns

Most individuals who live in the country can tell you the advantages of owning a shotgun. The urban guerrilla, if working by himself, should not be bothered with a shotgun, but get a pistol, which is much the better weapon. When guerrilla action has progressed to the point where cells have formed, and sabotage or ambush operations are being carried out, then the band should acquire several shotguns. A shotgun is a great weapon in many senses; when sawed-off it is a small but extremely effective weapon with a great deal of close range power, and it can easily be transformed into any number of other weapons, including brush cleaners and grenade launchers.

Converting a shotgun into a grenade launcher

A 12- or 16-gauge shotgun is propped up with a set of folding legs, so to form a tripod, with the butt of the gun being the third leg, at about a 45-degree angle. The angle can be varied, for aiming, by moving the legs back and forth. To build a grenade launcher, one must take an open shell and remove all the shot. Once this is done, replace it with a smooth cylindrical stick, which has been cut down to a close fit. When the shell is loaded into the gun, the stick should extend out of the muzzle of the gun. To the extended portion, a flat rubber base should be fixed and a "Molotov Cocktail" placed on it. This will send the burning bottles over a hundred yards with a good deal of accuracy. This is a good weapon for encirclement.

A "Molotov Cocktail" is a bottle filled with a flammable liquid such as gasoline, mixed with oil or soap powder to thicken it. A fuse, usually a rag soaked in gasoline, is attached to the cork, lit, and thrown. The bottle breaks on contact with another hard object, and the gasoline ignites, causing a burst of flame. These were used with a great degree of success in Hungary, against things as big as tanks.

The shotgun is where you can save some money, for as a general rule shotguns tend to be cheaper than rifles. The Sears Model 200 is an adequate, well-balanced, medium-priced weapon, with all the basic safety features necessary. A 20-gauge usually runs about $85.00 new. Since shotguns are not military weapons, your local sporting goods dealer will have good information about them, as long as you aren't black, Spanish, or a white freak.

Silencers

As almost everyone knows, silencers are illegal in virtually all the countries of the world, but then a true revolutionary believes that the government in power is illegal so, following that logic, I see no reason that he should feel restricted by laws made by an illegal body. More important than rationalizing illegalities are the precautions necessary when using illegal weapons. Silencers are very handy for snipers and night sabotage work, where the success of the entire mission relies on silence. There are many types of improvised silencers, which I will go into later in this section. A firearm silencer is defined legally as "any device for diminishing the explosive report of a portable weapon."

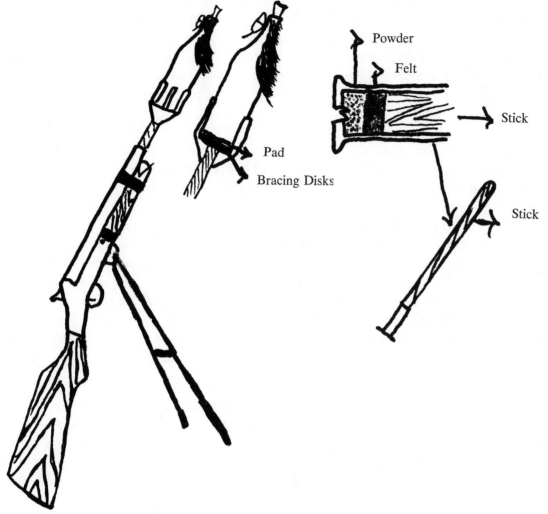

Figure 61. Converting a shotgun into a grenade launcher.

The really curious aspect of most legalities is the manner in which they are enforced. If you are arrested for possession of an illegal silencer (felony) you face charges not by the FBI, but rather by the Tobacco and Alcohol Division of the Internal Revenue Service, which is pretty strange.

The principles of firearm silencers differ to some degree with the type of weapon and the type of silencer used, but basically the compressed gas principle is the same. The silencer is constructed with an expansion chamber which will contain and distribute the compressed gas which follows the bullet. In most weapons, the gas escaping compression is what creates the explosive report. This containment and distribution are attained by using a series of baffles, coupled with absorbent material so to break up the high pressure. The sound of most low-caliber weapons (.22, .25, .32, etc.) comes directly from this gas under high pressure. However, in larger weapons with a higher caliber, the noisy gas is joined by another noise, that being a sonic boom. Any projectile that moves faster than 1,100 feet per second will experience a sonic boom. There have been devices created which will not only take care of the compressed gas, but will also reduce the speed of the bullet to a subsonic level, thus getting rid of the boom. This reduction in speed is made through several different methods. One which has been proven effective is drilling holes in the gun barrel, to bleed the weapon of some of its power. Another method (which is a great deal safer, as drilling a hole can ruin a gun completely) is simply to handload the cartridges to a lower velocity. The last method for reducing a projectile to a subsonic level is to force it to pass through semi-solid material. This should be accomplished with utmost care and skill.

The recent popularity of spy movies has given silencers a great deal of credit which is not due them. Since the National Firearms Act of 1934, there has been no civilian experimentation with silencers, so the type of silencers which are in illegal use today are basically the same ones that were used in the 30's. This in itself offers some major disadvantages, in that these devices are large and clumsy. The types of silencers used by James Bond and other super-spies are physical impossibilities, just because of their size.

There are other disadvantages to silencers which make them impractical for use on certain weapons; for example, the luger pistol operates on a recoil principle, and by placing a heavy silencer on the end of the barrel, you will cause the gun to malfunction, as the barrel will be too heavy to recoil. Another example of the impracticalities of certain silencers is the case of gas-operated weapons, where the barrel is drilled full of holes, or shortened to release the compressed gas. What may happen is that the gas will ease out under little or no pressure and the shot will not be fired.

How to build a silencer for a pistol

If one were to employ a silencer on an automatic weapon, he should be especially careful, since the absorbent material used is not manufactured to withstand the heat of a steady blast from an automatic weapon. All of these fac-

tors should be taken into consideration before attempting to build a device of this nature.

Following are illustrations and descriptions of a few basic firearm silencers, but I must repeat the necessity for caution, not only because of possible legal reprisals, but also because, if you do not know what you are doing, the chances are extremely great that you will blow your head off.

In Figure 62 is shown an autoloading military issue .22 caliber pistol. The barrel casing has been removed, and the barrel has been turned down to its minimum thickness. Four rows of eleven holes have been drilled to permit the compressed gases to bleed out, so making this a silent, subsonic weapon. To complete the building of this silencer, all one would have to do is wrap several layers of wire screening around the barrel and cover with an outer metal casing which would extend longer than the barrel itself. This section in front of the barrel is packed with washers stamped out of the same wire screen, and finally capped with a screw-on metal washer. This silencer will make a .22 sound like a BB gun.

On the next two pages I have illustrated an extremely simple silencer, which can be used both with automatic weapons and semi-automatic weapons. "A" is a Thompson Submachine Gun with the silencer attached, and "C" is the M-3 Submachine Gun with the silencer attached. "B" is a cross-section view of the Thompson silencer, which also applies to the M-3.

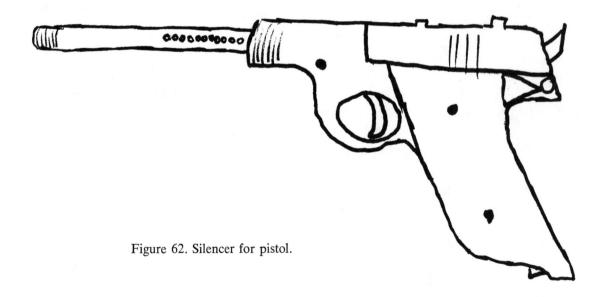

Figure 62. Silencer for pistol.

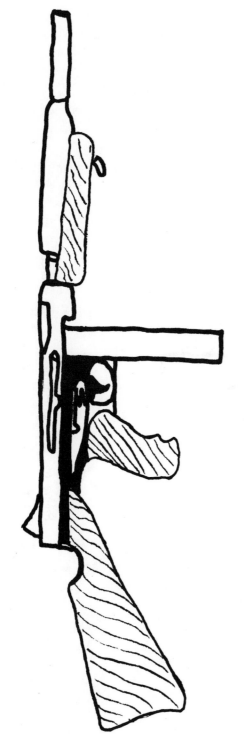

Figure 63. Thompson submachine gun with silencer.

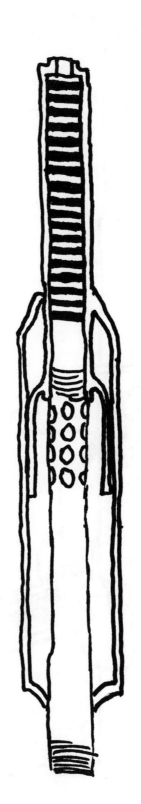

Figure 64. Cross-section view of Thompson submachine-gun silencer.

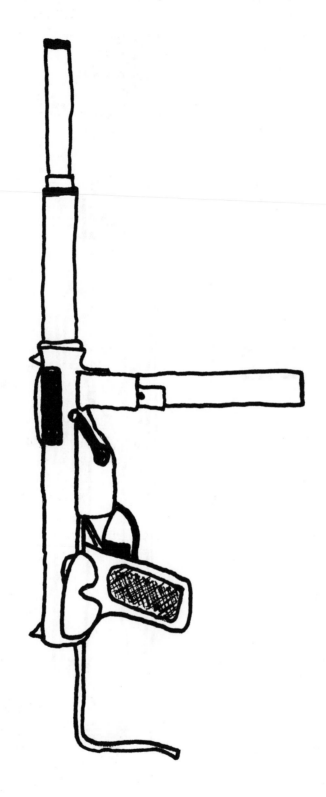

Figure 65. M-3 submachine gun with silencer.

In diagram "B," you can see that the silencer functions with a great similarity to the auto-loading .22 silencer in Figure 62. It is constructed with two tubes—a large rear one and a smaller front one, which join in the middle with an adapter. The larger rear tube encases the barrel, which has four rows of four holes drilled in it. Surrounding the barrel are several layers of bronze screening and then the large metal tube. The smaller connecting front tube houses 250 of the screen-type washers, with a screw-on cap at the end to keep the washers in place. The washers must have their holes large enough and in direct line with each other, so that the bullet can pass through without touching any of them. As a general rule for the construction of firearm silencers, one could say that it is unadvisable to bring the bullet into contact with the silencer itself. However, certain supersonic silencers do require this. The type of silencer works well, since it is used with weapons that employ .45 acp, which is subsonic and doesn't need to be reduced in velocity.

Most states have pretty strict regulations about the possession of machine guns—even small ones—so you had better check all the angles, before screwing yourself into jail.

How to build a silencer for a submachine gun

The Viet Cong have adapted this type of submachine-gun silencer for their combat situation and, in doing so, have made it much more effective and simple to build. The first and larger tube (160 mm. long and 40 mm. in diameter) is filled with bronze screening the same as pictured in Figure 63, except they have added oil-soaked cotton, and then attached it to the gun barrel. This oil-soaked cotton acts as a cooling agent, which is very important to consider when dealing with automatic weapons in a combat situation. The second smaller tube (170 mm. long and 30 mm. in diameter) is stuffed with a roll of bronze screening, which is much simpler than washers. The silencer is about 70 per cent effective, meaning that it cannot be heard over a distance of 300 to 400 yards, which is a fantastic advantage for the guerrilla fighter.

There are many claims for improvised silencers. At this point I have not had the chance to experiment with, or try, any of these, but many of them sound as if they should have some degree of validity.

1. Take a section of metal tubing and fill it with bottle caps, which have an "X" cut in the center of each and the flaps bent back, so as to form a small triangular passageway for the bullet.

2. A rubber nursing bottle nipple with an "X" slit in the top of the nipple, then placed over the end of the barrel, reportedly reduces the sound of the shot, but this type is only good for one shot.

3. One effective silencer was made from a row of washers attached to a welding rod and fitted with an outside casing.

4. It has been said that a balloon strung over an egg-beater-type wire frame was good for one shot.

Bows and arrows

A bow and arrow has been proven to be an effective weapon even today, with all our supertechnology. The great advantage to the bow and arrow is silence. One can snipe without being seen or heard. A long or so-called straight bow is large and bulky. Therefore, I recommend a crossbow if you are to use any. A crossbow can be purchased through a sporting goods store or through mail order, even though crossbows are illegal for hunting in many states. A crossbow is not a toy. It is a deadly weapon and should command the same respect as a firearm. Always unstring your bow after use. If it is a wooden bow, keep it in a dry place to prevent warpage. Check all arrows and bolts before purchasing them for warpage. This can be done by "sighting them." This entails looking down from the feathered end to the tip, watching for any curvature that might exist.

The crossbow illustrated in Figure 66 is a good one, although there are more powerful ones. It is capable of going almost completely through a large telephone book at 25

Figure 66. Crossbow.

yards. One word of caution about a bow and arrow set, and that is that you must practice carefully before attempting to use it as a weapon. Archery is a skill that is learned, and it is much harder than riflery. Although you don't have to worry about recoil with a bow, you do have to worry about the insides of your wrists. I have seen a guy take all the skin off the inside of his arm with a careless shot.

Fiberglass is better than wood, as it doesn't warp. Get a bow with over 50 pounds pull, as anything less is for target practice. The arrows or bolts themselves have many different points. Stick with a hunting tip.

Chemicals and gases

I saw the corpse of my daughter Annie incinerated, and her sexual organs squandered and divided after her death by the Police of France.

Antonin Artaud, *Artaud Anthology*

The development of tear gas was a long step forward in the history of civilization.

Robert Reynolds (President of Federal Laboratories, the world's largest producer of tear gas)

I was just rereading a manual on non-lethal police weapons for controlling mob action, and, just as every time before, it blew my mind. The police are really uptight about the recent rise in demonstrations and unrest. They have spent incredible amounts of money developing all types of weapons for control. They have a machine which can be driven into a riot area and in a matter of minutes fill a ten-block area, four feet deep, with a nontoxic colored foam. The foam will prevent movement on the part of the demonstrators, and the color will identify them later for the arrests. The police have also developed an even more frightening weapon. It consists of a truck with a loudspeaker on the top which can be driven into the riot area. A high-pitched sound, like a silent dog whistle, is broadcast from it. This high-pitched sound cannot be heard, but it manages to jumble the brain and render the individual helpless—unable to move or think. Although it's not permanent, it's still pretty frightening. The field in which these police scientists have made the most headway is with chemicals and gases. They have not stuck to non-toxic chemicals, but are using gases that permanently maim people. The redeeming feature is that these gases are not hard to make, and are available to everyone, although their possession is illegal in most states.

The most simple chemical agent is either common pepper or mustard powder. Both work pretty well at close range. If they are thrown into the eyes, or inhaled through the nose, they will cause confusion, temporary blindness, and an extreme burning sensation in the nasal passages. The major disadvantage of pepper or mustard powder is the manner in which they are projected. On the following pages is a method to produce an effective tear gas, which will act much more efficiently than either pepper or mustard.

Many states have made tear gas illegal to possess, but a form of pepper gas is still available in small penlike containers. These usually sell for under five dollars, and work very well—especially in an enclosed area. A direct spray from one of these devices will totally incapacitate a person. They are available in most novelty stores, particularly around Times Square in New York.

How to make tear gas in your basement

The method of making tear gas is so simple that anyone can do it. The two things to remember are care and caution. You will need a certain amount of equipment but, just like the chemicals, it is available from any hobby shop, or home chemical supplier. If you don't already own a gas mask, go out and get one. They are sold at Army-Navy stores for under ten dollars. Listed below are the materials necessary:

1. Ring stand	14. Rubber tubing
2. Alcohol lamp	15. Glass tubing
3. Flask (300-ml.)	16. Rubber stopper
4. Clamp	17. Collecting bottle
5. Rubber stopper	18. Glass tubing
6. Glass tubing	19. Rubber tubing
7. Clamp holder	20. Glass tubing
8. Rubber tubing	21. Rubber tubing
9. Condenser	22. Air trap bottle
10. Rubber tubing	23. Glass tubing
11. Ring stand	24. Rubber tubing
12. Clamp and clamp holder	25. Glass tubing
13. Rubber tubing	26. Beaker (300-ml.)

Method for preparing tear gas:

1. Work in a garage, or outside if possible—not in the kitchen.

2. Mix ten parts of glycerine with two parts of sodium bisulfate, in flask (No. 3), and heat. Do not fill more than

one-third of flask, as mixture froths when heated. When the frothing begins, adjust heat.

3. As soon as you see no more tear gas being generated, and solids beginning to be formed in the generating flask (No. 3), or a brown residue in the tube (No. 6), remove the heat source, *with your gas mask on,* and pour out the residue in flask. You must pour this outside. *Do not pour down sink or toilet.*

4. Remove collecting jar (No. 17) and stopper it quickly. What you have collected here is tear gas.

5. Do not attempt to make more than three ounces at one time.

6. Make sure all joints are tight.

Method to step up equipment:

1. Metal base ring stands (1 and 11) are placed on working surface.

2. Clamp and clamp holder (4 and 7) are placed onto ring stand (1).

3. Clamp and clamp holder (12) are placed on ring stand (11).

4. Generating flask (3) is placed in clamp (4).

5. Two pieces of rubber tubing (10 and 13) are connected to condenser (9).

6. Condenser (9) is placed into clamp (12).

7. Segment of glass tubing (6) is placed in rubber stopper (5).

8. Segments of glass tubing (15 and 18) are put into rubber stopper (16).

9. Segments of glass tubing (20 and 23) are put into rubber stopper (21).

10. Rubber stopper (5) is put into the mouth of the generating flask (3).

11. Rubber stopper (16) is put into mouth of collecting bottle (17).

12. Rubber stopper (21) is put into mouth of air trap bottle (22).

13. Connect glass tubing (6) with condenser (9) and with rubber tubing (8).

14. Connect condenser (9) with glass tubing (15) and with rubber tubing (14).

15. Connect glass tubing (18) with glass tubing (20) and rubber tubing (19).

16. Connect glass tubing (23) with glass tubing (24) and with rubber tubing (24).

17. Connect rubber tubing (13) to a faucet.

18. Put end of rubber tubing (10) into a sink or drain.

19. Fill beaker (26) three-quarters full of water, and place glass tubing (25) in the water.

20. Put ingredients into generating flask (3).

21. Turn on water to rubber tubing (13).

22. Light wick on alcohol heater (2) and place under generating flask (3).

The best method for putting tear gas into operation is to place it under pressure in a glass vial or bottle. Then throw the bottle at the target you have in mind. The glass will break on contact and allow the tear gas to escape. Other successful methods have been proven, including compressing in an atomizer, aerosol can, or seltzer bottles and the like.

Defense and medical treatment for gases

The problem with gas (offensively) is that it is so easy to defend against, and chances are very good that the people you intend to use it against are prepared for it. At this point in the struggle, any urban or rural guerrilla should have a gas mask. Everyone should understand the simple procedures for the treatment of a gas victim. Everyone should be able to identify the type of gas being used against him, so as to determine the type of treatment, and the seriousness of the situation. These factors I will go into on the next few pages.

There are five different types of gases used by the police at this point, and the effective forms of defense vary. A defense for one may cause more severe effects when used against another. Such is the case with vaseline. Vaseline works well against mace, since mace is a liquid, but it causes gases to adhere to the skin and thus results in more serious burns.

Police have been using canisters that do not explode on contact with the ground, but rather when picked up after the initial impact. This causes the gas to explode directly in the individual's face. Whereas a rubber gas mask is good protection against most types of gases, it is ineffective and

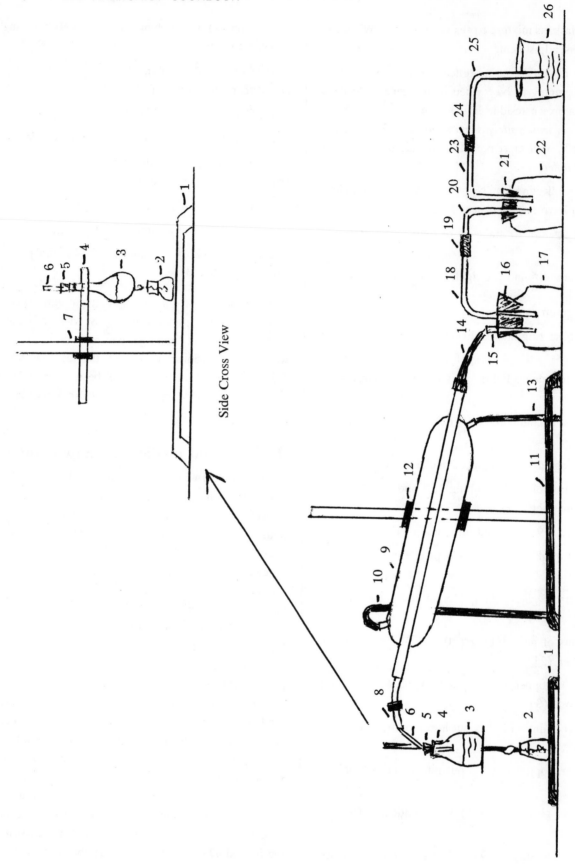

Figure 67. Equipment set up for preparing tear gas.

even dangerous if worn when nausea gas has been used. Wet paper towels and surgical masks can be used to ease breathing problems but are also ineffective against nausea gas. So the most important consideration before treating a gas or chemical victim is to determine the type of gas or chemical used.

CS tear gas: This gas is dispensed in various-sized canisters, plastic grenades, and fog machines, and can be sprayed over an entire area from a helicopter. When you are hit with this type of gas, you will suffer coughing, running nose and eyes, burning of the eyes, a reddening of the exposed area, nausea, and in some cases dizziness. To relieve the burning and running eyes, wash them out with one part boric acid and three parts water. If boric acid is not available, use normal tap water. Standard eye drops can be used effectively. The next step in the treatment of CS gas is to get the actual gas off your skin. This can be accomplished by applying mineral oil to the exposed portions of your skin. If mineral oil is unavailable, use water, but directly after you have applied the water, wipe the entire exposed area, except eyes, with alcohol. This will relieve the sting by substituting a cooling sensation. If the alcohol is not applied, the stinging and burning may last up to two hours, whereas the alcohol will cut the time down to a matter of minutes. A gas mask, or wet cloth or paper towel, can effectively be used against this form of gas.

CN gas: This is basically the same as CS gas, but a much milder form. It comes in the same type of container and has the same type of effect, but it is not quite as unpleasant. The treatment is just washing the exposed portions with water. In most cases, the mineral oil and alcohol will not be necessary.

Nausea gas: This is an extremely dangerous gas, as it is colorless and odorless. It does not affect the tear ducts, so chances are great that a person will not even know it has been used until it's too late. It comes in the same type of containers as the CS and CN gas do. The effect this gas has is pretty bad. I've never been hit with this stuff myself, but I have spoken to some friends from the army, who have. They told me that nausea gas is the worst there is. A person exposed to it vomits instantly on inhalation, but it is not a normal form of vomiting. It is a result of a muscle contraction and is referred to as projective vomiting. Projective vomiting is the ejection of the contents of the stomach over several feet. This can result in the ripping of the stomach or throat lining. As well as vomiting, the person experiences instant diarrhea. These are pretty disgusting symptoms, but on top of these the individual also loses the normal balance of his mind. He may find it extremely difficult to perform normal functions, such as walking or running. If a person has respiratory difficulties, he should be taken to a doctor immediately. There isn't much you can do about nausea gas yourself, except wait for the symptoms to go away. If the symptoms do not disappear or become more pronounced, get to a doctor. There is no protection against this type of gas. Gas masks, if worn, should be taken off as soon as you realize that it is nausea gas, as you might choke on your own vomit. The only effective protection is just running like hell, and getting out of the area. Because there is no effective form of protection against nausea gas, its use is somewhat limited; since not even the president can order the wind around.

Blister gas: This is even more strange and frightening than nausea gas but, thank God, it is a great deal rarer. I have had no experience with this form, but, from what I can gather, it is pretty foul. It causes blisters on the exposed portions of skin: They may come up in minutes after the initial exposure or they can take up to several days to appear. This type of gas does not affect the eyes or throat, so it may be difficult to know whether the gas is being used. The only protection against it is to cover up all portions of skin. This may include gloves, hats, bandages, long pants, etc. (girls should never wear skirts to demonstrations). The treatment for blisters is applying mineral oil and keeping the blistered area from the air. Try to get to a medic or doctor immediately. Anyone blistered should keep off the streets, as the cops or military will be able to identify anyone with blisters.

Mace: Mace is a liquid rather than a gas, and is used more on a person-to-person basis than in crowd control. It is made up of 10 percent CS gas, 70 percent a propellant agent (sodium bicarbonate), and 20 percent kerosene. The kerosene is the agent ingredient that causes the severe burning sensations. If you have been hit with mace, you know exactly what I am talking about. It feels as if you're thrown into a blast furnace, while your eyeballs are extracted from their sockets and submerged in a concentrated solution of sulfuric acid. The pain that mace causes is intense, and this in turn causes the breakdown of normal physical and mental functions, such as running. If you are sprayed in the mouth, it may lead to uncontrolled convulsions. The treatment for a mace victim is as follows: Wash out his eyes with the same boric acid solution described in the section on CS gas, wash all exposed portions of his body with water, then apply rubbing alcohol to dilute the kerosene and relieve the burning. The combination of ski goggles and a thin layer of vaseline covering the face has proven to work pretty well. The vaseline must be wiped off immediately after exposure.

The thing to remember is that all these gases and chemicals have been developed for use against Americans. The military isn't using mace in Vietnam, but mace is being used in Watts and Harlem. Millions of dollars are being spent every year to find new ways to control the people who supposedly control the government.

Figures 68 and 69 illustrate different forms of darts. These could be extremely effective for the guerrilla fighter, as they can be fired from an air gun with little or no sound. Figure 68 is especially interesting, as it shows the complete construction of a rapid injection dart, with a special compartment for the "drug of your choice."

There is an old saying that "ignorance is no excuse." Well, at this point one could take it a step further and say ignorance can be fatal. A young person today must have the technology and the know-how. Never before have self-sufficiency and education been so important, and they are virtually inseparable from survival.

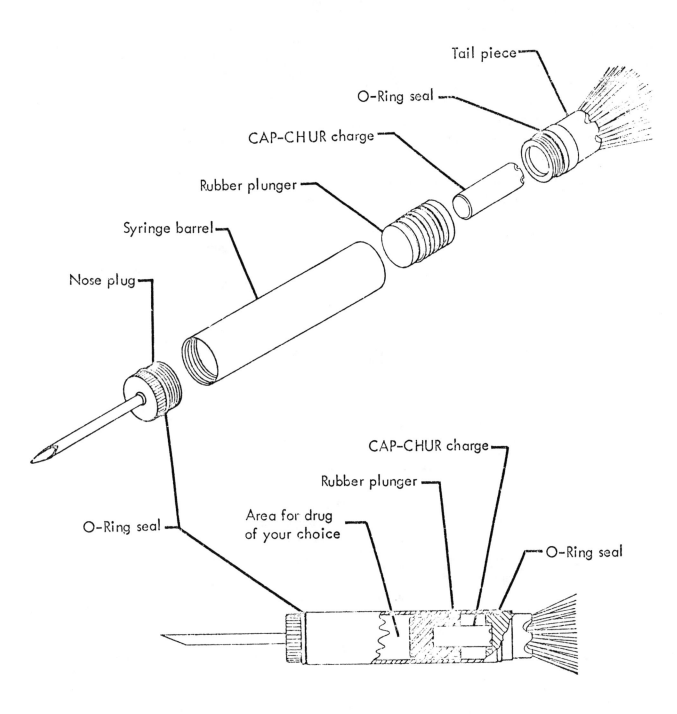

Figure 68. Darts for rapid injection.

DYE MARKER DART

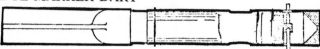

This dart is loaded with a nontoxic uranine dye—a bright yellow fluorescent color. It can be loaded with various liquids such as special stench liquids or vomit inducers.

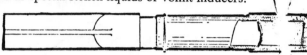

The uses of such a projectile are to mark or identify individuals in a crowd where contact and arrest are impractical. It has the effect of destroying anonymity.

HYPODERMIC SYRINGE PROJECTILE

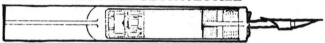

Hypodermic syringes in dart form for animal control. This projectile can accurately deliver and inject a 1cc dose into unapproachable animals.

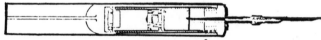

Pressurized ampules are available for loading by veterinarians. The serum is injected by compressed air behind a piston after the needle has come to rest in flesh. The dart's accuracy is a considerable factor in its usefulness.

TRAINING DART

This projectile is provided in similar weight and balance to the various "line" darts to give a similar trajectory pattern so that the trainee can get the feel of the gun without expending expensive rounds. It can be fired indefinitely at "soft" targets—a mat or pad is suggested as a backstop for training.

TEAR GAS DART

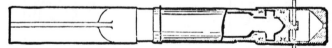

This dart is designed to carry 2.5 cc. of liquid tear gas that covers an area of 12 to 15″ in diameter. It has a safety spring clip. The clip is withdrawn on loading, making the projectile ready for firing.

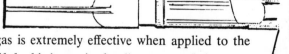

The tear gas is extremely effective when applied to the person even if the hit is not in the direct area of the eyes. It's practical to shoot at ranges from 10 to 50 yards.

Figure 69. Police projectiles

chapter four: Explosives and Booby Traps

Figure 70. The crazed anarchist.

The most heroic word in all languages is Revolution.

—Eugene Debs

This chapter is going to kill and maim more people than all the rest put together, because people just refuse to take things seriously. The formulas and recipes in here are real, they can be made by almost anyone, and they can be performed in the kitchen. I offer a serious note of caution. The people in the house on 11th Street (killed in New York City early in 1970 in an explosion caused by bombs they were making) did not know what they were doing. Not only did they kill themselves, but also some innocent people. Ignorance thus not only becomes fatal and inexcusable, but also criminal. If you are not absolutely sure of what you are doing, *do not do it*. The revolution has too many God-damn martyrs as it is.

Explosives, if used with care and all the necessary precautions, are one of the greatest tools any liberation movement can have. Ninety percent of all sabotage is based on some sort of demolitions, or booby traps. Most of the lethal weapons in the previous chapter rely on a small explosive charge. The actual application of explosives can be a really thrilling and satisfying experience. I have a friend who worked with demolitions in the Middle East, and he has told me on several occasions that an explosion for him was an experience very similar to a sexual orgasm. This may seem strange to anyone who has no experience with explosives, but in many regards it is absolutely true. An explosion is an amazing phenomenon. Coupled with the destruction of an object of popular hatred, it can become more than just a chemical reaction. It can take the shape of hope for a nation of oppressed people. It is a total sensual experience. It affects all the senses, and in primitive societies was considered a God, and worshiped. If you have read about any guerrilla struggles, or experienced any, you will realize that an explosion has many effects, especially when it is controlled by the oppressed group. It will confuse the enemy, cause destruction and death, impress and frighten the enemy with the power and technology of the people.

Maybe I should clarify some points for my own moral conscience. These recipes are not in this book for use by a minority. I do not place them here to be used by fringe political groups. They are included in this book to educate, since we have already decided that ignorance is inexcusable, fatal, and criminal. They are for the people, rich and poor, right and left, black, Spanish, white, middle-of-the-road liberals, young and old. This is the type of training the forces of fascism, communism, and capitalism get. It is my belief that all the people should have access to these skills, to be able to repel these oppressive forces.

Sometimes I wonder which side the so-called "liberation army" is on, meaning that I cannot understand any man who wishes to blow up department stores, unless he has an outstanding bill, but even then that's carrying capitalism a bit too far. The real problem comes from the fringe political factions, who at this point are so alienated from the real people of America that they think they are living in Russia in 1917. All of the faction groups cause great strife for the forces that are. No longer can the arthritic armchair politicos blame all the unrest on Cuban infiltrators, or Canadian saboteurs. They are confused, poor bastards. They really think that the Black Panthers were going to blow up the Botanical Gardens. If that type of reaction was observed under the controls of a psychology lab, I am sure they would have a name for it.

The important thing to remember is that this kind of reaction is madness, but an extremely clever and dangerous form. Madness creates its own fatal hubris, and will destroy itself; but sometimes it does need a push in the right direction.

There is a great misconception in some strata of our society that an explosion, wherever it goes off, is better than no explosion. I have spoken to many individuals who subscribe to this belief, holding that everyone is guilty of something and must be punished for it. The corporations which support the war should be bombed, the liberals who will not get off their asses should be shot, the politicians who don't care about the people must die, anyone who lives in the Middle West or South is a redneck and a potential threat to the revolution, etc. This may be hard to appreciate, but it is nevertheless true. Let us take as an example an individual who wished to destroy the Roman Catholic Church. He would not only be a fool, but a murderer, if he threw a bomb into a full church on Sunday morning. A much more intelligent and effective approach to the problem would be a well-placed rumor, defaming the Pope, so that the Catholic people themselves destroyed their own church.

When I use the term revolution, I do not use it in the same context or with the same meaning of Che Guevara, or Lenin, or anyone else. I see "the revolution" as a humanistic change, which may or may not incorporate violence. It must be a revitalization of the American system to take us back to the real moral and political principles adopted in 1776. Maybe I am not a revolutionary, but then it's all terminology, and more intolerance has sprung out of semantic misunderstandings than any other cause.

A freedom fighter, whether working within or outside the system, must be a pragmatic opportunist, meaning that he must be able to see his advantages, in any situation, regardless of how bad conditions may seem at first. A freedom fighter can never surrender, for if he does he becomes part of the problem. As for the guerrilla, the violent freedom fighter, there is no trial in times of trouble—just torture and death.

There are individuals, in our society, who claim that we cannot exist without oppression and regulation, because we are children. I agree that we are children, because we have always had supervision, and have never been allowed the freedom to see ourselves in a different light. We are all children of the humanistic revolution, and, whether certain individuals like it or not, American children are growing up, fast.

Explosives fall into two basic classes. The first is high explosives, which include dynamite, TNT, nitroglycerine, and plastique. The second class is low explosives, which have less of an explosive report and power than the higher class. The low explosives include smokeless powder, black powder, and other less powerful chemical reactions. I will deal with each class separately, starting first with high explosives, and then going on to the lower ones. Following this, I have included a very important section, that must be read. This is the safety precautions for and methods of handling the different forms of explosives. Following the safety precautions is a section on actual application of demolitions and booby traps. I would like to make it clear that no part of this chapter should be used without first reading and studying the rest of it.

How to make nitroglycerin

Almost all modern explosives are a derivative of a nitric acid base. Although fuming nitric acid (98 percent solution in water) is not an explosive in itself, it is explosive when mixed with many other compounds. This process of mixing a compound with nitric acid chemically is called the nitrating principle. The best-known nitrating agent is glycerin, but many others can be and are used. Mercury, sugar, cork, wheat germ, sawdust, starch, lard, and indigo are all common nitrating agents and are used in modern industry. For example when sawdust is nitrated, it be-

comes nitrocellulose, and is used in smokeless powder. Mercury fulminate (nitrated mercury) is a very powerful and effective detonator.

The next recipe is for nitroglycerin. Nitroglycerin is a high explosive, with an incredibly unstable nature. It can explode for the most minute reasons, such as a change of one or two degrees in temperature, or a minor shock. Because of nitroglycerin's unstable nature, I would suggest that only people with an extensive background training in both chemistry and explosives try this procedure.

Nitroglycerin $C_3H_5(NO_3)_3$.

1. Fill a 75-milliliter beaker, to the 13-ml. level, with fuming red nitric acid, of 98 percent concentration.

2. Place beaker in an ice bath and allow to cool below room temperature.

3. After it is cooled, add to it three times the amount of fuming sulfuric acid (99 percent H_2SO_4). In other words, add to the now-cool fuming nitric acid 39 milliliters of fuming sulfuric acid. When mixing any acids, always do it slowly and carefully to avoid splattering.

4. When the two are mixed, lower their temperature, by adding more ice to the bath, to about 10 or 15 degrees Centigrade. This can be measured by using a mercury-operated Centigrade thermometer.

5. When the acid solution has cooled to the desired temperature, it is ready for the glycerin. The glycerin *must be added in small amounts using a medicine dropper*. Glycerin is added, slowly and carefully, until the entire surface of the acid is covered with it.

6. This is a dangerous point, since the nitration will take place as soon as the glycerin is added. The nitration will produce heat, so the solution *must be kept below 30 degrees C*. If the solution should go above 30 degrees, the beaker should be taken out of the ice bath and the solution should be carefully poured directly into the ice bath, since this will prevent an explosion.

7. For about the first ten minutes of the nitration, the mixture should be gently stirred. In a normal reaction, the nitroglycerin will form as a layer on top of the acid solution, while the sulfuric acid will absorb the excess water.

8. After the nitration has taken place and the nitroglycerin has formed at the top of the solution, the entire beaker should be transferred very slowly and carefully to an-

other beaker of water. When this is done, the nitroglycerin will settle to the bottom, so that most of the acid solution can be drained away.

9. After removing as much acid as possible without disturbing the nitroglycerin, remove the nitroglycerin with an eyedropper and place it in a bicarbonate of soda (sodium bicarbonate) solution. The sodium bicarbonate is an alkali and will neutralize much of the acid remaining. This process should be repeated as many times as necessary using blue litmus paper to check for the presence of acid. The remaining acid only makes the nitroglycerin more unstable than it normally is.

10. The final step is to remove the nitroglycerin from the bicarbonate. This is done with an eye dropper, slowly and carefully. The usual test to see if nitration has been successful is to place one drop of the nitroglycerin on a metal plate and ignite it. If it is true nitroglycerin, it will burn with a clear blue flame. *Caution:* Nitroglycerin is extremely sensitive to decomposition, heating, dropping, or jarring, and may explode even if left undisturbed and cool. *Know what you are doing before you do it.*

How to make mercury fulminate

When employing the use of any high explosive, an individual must also use some kind of detonating device. Blasting caps are probably the most popular today, since they are very functional and relatively stable. The prime ingredient in most blasting caps and detonating devices in general is mercury fulminate. There are several methods for preparing mercury fulminate.

Method No. 1 for the preparation of mercury fulminate:

1. Take 5 grams of pure mercury and mix it with 35 ml. of nitric acid.

2. The mixture is slowly and gently heated. As soon as the solution bubbles and turns green, one knows that the silver mercury is dissolved.

3. After it is dissolved, the solution should be poured, slowly, into a small flask of ethyl alcohol. This will result in red fumes.

4. After a half hour or so, the red fumes will turn white, indicating that the process is nearing its final stage.

5. After a few minutes, add distilled water to the solution.

6. The entire solution is now filtered, in order to obtain the small white crystals. These crystals are pure mercury fulminate, but should be washed many times, and tested with litmus paper for any remaining undesirable acid.

Method No. 2 for the preparation of mercury fulminate:

1. Mix one part mercuric oxide with ten parts ammonia solution. When ratios are described, they are always done according to weight rather than volume.

2. After waiting eight to ten days, one will see that the mercuric oxide has reacted with the ammonia solution to produce the white fulminate crystals.

3. These crystals must be handled in the same way as the first method described, in that they must be washed many times and given several litmus paper tests.

Many other fulminates can be made in the same manner as above, but I will not go into these, since most are extremely unstable and sensitive to shock. All fulminates, including mercury fulminate, are sensitive to shock and friction, and in no circumstances should they be handled in a rough or careless manner.

How to make blasting gelatin

One of the nearly perfect explosive compounds, in the sense of chemical combustion rather than stability, is blasting gelatin. This was discovered by Nobel, and is a very primitive form of plastique, as we know it today. It is made by mixing a small amount of nitrocellulose (nitrated sawdust) with a larger amount of nitroglycerin. This creates a stiff, plastic substance which has power as an explosive greater than either of its ingredients. A person attempting to make this should use 92 percent nitroglycerin and 8 percent nitrocellulose, and pray. If you don't want to mess with making nitrocellulose and have access to guncotton, it can be substituted. Any recipe listed in this chapter which employs unstable or sensitive explosive compounds, such as nitroglycerin, should be left alone by all those who do not have access to a laboratory or previous training. This book is not enough training to mess with these compounds.

Formulas for the straight dynamite series

Probably one of the single greatest breakthroughs in explosives came by accident, when Nobel discovered a primitive form of dynamite. One of the primary ingredients of dynamite is nitroglycerin, which has great explosive power, although it has the disadvantage of being ultrasensitive to heat and shock. What dynamite does is to combine the high explosive power of nitroglycerin with a stabilizing agent, to render it powerful but safely usable. Nobel developed what is called today the straight dynamite series, which is nothing more than nitroglycerin and a stabilizing agent. The most common straight dynamite formulas follow (nitroglycerin will be referred to as NG):

1) NG	32
sodium nitrate	28
woodmeal	10
ammonium oxalate	29
guncotton	1

2) NG	24
potassium nitrate	9
sodium nitrate	56
woodmeal	9
ammonium oxalate	2

3) NG	35.5
potassium nitrate	44.5
woodmeal	6
guncotton	2.5
vaseline	5.5
powdered charcoal	6

4) NG	25
potassium nitrate	26
woodmeal	34
barium nitrate	5
starch	10

5) NG	57
potassium nitrate	19
woodmeal	9
ammonium oxalate	12
guncotton	3

6) NG	18
sodium nitrate	70
woodmeal	5.5
potassium chloride	4.5
chalk	2

7) NG	26
woodmeal	40
barium nitrate	32
sodium carbonate	2

8) NG	44
woodmeal	12
anhydrous sodium sulfate	44

9) NG	24
potassium nitrate	32.5
woodmeal	33.5
ammonium oxalate	10

10) NG	26
potassium nitrate	33
woodmeal	41

11) NG	15
sodium nitrate	62.9
woodmeal	21.2
sodium carbonate	.9

12) NG	35
sodium nitrate	37
woodmeal	27
ammonium oxalate	1

13) NG	32
potassium nitrate	27
woodmeal	10
ammonium oxalate	30
guncotton	1

14) NG	33
woodmeal	10.3
ammonium oxalate	29
guncotton	.7
potassium perchloride	27

15) NG	40
sodium nitrate	45
woodmeal	15

16) Ng	47
starch	50
guncotton	3

17) Ng	30
sodium nitrate	22.3
woodmeal	40.5
potassium chloride	7.2

18) Ng	50
sodium nitrate	32.6
woodmeal	17
ammonium oxalate	.4

19) NG	23
potassium nitrate	27.5
woodmeal	37
ammonium oxalate	8
barium nitrate	4
calcium carbonate	.5

The figures given in the right column are percentage parts, adding up to a sum of 100 percent. Percentage parts are always based on a weight ratio rather than volume. When preparing any high-explosive formula, be sure you know what you are doing. Have the correct equipment, and the correct chemicals. Many of these chemicals are sold under brand names, which are more familiar than their chemical names, but, before assuming anything, read the ingredients, and take nothing for granted.

These formulas listed above are for straight dynamite. Straight dynamite is a very primitive form of what we know today as dynamite. Later ammonium nitrate was added to the dynamite. This substance produced a greater explosive action, but less velocity. The intensification of the explosive action results because ammonium nitrate furnishes more oxygen for the dynamite. Ammonium nitrate has not only been used in dynamite, but also in many other different explosive compounds, including NG., picric acid, and coal dust. Ammonium nitrate when mixed with these substances creates the cheapest form of high explosive known to man.

How to make chloride of azode

A good example of how ammonium nitrate can be chemically mixed with other substances, and impart its explosive qualities to these otherwise nonexplosive materials, is in the preparation of chloride of azode.

1. A quantity of chlorine gas is collected in a small glass beaker, and placed upside down on another glass beaker containing a water solution of ammonium nitrate.

2. Now the solution of ammonium nitrate is heated gently. While it is being heated, the surface of the solution will become oily, and finally small droplets will form and sink to the bottom of the beaker.

3. After this process is finished, remove the heat and drain off excess ammonium nitrate solution. The droplets that remain at the bottom of the beaker are chloride of azode of nitrochloride. Nitrochloride explodes violently when brought into contact with an open flame, or when exposed to temperatures above 212 degrees F.

There are hundreds and hundreds of formulas for the use of ammonium nitrate, in different explosive compounds. The ones on the following pages are only the major, or well-known, ones. For further information, a chemistry manual or handbook of explosives can be useful.

Formulas for ammonium nitrate compounds

1) ammonium nitrate 60
potassium nitrate 29.5
sulfur flour 2.5
charcoal powder 4
woodmeal 4

2) ammonium nitrate 34
potassium nitrate 34
T.N.T. 17
ammonium chloride 15

3) ammonium nitrate 59
woodmeal 10
nitroglycerin 10
sodium chloride 20
magnesium carbonate 1

4) ammonium nitrate 70
ammonium sulfate 9
nitroglycerin 6
barium sulfate 7
dextrin 8

5) ammonium nitrate 88
charcoal powder 12

6) ammonium nitrate 75
aluminum powder 25

7) ammonium nitrate 94
potassium nitrate 2
charcoal powder 4

8) ammonium nitrate 64
T.N.T. 15
sodium chloride 21

9) ammonium nitrate 60
woodmeal 10
nitroglycerin 10
sodium chloride 20

10) ammonium nitrate 35
potassium nitrate 33
T.N.T. 12
ammonium chloride 20

11) ammonium nitrate 87
charcoal powder 13

12) ammonium nitrate 92.5
potassium bichromate 2
naphthalene 5.5

13) ammonium nitrate 70
ammonium sulfate 9
nitroglycerin 6
barium sulfate 7
dextrin 8

14) ammonium nitrate 65.5
T.N.T. 15
sodium chloride 5
potassium chloride 14.5

15) ammonium nitrate 68
woodmeal 8
nitroglycerin 9
potassium chloride 15

16) ammonium nitrate 76
woodmeal 2
T.N.T. 16
potassium perchloride 6

17) ammonium nitrate 73
barium nitrate 19
potato starch 8

18) ammonium nitrate 80
woodmeal 10
nitroglycerin 10

19) ammonium nitrate 63.5
sulfur flour 2
charcoal flour 18.5
ammonium sulfate 7.5
water 1
copper sulfate 7.5

20) ammonium nitrate 65
sulfur flour 2
charcoal powder 20
rice starch 9
paraffin wax 3
water 1

21) ammonium nitrate 85
cellulose residue 15

22) ammonium nitrate 88
dinitronaphthalene 12

23) ammonium nitrate 80.75
charcoal powder 4.25
pyro powdered
aluminum 15

24) ammonium nitrate 88
charcoal powder 4
pyro powdered
aluminum 8

25) ammonium nitrate 80
charcoal powder 2
pyro powdered
aluminum 18

26) ammonium nitrate 89
ammonium sulfate 6
aniline hydrochloride 5

27) ammonium nitrate 70
sodium nitrate 20
nitrated resin 10

28) ammonium nitrate 90
charcoal powder 6
pyro powdered
aluminum 4

29) ammonium nitrate 94.5
charcoal powder 2.5
pyro powdered
aluminum 3

30) ammonium nitrate 75
copper oxalate aniline 20
powdered sugar cane 5

31) ammonium nitrate 70
sodium nitrate 25
nitrated resin 5

32) ammonium nitrate 91
potassium nitrate 4
resin 5

33) ammonium nitrate 94
aniline hydrochloride 6

34) ammonium nitrate 90
nitrated resin 10

35) ammonium nitrate 95.1
resin 4.9

36) ammonium nitrate 83.5
dinitrobenzene 16.5

37) ammonium nitrate 84
ammonium nitrocreasol
sulphonate 16

38) ammonium nitrate 87
sodium creasol
sulphonate 13

39) ammonium nitrate 86
charcoal powder 2.5
pyro powdered
aluminum 8
potassium bichromate 3.5

40) ammonium nitrate 70
charcoal powder 20
zinc dust 5
pyro powdered
aluminum 5

41) ammonium nitrate 60
sodium creasol
sulphonate 10
sodium sulphonate 30

42) ammonium nitrate 89.5
T.N.T. 5
wheat flour 5.5

43) ammonium nitrate 65
T.N.T. 6
sodium chloride 20
wheat flour 4
rye flour 5

44) ammonium nitrate 66
T.N.T. 15
sodium chloride 10
wheat flour 4
rye flour 5

45) ammonium nitrate 78
T.N.T. 8
calcium silicide 14

46) ammonium nitrate 81
T.N.T. 17
wheat flour 2

47) ammonium nitrate 85
T.N.T. 15

48) ammonium nitrate 78.5
tetryl 21.5

49) ammonium nitrate 80
T.N.T. 12
nitroglycerin 4
rye flour 4

50) ammonium nitrate 38.5
potassium nitrate 29.5
T.N.T. 10
ammonium chloride 22

51) ammonium nitrate 34.3
sodium nitrate 33.3
T.N.T. 12.2
ammonium chloride 20.2

52) ammonium nitrate 35
potassium nitrate 33
ammonium chloride 20
tetryl 12

53) ammonium nitrate 88
T.N.T. 8
mononitronaphthalene 4

54) ammonium nitrate 89
ammonium oxalate 1
T.N.T. 10

55) ammonium nitrate 80
woodmeal 10
nitroglycerin 10

56) ammonium nitrate 88
T.N.T. 10
graphite 2

57) ammonium nitrate 61
T.N.T. 15
sodium chloride 15
wheat flour 4
rye flour 5

58) ammonium nitrate 77
woodmeal 3
T.N.T. 12
nitroglycerin 3
guncotton 5

59) ammonium nitrate 47.5
potassium nitrate 24
T.N.T. 10
ammonium chloride 18.5

60) ammonium nitrate 57
T.N.T. 15
sodium chloride 21
graphite 7

61) ammonium nitrate   38
    potassium nitrate   35.5
    ammonium oxalate   10.5
    sulfur flour   4.5
    charcoal   11.5

The formulas listed above are for high explosives. They are not for cherry bombs or Roman candles. The ingredients that make up these formulas have several functions: The first is the explosive agent itself, the second is the stabilizing agent, and the third is a texturizer (paraffin). Below are listed the most important and common ingredients that are used to form an explosive compound, and a description of their purpose and function.

Ammonium Nitrate .... An extremely unstable, white explosive, usually in crystalline form.

Aluminum .... A silver metallic powder, when in pyro grade, it is a major ingredient in many ammonal explosive compounds.

Ammonium oxalate ...... A very valuable stabilizing agent, especially for NG.

Barium nitrate .... Nitrated barium, in white crystalline powdered form.

Charcoal Powder .... A fine black powder, which is extremely absorbent, and used extensively in pyrotechnics.

Guncotton .... Nitrated cellulose (sawdust) is fairly stable, but usually used with other ingredients rather than alone. It is about 13-14 percent nitrogen.

Naphthalene .... This is a sensitizing agent that is normally in a white crystalline form.

Paraffin .... This is a primary ingredient in plastique, and acts as a texturizer.

Potassium nitrate .... An explosive compound in itself, which is stable. It is usually in a white crystalline form.

Potassium perchloride ... A white powder used as an igniting agent in high explosives. It is an extremely common ingredient in low explosives.

Resin .... A gummy substance, which is flammable, and used in high explosives as an igniting agent.

Sodium carbonate .... This white crystalline powder acts to neutralize acid, which may make the explosive more unstable than it normally is.

Sodium chloride .... This is nothing more than ordinary table salt, and is used as a cooling agent in many high explosives.

Sodium nitrate .... A stable explosive compound which has the advantage of being water-absorbent.

Sodium sulfate .... A stabilizing powder, which is water-resistant.

Starch .... This can be either potato or corn starch, and acts as an absorbent in many explosive compounds.

Sulfur .... A yellow crystalline powder, which should be used in flour form only.

Vaseline .... A clear petroleum jelly used in a similar manner as paraffin, as a plasticizer, for many forms of exploding gelatins and plastic explosives.

Formulas for gelatin dynamites

The following few pages have some of the most important formulas for gelatin and semi-gelatin dynamites. As with most of the explosive substances in this chapter, there are hundreds of different recipes. Each chemist claims he's got the most powerful and safest recipe. What I have attempted to do is collect the most common industrial and military formulas, since these function in the correct context that this book is written.

1) nitroglycerin   12
   guncotton   .5
   ammonium nitrate   87.5

2) nitroglycerin   88
   potassium nitrate   5
   tetryl   7

3) nitroglycerin   9.5
   guncotton   .5
   ammonium nitrate   59
   woodmeal   6
   ammonium oxalate   10
   sodium chloride   15

4) nitroglycerin   9.5
   guncotton   .5
   ammonium nitrate   59.5
   woodmeal   6
   ammonium oxalate   5
   sodium chloride   19.5

5) nitroglycerin   24
   guncotton   1
   ammonium nitrate   75

6) nitroglycerin   12
   ammonium nitrate   87.5
   collodion cotton   .5

7) nitroglycerin   71
   ammonium nitrate   23
   collodion cotton   4
   charcoal powder   2

8) nitroglycerin   75
   guncotton   5
   potassium nitrate   15
   woodmeal   5

9) nitroglycerin	12
guncotton	.5
ammonium nitrate	82.5
potassium nitrate	5

10) nitroglycerin	30
guncotton	1
ammonium nitrate	68
sodium chloride	1

11) nitroglycerin	9.5
ammonium nitrate	67.5
woodmeal	8
sodium chloride	15

12) nitroglycerin	25
ammonium nitrate	62
tetryl	1
charcoal powder	12

| 13) nitroglycerin | 80 |
| ethylene glycol dinitrate | 20 |

| 14) nitroglycerin | 60 |
| dinitrotoluene | 40 |

15) nitroglycerin	60
guncotton	4
potassium nitrate	28
woodmeal	8

16) nitroglycerin	29
guncotton	1
ammonium nitrate	65
potassium nitrate	5

17) nitroglycerin	55
guncotton	3
potassium nitrate	18
woodmeal	7
anhydrous magnesium sulfate (Epsom salts)	17

18) nitroglycerin	27
guncotton	.7
ammonium nitrate	30
sodium nitrate	30
charcoal powder	11
barium sulfate	1.3

19) nitroglycerin	29
guncotton	1
ammonium nitrate	70

How to make TNT

Probably the most important explosive compound in use today is TNT (trinitrotoluene). This and other very similar types of high explosives are all used by the military, because of their fantastic power—about 2.25 million pounds per square inch, and their great stability. TNT also has the great advantage of being able to be melted at 82 degrees F., so that it can be poured into shells, mortars, or any other projectiles. Military TNT comes in containers which resemble dry cell batteries, and are usually ignited by an electrical charge, coupled with an electrical blasting cap, although there are other methods.

Preparation of TNT

1. Take two beakers. In the first, prepare a solution of 76 percent sulfuric acid, 23 percent nitric acid, and 1 percent water. In the other beaker, prepare another solution of 57 percent nitric acid and 43 percent sulfuric acid (percentages are on a weight ratio rather than volume).

2. Ten grams of the first solution are poured into an empty beaker and placed in an ice bath.

3. Add ten grams of toluene, and stir for several minutes.

4. Remove this beaker from the ice bath and gently heat until it reaches 50 degrees C. The solution is stirred constantly while being heated.

5. Fifty additional grams of the acid, from the first beaker, are added and the temperature is allowed to rise to 55 degrees C. This temperature is held for the next ten minutes, and an oily liquid will begin to form on the top of the acid.

6. After 10 or 12 minutes, the acid solution is returned to the ice bath, and cooled to 45 degrees C. When reaching this temperature, the oily liquid will sink and collect at the bottom of the beaker. At this point, the remaining acid solution should be drawn off, by using a syringe.

7. Fifty more grams of the first acid solution are added to the oily liquid while the temperature is *slowly* being raised to 83 degrees C. After this temperature is reached, it is maintained for a full half hour.

8. At the end of this period, the solution is allowed to cool to 60 degrees C., and is held at this temperature for another full half hour. After this, the acid is again drawn off, leaving once more only the oily liquid at the bottom.

9. Thirty grams of sulfuric acid are added, while the oily liquid is gently heated to 80 degrees C. All temperature increases must be accomplished slowly and gently.

10. Once the desired temperature is reached, 30 grams of the second acid solution are added, and the temperature is raised from 80 degrees C. to 104 degrees C., and is held for three hours.

11. After this three-hour period, the mixture is lowered to 100 degrees C. and is held there for a half hour.

12. After this half hour, the oil is removed from the acid and washed with boiling water.

13. After the washing with boiling water, while being stirred constantly, the TNT will begin to solidify.

14. When the solidification has started, cold water is added to the beaker, so that the TNT will form into pellets. Once this is done, you have a good quality TNT.

Note: The temperatures used in the preparation of TNT are exact, and must be used as such. Do not estimate or use approximations. Buy a good centigrade thermometer.

How to make tetryl

The next two recipes are for the preparation of tetryl and picric acid, both of which are commonly used in compounds containing TNT.

Method for the preparation of tetryl:

1. A small amount of dimethyllaniline is dissolved in an excess amount of concentrated sulfuric acid.

2. This mixture is now added to an equal amount of nitric acid. The new mixture is kept in an ice bath, and is well stirred.

3. After about five minutes, the tetryl is filtered and then washed in cold water.

4. It is now boiled in fresh water, which contains a small amount of sodium bicarbonate. This process acts to neutralize any remaining acid. The washings are repeated as many times as necessary according to the litmus-paper tests. When you are satisfied that the tetryl is free of acid, filter it from the water and allow it to dry. When tetryl is detonated, it reacts in very much the same way as TNT.

How to make picric acid

Method for the preparation of picric acid:

1. Phenol is melted and then mixed with a concentrated solution of sulfuric acid. The mixture is constantly stirred and kept at a steady temperature of 95 degrees C., for four to six hours, depending on the quantities of phenol used.

2. After this, the acid-phenol solution is diluted with distilled water, and an equal excess amount of nitric acid is added. The mixture of the nitric acid will cause an immediate reaction, which will produce heat, so the addition of the acid must be performed slowly, but more importantly the temperature of the solution must *not go above* 110 degrees C.

3. Ten or so minutes after the addition of the nitric acid, the picric acid will be fully formed, and you can draw off the excess acid. It should be filtered and washed in the same manner as above, until the litmus paper tests show that there is little or no acid present. When washing, use only cold water. After this, the picric acid should be allowed to partially dry.

Picric acid is a more powerful explosive than TNT, but it has disadvantages. It is much more expensive to make, and is best handled in a wet 10 per cent distilled water form, as picric acid becomes very unstable when completely dry. This compound should never be put into direct contact with any metal, since instantly on contact there is a formation of metal picrate, which explodes spontaneously upon formation.

How to make low explosives

Up to this point, I have referred only to high explosives, but there are many formulas and recipes for low explosives, which, although they do not have the power or impact of the high explosives, are generally speaking safer to use and handle. It may seem at first that an explosive compound that has less power is a disadvantage, but this is not true. If a high-explosive charge were used to set off a bullet in a gun, the gun would probably explode in the user's face. Therefore, low explosives have a definite purpose and use, and are not interchangeable with high explosives. Although I stated above that, generally speaking, low explosives are more stable than high explosives, there are some low-explosive compounds that are as dangerous as high-explosive compounds, if not more so. Below is a chart of the most common low-explosive combinations and their stabilities and merit.

Potassium and sodium nitrate gunpowders: These are without a doubt one of the safest low explosives to handle. They are especially good when packed into a tight container, and exploded under pressure.

Smokeless powder: This type of low explosive is much like the one mentioned above, in the sense that it is extremely stable, but it is much more powerful. It also needs the element of pressure in the actual demolition work.

Potassium chlorates with sulfates: Any mixture of potassium or sodium chlorates should be avoided at all costs, since most combinations will explode immediately, on formation, and those that don't are extremely unstable and likely to explode at any time.

Ammonium nitrate with chlorates: This is similar to the compounds discussed above. These are extremely hazardous compounds, with very unstable ingredients.

Potassium chlorate and red phosphorus: This combination is probably the most unstable and highly sensitive of all the low explosives. It will explode immediately and violently upon formation, even in the open when not under pressure.

Aluminum or magnesium with potassium chlorate or sodium peroxide: Any of these combinations, although not quite as unstable as the one discussed above, is still too sensitive to experiment or play around with.

Barium chlorate with shellac gums: Any mixture employing either barium or barium nitrate and carbon, or barium chlorate and any other substance, must be given great care. Barium nitrate and strontium nitrate mixed together form a very sensitive explosive, but the danger is greatly increased with the addition of charcoal, or carbon.

Barium and strontium nitrate with aluminum and potassium perchlorate: This combination is relatively safe, as is the combination of barium nitrate and sulfur, potassium nitrate, and most other powdered metals.

Guanidine nitrate and a combustible: This combination of guanidine nitrate and a combustible (i.e. powdered antimony) is one of the safest of all the low explosives.

Potassium bichromate and potassium permanganate: This is a very sensitive and unstable compound, and should be avoided, as it is really too hazardous to work with or handle.

The low-explosive reaction is based on the principle of a combustible material combined with an oxidizing agent, in other words combining a material that burns easily with another material which in the chemical reaction will supply the necessary oxygen for the combustible's consumption. Listed below are the most common low-explosive combinations of oxidizing agents and combustibles. The first ingredient listed is the oxidizer, and the second is the combustible:

1. Nitric acid and resin.
2. Barium nitrate and magnesium.
3. Ammonium nitrate and powdered aluminum.
4. Barium peroxide and zinc dust.
5. Ammonium perchlorate and asphaltum.
6. Sodium chlorate and shellac gum.
7. Potassium nitrate and charcoal.
8. Sodium peroxide and flowers of sulfur.
9. Magnesium perchlorate and woodmeal.
10. Potassium perchlorate and cane sugar.
11. Sodium nitrate and sulfur flour.
12. Potassium bichromate and antimony sulfide.
13. Guanidine nitrate and powdered antimony.
14. Potassium chlorate and red phosphorus.
15. Potassium permanganate and powdered sugar.
16. Barium chlorate and paraffin wax.

The combinations that are most unstable and sensitive are Nos. 3, 5, 7, 13, 14, 15, 16. These should be avoided.

Formulas for black powder

Gunpowder is the great-granddaddy of all the rest of the high- and low-power explosives, and still to this day is one of the most important explosives. As with all the rest of the explosive formulas, it seems everyone has his own recipe, which he claims to be the best. I have collected 11 of the safer, more functional, methods of preparing gunpowder. The most important thing to remember when dealing with black powder is its incredible sensitivity to sparks. *Note:* A cook, a book does not make.

1) potassium perchlorate	69.2	2) potassium chlorate	75
sulfur	15.4	charcoal	12.5
charcoal	15.4	sulfur	12.5

3) potassium nitrate	70.4	4) potassium nitrate	79
sulfur	19.4	sulfur	3
sodium sulfate	10.2	straw charcoal	18

5) potassium nitrate	64	6) potassium nitrate	70.6
sulfur	12	sulfur	23.5
lamp black	7	antimony sulfate	5.9
sawdust	17		

7) potassium nitrate	50	8) potassium nitrate	37.5
ammonium perchlorate	25	starch	37.5
sulfur	12.5	sulfur	18.75
powdered willow charcoal	12.5	antimony powder	6.25

9) barium nitrate	75	10) guanidine nitrate	49
sulfur	12.5	potassium nitrate	40
charcoal	12.5	charcoal	11

| 11) sodium peroxide | 67 |
| sodium thiosulphate | 33 |

When preparing black powder for use in firearms, it is important to keep in mind that these formulas are more powerful than ordinary potassium nitrate gunpowder, and for that reason smaller quantities should be used. The correct amount can only be discovered by trial-and-error experimentation, but caution must be taken to prevent overloading.

Although black powder is one of the safest explosives, it has disadvantages: It is extremely sensitive to sparks; and it leaves a messy residue in gun barrels, which necessitates frequent cleaning. The advantage of smokeless powder is that it is an extremely stable high-powered explosive in the low-explosive class, which gives off only gaseous products upon explosion. The first type of smokeless powder used by the army was basically nitrocellulose with a small amount of diphenylamine, for stabilizer. Smokeless powder is perhaps the safest of any explosive compound discussed in this chapter, and for that reason is extremely popular today.

How to make smokeless powder

1. Boil cotton for 30 minutes, in a 2 percent solution of sodium hydroxide.

2. Wash the cotton in hot water and allow it to dry.

3. Mix slowly and carefully at 25 degrees Centigrade, 250 cc. of concentrated sulfuric acid, 150 cc. of concentrated nitric acid, and 20 cc. of water. They must be kept at 25 degrees C.

4. Next place the dried cotton in the acid solution, and stir well with either a glass or porcelain rod (do not use metal). This should be done for 35 minutes.

5. After nitration, the acids are washed away, and the cotton is washed in boiling water five times, each time for 25 minutes. The cotton is given several tests with litmus paper. If the litmus test proves that there is still some acid present, a 2 percent solution of sodium bicarbonate should neutralize whatever is left. This is important, since any remaining acid acts as an impurity to make the explosive more unstable.

How to make nitrogen tri-iodide

Probably the most hazardous explosive compound of all is nitrogen tri-iodide. Strangely enough, it is very popular with high school chemists, who do not have the vaguest idea of what they are doing. The reason for its popularity may be the ready availability of the ingredients, but it is so sensitive to friction that *a fly landing on it, has been known to detonate it*. The recipe has only been included as a warning and as a curiosity. *It should not be used.*

Preparation for making nitrogen tri-iodide:

1. Add a small amount of solid iodine crystals to about 20 cc. of concentrated ammonium hydroxide. This operation must be performed very slowly, until a brownish-red precipitate is formed.

2. Now it is filtered through filter paper, and then washed first with alcohol and secondly with ether.

Tri-iodide must remain wet, since when it dries it becomes supersensitive to friction, and a slight touch can set it off. *This is an extremely unstable compound and should not be experimented with.*

Formulas for different-colored smoke screens

An interesting aspect of explosives is the extra ingredients which can be added to give the explosion characteristics it would not normally have. A smoke bomb is like this, in the sense that it is not only useful to create confusion and chaos, but also for smoking persons out of an enclosed area, as well as signaling.

Formulas for the preparation of a black smoke screen:

1) magnesium powder	19	2) magnesium powder	20
hexachloroethane	60	hexachloroethane	60
naphthalene	21	naphthalene	20

3) hexachloroethane	55.8	4) black powder FFF	50
alpha naphol	14	potassium nitrate	10
athracene	4.6	coal tar	20
aluminum powder	9.3	powdered charcoal	15
smokeless powder	14	paraffin	5
naphthalene	2.3		

Formulas for the preparation of a white smoke screen:

1) potassium chlorate	44	2) zinc dust	28
sulfur flour	15	zinc oxide	22
zinc dust	40	hexachloroethane	50
sodium bicarbonate	1		

| 3) zinc dust | 66.67 |
| hexachloroethane | 33.33 |

Formulas for the preparation of a yellow smoke screen:

1) potassium chlorate	25	2) potassium chlorate	30
paranitraniline	50	naphthalene azodimethyl	
lactrose	25	aniline	50
		powdered sugar	20

3) potassium chlorate	21.4
naphthalene	
azodimethyl aniline	2.7
auramine	38
sodium bicarbonate	28.5
sulfur flour	9.4

Formula for the preparation of a green smoke screen:

1) potassium nitrate	20
red arsenic	20
sulfur flour	20
antimony sulfide	20
black powder FFF	20

Formulas for the preparation of a red smoke screen:

1) potassium chlorate	20	2) potassium chlorate	26
lactose	20	diethylaminorosindone	
paranitraniline red	60		48
		powdered sugar	26

3) potassium chlorate	27.4	4) potassium	
methylaminoanthra-		perchlorate	25
quinone	42.5	antimony sulfide	20
sodium bicarbonate	19.5	rhodamine red	50
sulfur flour	10.6	dextrin	5

Household substitutes

On the next few pages I have included a chart of the chemicals' names and their more common household names. This chart is not entirely correct, although it may seem so. The household substitutes must be checked before using to be absolutely certain they are what you want. Be sure that the chemical you want is alone, since if it is included in the household substitute, but not isolated, the extra ingredients may counteract the desired results.

CHEMICAL NAME	HOUSEHOLD SUBSTITUTE
acetic acid	vinegar
aluminum oxide	alumia
aluminum potassium sulfate	alum
aluminum sulfate	alum
ammonium hydroxide	ammonia
carbon carbonate	chalk
calcium hypochloride	bleaching powder
calcium oxide	lime
calcium sulphate	plaster of Paris
carbonic acid	seltzer
carbon tetrachloride	cleaning fluid
ethylene dichloride	Dutch fluid
ferric oxide	iron rust
glucose	corn syrup
graphite	black lead (pencil lead)
hydrochloric acid	muriatic acid
hydrogen peroxide	peroxide
lead acetate	sugar of lead
lead tetroxide	red lead
magnesium silicate	talc
magnesium sulfate	Epsom salts
naphthalene	mothballs
phenol	carbolic acid
potassium bitartrate	cream of tartar
potassium chromium sulfate	chrome alum
potassium nitrate	saltpeter
silicon dioxide	sand
sodium bicarbonate	baking soda
sodium borate	borax
sodium carbonate	washing soda
sodium chloride	salt
sodium hydroxide	lye
sodium silicate	water glass
sodium sulfate	Glauber's salt
sodium thiosulfate	photographer's hypo
sulfuric acid	battery acid
sucrose	cane sugar
zinc chloride	tinner's fluid

Safety precautions

The next few pages are the most important in this chapter. More people, young and old, political and apolitical, have executed themselves with some form of explosives than I would care to state here. The safety procedures for all explosives are nothing more than common sense and reasoning. Yes, smokeless powder is stable, but if you put it in the oven, it will explode. That may sound stupid, but a 14-year-old in Ohio did it two years ago and killed himself. Plastique is a very stable explosive compound, but it needs to be softened before use. Some guy in New Jersey softened his plastique with a hammer, and he is no more. TNT can be burned and it will not explode—most of the time—whereas gunpowder will ignite with the smallest spark. *Moral:* Read the next few pages and study them, do not assume anything.

Safety precautions for the storing of explosives:

1. The most important factor in picking a storage place is its location. You will want the place close enough to be under your surveillance, but not close enough to be a hazard to you or your family. All explosive magazines or dumps must have secure locks on all the doors.

2. Do not store blasting caps, electrical caps, or primers in the same container or even the same magazine with any other form of high or low explosives.

3. Do not store fuses or fuse lighters in a wet or damp place, or near the storage of flammables such as oil, gasoline, cleaning solvents, or paints. Fuses should also be kept away from radiators, steam pipes, stoves, or any other source of heat, because the very nature of nonelectrical fuses is such that any one of these things could start a large fire.

4. Metals should be kept absolutely away from explosives, meaning that metal tools should not be stored in the same magazine with explosives.

5. In no circumstances, allow any open flame or other fire, including a lighted cigarette, around an explosive storage dump.

6. Spontaneous combustion is a real problem when storing explosives. For this reason, do not allow leaves, grasses, brush, or any debris to collect or accumulate around the explosives storage area.

7. Do not discharge weapons near an explosive magazine. Do not shoot into the storage dump. Keep the shooting away from the explosives.

8. Certain types of explosives require certain types of storage, including temperature regulation and other controls. Be sure that you understand all aspects of the compound's nature before handling or storing it.

9. At all times use common sense, and allow only qualified persons to be near or handle explosives.

Safety precautions for handling explosives:

1. When transporting explosives, know what the federal and state laws and regulations are. Many of these regulations are just common-sense protection for yourself.

2. Make sure that any vehicle used to transport explosives is in proper working order and equipped with a tight wooden or nonsparking metal floor, with sides and ends high enough to prevent the explosives from falling off. The load in an open-bodied truck should be covered with a waterproof and fire-resistant tarpaulin. Wiring should be fully insulated so as to prevent short circuiting, and at least two fire extinguishers should be carried. The truck should be plainly marked, if possible.

3. In no circumstances allow metals of any sort, except the nonsparking type, to come into contact with the explosive casing. Metal, flammable, or corrosive substances should not be transported with explosives.

4. Never in any circumstances allow smoking around any explosive, regardless of its stability.

5. Do not allow unauthorized persons to go near the explosives. This is for two reasons; first, because they might not know what they are doing and accidentally set off an explosion, and secondly, because they might be undercover agents from the enemy.

6. When loading or unloading explosives, do it with the utmost care. Whenever dealing with explosives, in any capacity, do not rush. Take your time and exercise extreme caution.

7. If you must transport both high explosives and blasting caps in the same vehicle, be sure that they are completely separate from one another.

Safety precautions when using explosives:

1. When opening a case of explosives, in no circumstances use a metal crowbar or wedge. Use a wooden wedge or nonmetallic tool.

Figure 71. Opening explosives.

2. Do not smoke or allow anyone to smoke. Do not carry an open flame, or any other form of heat source or fire near an area where explosives are being used.

3. Do not place explosives where they may be exposed to a flame, excessive heat, sparks, or shock.

4. Replace the cover or close the top of the explosives container after use.

5. Do not carry explosives in your pocket or on your person at any time. Even when on a mission of sabotage, it is better to carry explosives in a separate container.

6. When making up primers or crimping blasting caps, do not do it near any other explosives, high or low.

7. Blasting caps, although they may look like firecrackers, are a powerful explosive charge and must be treated accordingly.

8. Never insert anything but a fuse into a blasting cap. Since blasting caps, to be functional, must be sensitive, a great degree of care must be used in handling them.

9. Never experiment with, disassemble, strike, tamper with, or in any way try to remove the contents of a blasting cap. Do not try to pull the wires out of an electrical blasting cap.

10. When handling explosives, the only persons who should be present are those who are absolutely necessary. All unnecessary and unauthorized persons should be cleared from the area. This, of course, includes animals and children.

11. Do not handle explosives, or stay in an area where explosives are being stored, when an electrical storm is approaching. Clear the area and retire to safety.

12. Inspect all equipment before use, and never use any equipment that appears damaged or deteriorated.

13. Never attempt to reclaim any explosive or blasting material that has been water-soaked.

Safety precautions to be taken when drilling:

1. Check what you are about to drill into, to be sure there is not a charge already there. Never drill into an explosive charge.

2. Never stack surplus explosives near the drilling area.

3. Since the act of drilling is based on the principles of friction, heat will be created. Never load a bore hole without first checking the temperature. Also check to see if any pieces of burning material are present. Temperatures above 150 degrees F. are extremely dangerous.

4. A common practice in demolitions is what is called springing a bore hole. This is when a small explosive is used to enlarge a bore hole, so that a much larger explosive charge can be placed in it. This should require extreme caution. Check to see if there are any other charges nearby.

5. Never force explosives into a bore hole. Recheck your hole and clear the obstruction before attempting to reload.

6. Never force a blasting cap or electrical blasting cap into a stick of dynamite. Use the hole made by the punch.

7. Do not tamper in any manner with the primer.

8. Figure out what quantity of explosives you will need, according to the formulas given later in the chapter, and then put in that amount. Do not use more than necessary.

Safety precautions to be taken when tamping:
(Tamping is the process of placing materials, such as sandbags, around the explosives so as to send the force of the explosion in one certain direction.)

1. Tamping is a gentle process and should never be performed violently.

2. When using tamping tools, be sure that these are made of wood or some other nonmetal sparkfree material.

3. When tamping a bore hole that has recently been drilled, use clay, sand, dirt, or some other noncombustible material.

4. Take extreme care not to damage or injure the fuse or electrical blasting cap wire when tamping.

5. One should always tamp if possible, since it cuts down the amount of explosives necessary.

Safety precautions to be taken when detonating electrically:

1. Do not uncoil the wires of an electrical blasting cap, or employ their use, during a thunderstorm, dust storm, or when any other source of static electricity is present.

2. Be very careful about the use of electrical blasting material near a radio frequency transmitter. Consult *Radio Frequency Hazards,* a pamphlet issued by the Institute of Makers of Explosives.

3. Keep your firing circuit completely insulated from all conductors except the one circuit you intend to use. This means extreme care in insulation against the ground, bare wires, rails, pipes, or any paths of stray current.

4. Keep all cables, wires, or other electrical equipment away from electrical blasting caps, except at the time of the blast, and for the purpose of that blast.

5. Be very careful in the use of more than one blasting cap. Never use more than one type of blasting cap in a single operation.

6. Use the correct current stated by the manufacturer to set off electrical blasting caps. Never use any less.

7. Be sure that all the ends of the wires which are to be connected are bright and clean.

8. Keep the electrical cap wires or lead wires short-circuited until ready to fire.

Safety precautions to be taken when using a fuse:

1. Handle the fuse carefully. Avoid damaging the covering. In cold weather, warm the fuse slightly before using. Avoid cracking the waterproof outer coating.

2. Never use a short fuse. Always use a fuse which is over two feet in length. Be absolutely sure you know the burning speed of the fuse, and have calculated the amount of time you will need to get to safety.

3. When placing the fuse in the blasting cap, cut off an inch or so to insure dryness. Cut straight across the fuse with a clean new razor blade. Once the fuse is in place, do not twist, pull, or otherwise cause friction.

4. Once the fuse is in place, it is necessary to crimp the fuse into the blasting cap. Crimping is the procedure of attaching a nonelectrical blasting cap to a fuse, by bending the ends of the cap around the fuse. This must be done only with a special tool, called a crimper. Although crimpers may look like pliers, they are not, and pliers must not be used. When crimping, be absolutely sure you know what you are doing, since, if you squeeze the explosive within the cap rather than the ends, there is a good chance you will blow your hand off.

5. Do not light the fuse until you are sure that the sparks that come from it will not set off the explosive until the fuse has burned down.

Safety precautions to be taken when firing explosives:

1. Never hold an explosive in your hands, when lighting.

2. Before exploding any charge, make sure a complete check of the area has been made, and sufficient time and warning have been given.

3. Do not return to the area of the blast until all the smoke has cleared.

4. Do not attempt to investigate a misfire too soon. Wait

at least one hour, and be sure, if you are using an electrical circuit, that you have disconnected it.

5. Never drill out misfires.

6. Never abandon any explosives.

7. Do not leave any explosive equipment, packing material, or empty cartridges where children or animals can get at them.

Basic formulas for demolitions use

1. Computation of minimum safety distance

For charges less than 27 pounds, the minimum safety distance is 900 feet. Over 27 pounds, the minimum safety distances can be figured by using the following formula:

$$300 \times \sqrt[3]{\text{pounds of explosive (T.N.T.)}}$$

2. Steel cutting

When cutting, with explosives, part of a steel structure, determine the area in square inches of the member to be cut. This area is then labeled "A," and one can use the following formula:

$$P = \frac{3}{8}A$$

P=the number of pounds of T.N.T. necessary.

3. Steel cutting

When a steel member is not part of a greater structure, a different formula is used. This is based on the diameter of the individual member.

$$P = D^2$$

P = the amount of T.N.T. required, and D is the diameter of the piece of steel.

4. Train rails

To cut rails that weigh less than 80 pounds, use one-half pound of explosives. To cut rails that weigh over 80 pounds, use a full pound of explosives.

5. Timber cutting

When the charge is to be external and untamped, the formula is as follows:

$$P = \frac{C^3}{30}$$

P equals the pounds of explosives required, and C equals the circumference of the tree in feet (this formula is given for plastique). When figuring an internal tamped charge, the formula is:

$$P = \frac{D^2}{250}$$

P equals the pounds of explosives, and D equals the diameter of the tree in inches.

Some important principles

A basic rule to follow in all calculations having to do with explosive compounds is to round off the amount to the next highest unit package. At times you may use a little more than necessary, but you will be assured of success. Another rule when calculating charges is to add one-third more explosives if you do not intend to tamp. If a formula is given for plastique (composition 4), as was done for both timber-cutting formulas, you are able to compute poundage in T.N.T. by adding one-third to the weight of the plastique.

When using the principle of cratering to destroy a paved surface with explosives, use several charges rather than just one. The use of a bore hole is especially effective here. It is pointless to attempt cratering a roadway without tamping, since most of the destructive force of your charge will go straight up in the air.

In the first two sections of this chapter, I have discussed explosives chemically and written about their safe handling. In the third section, I intend to go into their specific application. Bombs, like spies, have no allegiance, even to their creators.

Bombs and booby traps incorporate more than just technical knowledge, they are based on human nature. To create an effective booby trap, one must have a primitive insight into his enemy's actions, thoughts, and methods. Before I get into the nitty-gritty of constructing booby traps, bombs, land mines, grenades, etc., it is important to explain the basic working principles and mechanisms behind these devices.

In the acquisition of equipment I would recommend purchasing or stealing, rather than making your own. Manufactured equipment is much safer to work with, and usually more effective. Once you have your explosive compound, you will need a way to set it off, or detonate it. With all high explosives, you will need a detonator or blasting cap, unless you decide to lace the fuse into the explosive, although this is not recomended. A blasting cap is a low-explosive compound that is connected to a high explosive, for the purpose of detonating it. There are two types of blasting caps—electric and nonelectric.

To use a nonelectrical blasting cap, one gently pushes the fuse into the hollow end, until it is fully in. He then crimps the hollow metal end around the fuse, and puts it into the high explosive. When the fuse burns down, it ignites the flash charge. That in turn explodes the priming

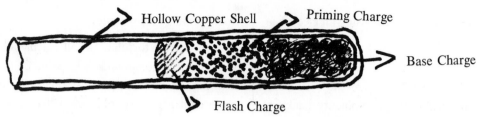

Figure 72. Nonelectrical blasting cap.

charge, which detonates the base charge, and finally creates enough heat to set off the high-explosive charge. The fuse is ordinary safety fuse or detonating cord.

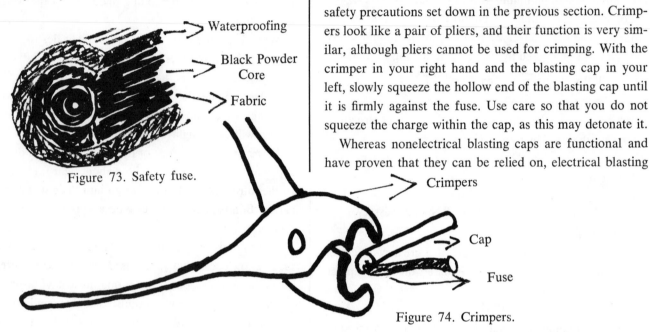

Figure 73. Safety fuse.

When the fuse is put into the blasting cap, it is necessary to seal it. This act of sealing is called crimping. When involved with this sort of thing, one must use the standard safety precautions set down in the previous section. Crimpers look like a pair of pliers, and their function is very similar, although pliers cannot be used for crimping. With the crimper in your right hand and the blasting cap in your left, slowly squeeze the hollow end of the blasting cap until it is firmly against the fuse. Use care so that you do not squeeze the charge within the cap, as this may detonate it.

Whereas nonelectrical blasting caps are functional and have proven that they can be relied on, electrical blasting

Figure 74. Crimpers.

caps offer a much greater variety of uses. The basic principle of the electrical blasting cap is that an electrical charge moves through an insulated wire until it reaches a small section of that same wire which is not insulated and which is surrounded by a primary flash charge. The heat from the electrical charge will explode the flash charge, which in turn will set off a series of minor explosions, finishing up with the high explosive.

Both types of blasting caps should be placed within the high explosive itself. This is easy when working with plastique or a pliable substance. Manufactured T.N.T. has

a small hole designed at the top for just this reason, but in dynamite one has to make his own hole. This hole should be made with a wooden or nonsparking metal object. The ends of the crimpers, illustrated on the previous page, are ideal. The hole can be made in one of two ways: the first is bored carefully and gently straight down from the top of the stick, to exactly the length of the cap itself; the second type of hole is made from the side in a downward diagonal direction. Both of these methods have proven effective.

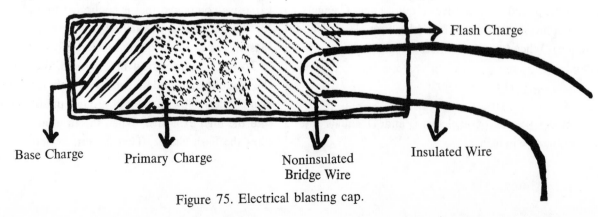

Figure 75. Electrical blasting cap.

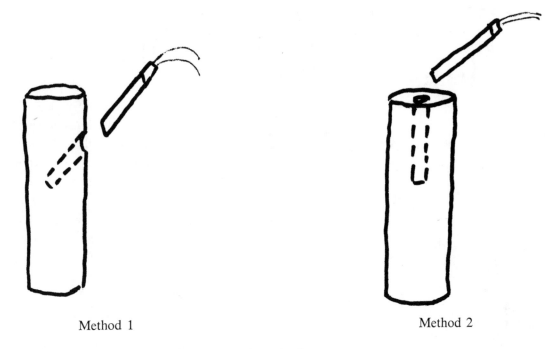

Method 1   Method 2

Figure 76. Priming dynamite electrically.

Another method of priming dynamite, which is not as reliable as either nonelectrical or electrical blasting caps, is called "lacing." The principle behind most detonating devices is simply to create a temperature which is hot enough to ignite the high explosive. This increase in temperature can be accomplished with a relatively good degree of success by weaving the fuse throughout the high explosive so that, as the fuse burns down, the heat created from the burning process is captured and held within the high explosive until the detonation temperature is reached.

There are different methods of lacing, depending on what type of high explosive you happen to be working with. For dynamite, the most common and most functional method is literally to sew the detonation cord into the stick. This preparation entails the individual's making several holes directly through the dynamite itself. This hole-making should be performed just as the planting of the blasting cap was handled. The holes must be dug gently and slowly with a nonmetallic instrument. "Lacing" should be done only when there is no alternative, and blasting caps are not available.

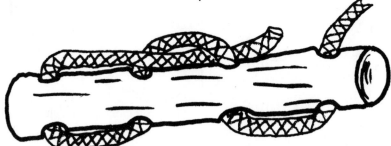

Figure 77. Lacing dynamite.

When using TNT, you can lace it by wrapping the detonating cord around the body of the explosive at least five or six times, and then tying it off with a clove hitch. This will result in a great amount of heat being transferred into the TNT from the fuse, and its detonation.

Plastique can also be ignited in this fashion, by employing a heavy-duty detonation cord, and tying a double knot in one of its ends. This large knot is then buried deep in the center of the composition. It must be at least one inch from any side.

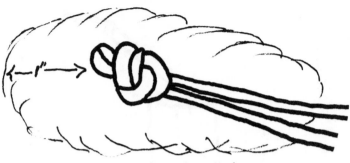

Figure 78. Lacing plastique.

Tamping

Tamping is nothing more than an operation performed before the explosion, to regulate and direct the destructive power of the explosion. In other words, if a pound of black powder is ignited with a match, the explosion will occur but most of the destructive force will take the path of least resistance—into the atmosphere. Now, if the same pound of black powder was placed within a steel pipe, and sealed at both ends, except for a tiny hole for the fuse, the explosion could be regulated with ease. This tamping operation is necessary for any forms of demolitions in order that the operation be successful. A stick of dynamite placed on a concrete roadway untamped, when exploded will create a very small crater, perhaps a few inches. If this same stick of dynamite were tamped, by placing several sandbags on top of it and around it, the explosion would create a much greater crater. This tamping operation is absolutely necessary for the demolition of a large structure or building.

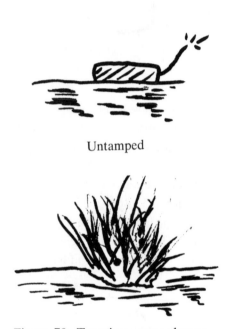

Untamped

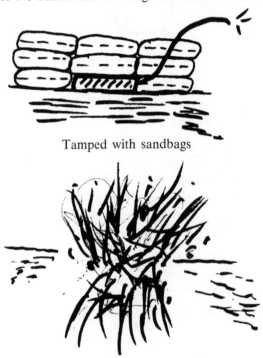

Tamped with sandbags

Figure 79. Tamping crater charges.

1. When attempting to sever a steel rod or pole, through the use of explosives, place a charge on each side, leaving a small gap between the butts of the explosives.

2. When cutting a chain, place the explosive charge on one side and tape it securely into place.

3. When cutting any odd-shaped object, the best explosive to use is plastique, because of its flexibility. It is especially useful and effective when cutting heavy metal cables. The compound should be placed around the side of the cable that is to be cut, about a half-inch thick.

When sabotaging railroad tracks with explosive, use plastique if available, since this is the easiest substance to use when trying to sever objects of irregular shapes. The most common way of cutting train tracks is by placing a charge of high explosives on either side of the "I" beam track, so as to have the forces of the two explosions act upon each other, thus causing the middle object maximum destruction.

Another method which has proven equally effective is placing a charge between the rail and the switch. The switch is one of the weakest points along the line, and a

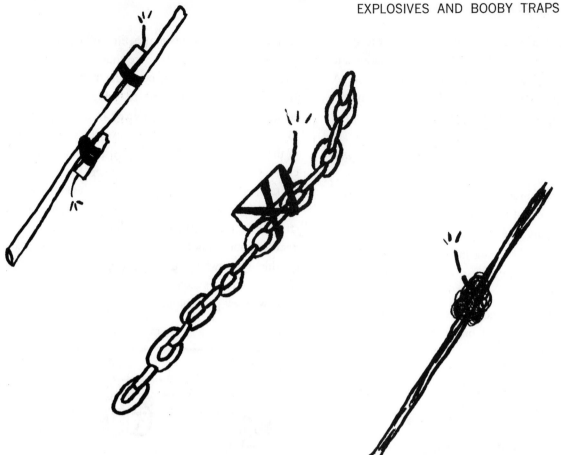

Figure 80. Using explosives to cut through materials.

relatively small charge will not only sever the switch and rail, but will also rip up the ties and the railroad bed. Tamping with sandbags can and should be used if at all possible, since the extent of the damage is multiplied several times by the addition of the sandbags. Tamping can be useless if you are on a silent lightning-fast mission. In this case, a two-pound charge of TNT carefully placed between the switch and rail will almost certainly do the trick without tamping. The best procedure when engaged in this type of sabotage is to repeat the acts every three-quarters of a mile or so, so as to delay the repairmen and create confusion.

Placement of charges

In demolition work, the greatest problem is the actual placement of the charges. When an individual is working on a large structure such as a building or a bridge, it is imperative that he have an understanding of the directional force of explosives, and the structure's weaknesses. These large-type structures are built to bear up under abnormal stress, so the chances are good, unless the charges are placed correctly, that the sabotage will have little or no effect.

When attempting the demolition of a building, the first

Figure 81. Railroad Sabotage

Figure 82. Type of placement and tamping necessary to destroy large buildings.

thing to do is to determine the weakest point in the structure. This is the point where a charge can be placed and well-tamped, and will result in maximum destruction. A large building will usually take more than just one charge. The best bet is to place large explosive charges on either side of a weak point in the foundations. These charges should be tamped from the outside, so as to drive the force inward.

There are several basic methods of planting explosives. The advantage to most of the ones listed below is that they have a natural tamping factor, built-in.

1. Bury the explosive beneath the object of destruction.

2. Drill a bore hole into the object and fill with explosives.

3. Form a brace to hold the explosives tight against the object of destruction. A good brace can be made from wood placed on a diagonal, with one end jammed into the ground.

4. Place a charge out in the open, with the tamping material surrounding it, and directing its force.

Bridge destruction

Bridges are much harder to destroy than buildings, and this is for several reasons:

1. Most of the bridges to be destroyed will be far larger than the buildings.

2. They are built strongly, to last for long periods of time.

3. They have many reinforcements that are not visible.

4. Everyone realizes the strategic importance of bridges, therefore everyone should realize how well guarded they are.

An important factor to bear in mind, when working on bridge demolition, is the extent of real damage desired. Total destruction of a bridge is useless, a waste of good explosives. It may even be harmful, since there may come a time when a friendly force will need the use of that bridge. Bridge destruction should therefore be considered a tactical-delay operation. It will slow the enemy down, and cause them much expense and time to rebuild. Since types of charges differ for different types of bridges, I will go into specific types of bridge demolitions.

Stringer bridges are the most common type of concrete, steel, or timber bridges in existence. They are usually one

or more spans, but this makes little difference in the actual placement of charges. If more than one span is to be destroyed, one should just copy the first placement on the second span. The stringer-type bridge is on basically two or three steel "I" beams, referred to as stringers. The obvious method is to attempt to sever these primary aspects of the entire structure. This can be accomplished by placing charges on either side of each stringer. Each charge should be tamped either with sandbags or a wooden brace. The result of placing all the charges on the same side of the stringer is the twisting and forced warping of the steel beams beyond any future use. When dealing with a bridge of this type which incorporates more than one span, place the charges along the joints of the stringer, since this is the weakest point along the line.

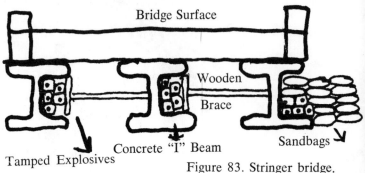

Figure 83. Stringer bridge.

A *slab bridge* is a simple structure, consisting of a flat slab of either concrete or timber held together in such a way that it forms one continuous slab. These are the easiest bridges to destroy, since all that is required is a diagonal line of explosive charges placed either under, or drilled into, the structure itself. If the charges are placed be-

Figure 84. Slab bridge.

neath the bridge, they should be attached by some means, and tamping should be used.

The *T-beam bridge* is very similar to the stringer-type bridge, except it is without the bottom reinforcements. This doesn't mean that the T-beam type is any weaker or easier to destroy. This type of bridge is based on three or four concrete or steel T-beams, with a large slab of concrete covering them. The space between the T-beams on the underneath of the bridge is ideal for the placement of explosive charges, since 75 percent of the tamping has al-

ready been constructed, by the very nature of the bridge itself. This type of bridge may have more than one span but, since bridge destruction is only a tactical-delay operation, the destruction of one span should be enough. If you wish to destroy more than one span, just repeat the same operation, on the second span, paying close attention to the joints. Like the stringer-type bridge, the charges are placed beneath the bridge, between the beams themselves. A steel or wooden platform should be constructed to so hold the explosives, and direct their force upward into the bridge.

Figure 85. T-beam bridge.

The *concrete cantilever bridge* is probably better known as a causeway. It is usually a very low bridge, with many segments or spans supported by a series of concrete columns. The same basic procedure should be followed as previously outlined, in that one should look for the weakest point in the entire structure, and fix the charges at that point. The weakest point in most structures is the place where two objects join, so the explosive charges should be

placed along the joints of the separate sections or spans. Place charges of explosives at the foot of the corresponding column to insure destruction. The charges placed at the foot of the columns should all be tamped and placed on the same side of the respective columns, so as to encourage maximum destruction. This type of bridge has many spans, but usually it is only necessary to destroy several of the middle sections, as shown below.

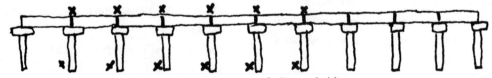

Figure 86. Concrete cantilever bridge.

The "X"s mark the location of the explosive charges. All charges placed at the foot of the columns should be situated on the same side, so as to channel the movement of the destructive force in one direction.

The *truss bridge* is usually used for railroad crossings, and is built of steel. This type of bridge is one of the strongest in the world, and offers many problems for the

saboteur. The best method is to run several different explosions at thirty-minute intervals, so that one can see exactly what needs destruction, but this is not feasible for the guerrilla operation. Figure 87 is a diagram of this type of bridge. The "X"s show the location of five charges, which can be placed hastily and are reasonably effective. Be very careful when attempting a sabotage operation of this type, especially with a truss bridge, since, as it is a train crossing, it will undoubtedly be guarded heavily.

Figure 87. Truss bridge.

Suspension bridges are, generally speaking, the largest bridges in the world, and accordingly the strongest. It is a good idea to allow yourself three or four separate charges with a time lapse between them. If this not possible, concentrate your charges on the main cables, and the center section of the bridge. Six—no less important—charges should be placed on the two towers at either end of the bridge and tamped down. "X"s mark the location of the explosive charges in Figure 88.

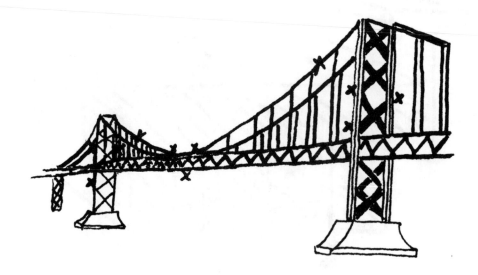

Figure 88. Suspension bridge.

Detonators

The most common time-delay device is an ordinary safety fuse. These fuses usually consist of a black-powder core surrounded with a fabric and then a layer of waterproof material. Although there are many different types, it can generally be said that safety fuses burn between 30 and 45 seconds per foot; however, check these figures when you make your purchase. Fuses can be bought from any mail-order pyrotechnics company. Two with whom I have dealt are:

Ecco Products
Box 189
Northvale, New Jersey 07647

Westech Corporation
P.O. Box 8193
Salt Lake City, Utah 84108

Double-coated waterproof fuse usually sells for 20 to 25 dollars for a thousand to fifteen hundred feet. I would ad-vise purchasing this equipment, since homemade fuses are not to be trusted.

Bombs can be detonated in many ways. The detonation and use of certain devices are based mainly on the cleverness and imagination of the saboteur. In the following section I have discussed several basic forms of detonators, both nonelectric and electric. However, there is an infinite number of variations, which may be better suited to individual situations.

The first type is referred to either as a tension-release, or a wiretrip device. It operates on the principle of releasing the tension caused by a wound spring, on the firing pin, and allowing it to strike and set off a nonelectrical blasting cap. The nonelectrical blasting cap will in turn generate the necessary heat to ignite the T.N.T. or dynamite. This can be implemented in many ways. Two simple methods are illustrated in Figures 89 and 90. A common method in which the wire-trip device can be employed is stretching a trip wire about six inches above the ground. Another equally popular method of employing the tension-release device is attaching the taut wire to the back of a door, so that, when the door is opened, the tension is released, and the explosive ignites.

A device very similar to the last one is the pull-trigger electric detonator. It functions in the same manner, in that a safety pin is removed from the striker or firing pin, causing it to move forward and connect with a metal plate. This connection with the metal plate completes the electrical circuit. The batteries have been connected by wires to an electrical blasting cap, a metal plate, and finally to the firing pin. (See Figure 91.) Although professional supplies for this equipment are available at reasonable prices, the diagram shows the detonating device constructed from household items. The construction of this device is as follows: Two flashlight batteries are connected to each other, and then one wire is run from one end of the batteries to the electrical blasting cap, the other wire from the opposite end of the batteries to the metal plate. A third wire is run from the blasting cap to the firing pin. This now completes the fully cocked device.

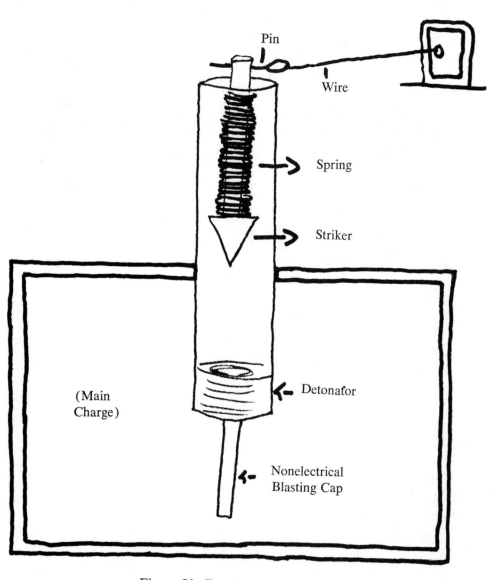

Figure 89. Tension-release detonator.

In the same manner as the explosive in Figure 89 is detonated, so is the common military grenade. The principle of a tension release is the same. After the pin is pulled out of the military grenade, the spring is free to react, causing the primer to ignite the lead-spitter fuse, and it in turn will ignite the lead oxide and pentolite. The pentolite will release enough heat to ignite the T.N.T. and cause the fragmentation of the metal casing.

The next type of detonating device I am going to discuss is called the pressure-trigger device. It is based on the application of pressure rather than its release, as in the previous devices. This mechanism is primarily used when an electrical circuit is employed. The plunger is pushed down; it forces one thin metal plate against another thicker metal plate. The batteries are connected, via the blasting cap, to each of these metal plates. Therefore, when they touch, the electrical circuit is complete, and the explosive will ignite.

This type of device has several important advantages. First of all, it can be constructed away from the area it will be used in. This will cut installation time down to seconds. Later in the chapter, I discuss a type of booby trap that can be rigged into the ignition system of a car. Although the ignition-system booby trap works very well, it takes time to install. This pressure-trigger device will act almost in the same manner if placed beneath the driver's seat, and can be installed in a lot less time. (See Figures 92 and 93.)

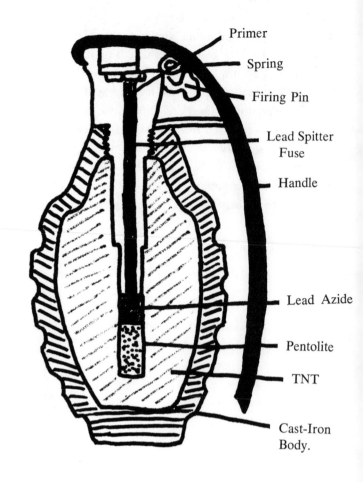

Figure 90. Military grenade.

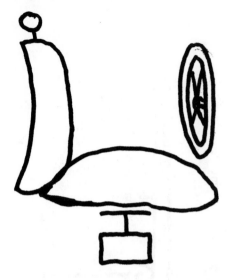

Figure 92. Pressure-trigger device under driver's seat.

Release of pressure detonators

The next type of detonating device I will discuss is called a release-of-pressure mechanism. This device employs exactly the same principles as the pressure-trigger device, except in reverse. The movement of the pressure plate, rather than down, is now up. This can be used effectively when a weight is placed on the pressure plate. Then when it is removed, the explosives will be ignited. To construct, use a heavy-duty spring beneath the first metal plate, as shown in Figure 93. Connect a wire from the blasting cap to the first metal plate. The second wire is then stretched from the bottom of battery "A," to the second metal plate. The third wire is run from the electrical blasting cap to the top of battery "B." When this is accomplished, the booby trap is fully cocked. When the weight on the pressure plate is removed, the spring will force the second metal plate against the first metal plate, thus completing the electrical circuit and exploding the device.

Figure 95 shows a booby trap which incorporates a tension-release device. When the tension, resulting from a wire pulling on a pliable metal strip, is released, the metal strip will snap back into another metal strip. Since the wires from the batteries and blasting cap are connected to either metal strip, when they touch, the circuit will be complete and it will detonate the explosive charge. This type of detonator is especially effective when attached to drawers, doors, or any movable objects.

Time delay devices

There are three different types of time-delay devices:

1. Metal strip under tension until it breaks.

2. Chemical action that will, after a period of time, produce enough heat to detonate the explosive charge.

3. An alarm clock set for a certain time, so that when it rings it will complete an electrical circuit, thus detonating an electrical blasting cap. The first method, metal under tension until breakage, I will not discuss, since it is extremely hazardous and unreliable. You can have little or no control over timing, and such devices are notorious for backfiring.

The chemical-action time-delay methods have proven to be pretty reliable. Most of this action incorporates the amount of time taken by a certain solution of acid to eat its way through another substance. The time length can be determined by the concentration of the acid and by the substance to be eaten through.

An example of this type of chemical action is the Nipple Time Bomb, which is very effective. One must obtain a short section of steel pipe and cap each end accordingly. Place inside the steel pipe a stick of dynamite, and drill a quarter-inch hole at one end of the cap. Now, into this hole you must place a small amount of potassium chlorate and gunpowder. Now, separately from the pipe, take a small glass vial and fill it with a concentrated sulfuric acid solution, then stop up the end with a paper or cork stopper. To arm the bomb, place the vial of acid upside down in the hole at the top of the pipe. Now, when the acid has eaten its way through the stopper, it will come into contact with the potassium chlorate and gunpowder. The mixture of these chemicals will cause a minor explosion, but it will be large enough to produce the heat necessary to detonate the dynamite. The detonation time is usually between three and six hours. If a solution of sulfuric acid and glycerin is used, rather than just pure sulfuric acid, the time delay will be up to five or six days. (See Figure 96.)

Figure 97 is a diagram of an incendiary time bomb. This is very similar to the Nipple Time Bomb, in that it relies on the same chemical action, but without the dynamite. The procedure is very simple. A cardboard or iron tube is filled with a mixture of three-quarters potassium chlorate and one-quarter sugar, and then sealed. At one end a hole is made. Into that hole is placed an inverted vial of sulfuric acid, with a paper or cork stopper. When the acid has eaten its way through the stopper, it will come into contact with the potassium chlorate-sugar mixture. This will result in a very hot, powerful fire.

The Magnifying-Glass Bomb, illustrated in Figure 98,

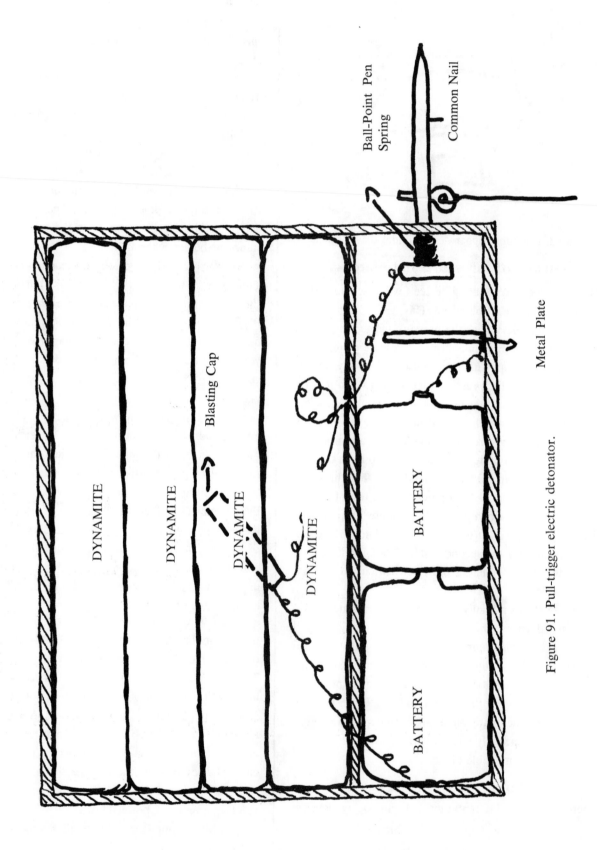

Figure 91. Pull-trigger electric detonator.

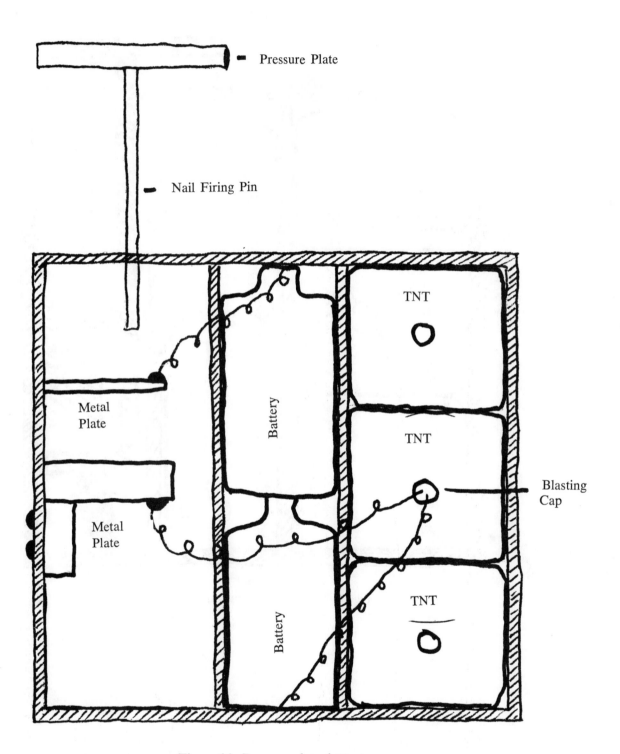

Figure 93. Pressure-plate detonator.

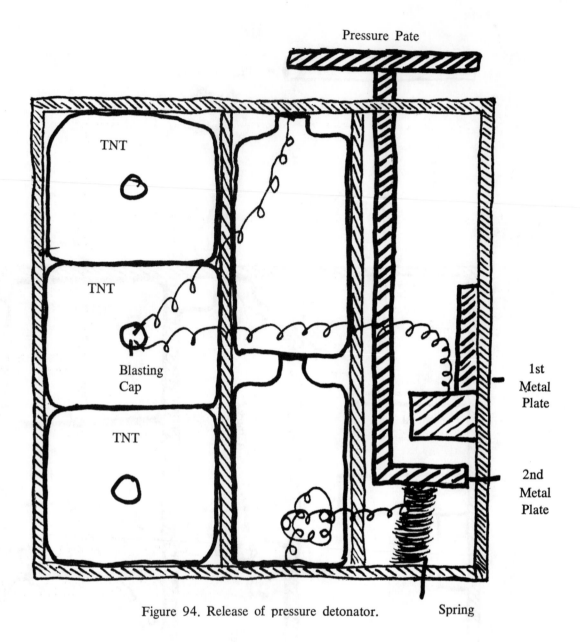

Figure 94. Release of pressure detonator.

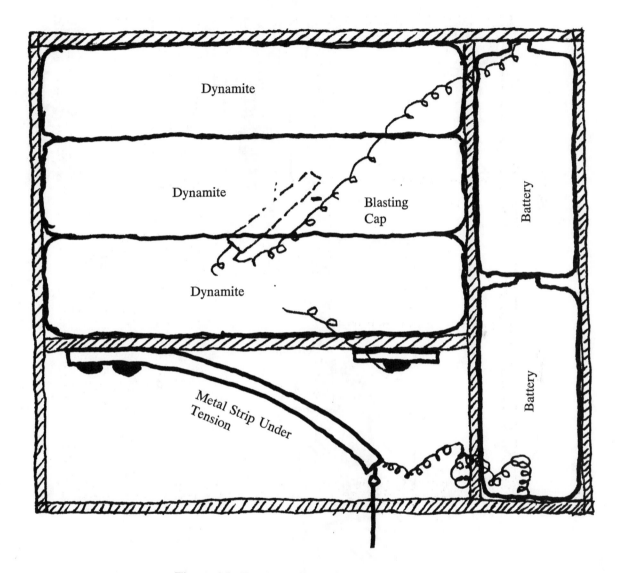

Figure 95. Tension-release detonator.

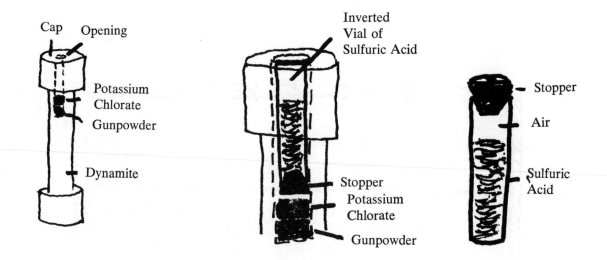

Figure 96. Nipple time bomb.

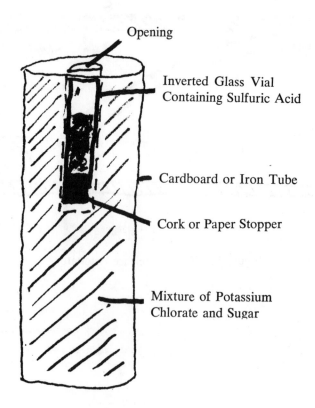

Figure 97. Incendiary time bomb.

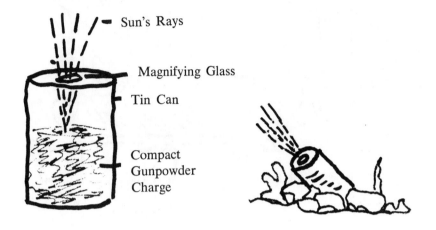

Sun's Rays

Magnifying Glass

Tin Can

Compact
Gunpowder
Charge

Figure 98. Magnifying-glass bomb.

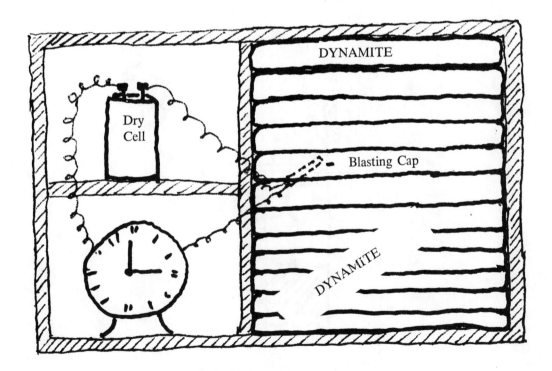

Figure 99. Alarm-clock time bomb.

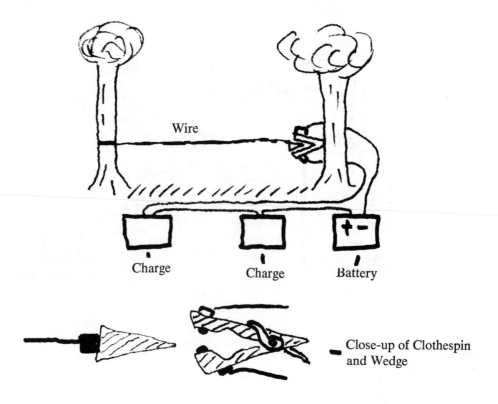

Wire

Charge   Charge   Battery

Close-up of Clothespin
and Wedge

Figure 100. Road trap.

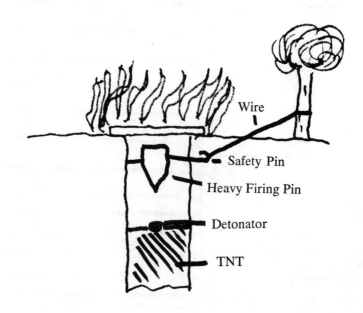

Wire

Safety Pin

Heavy Firing Pin

Detonator

TNT

Figure 101. Walk trap.

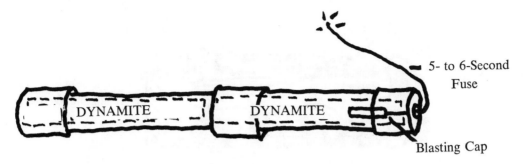

Figure 102. Bangalore torpedo.

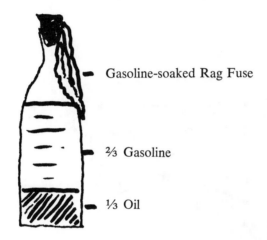

Figure 103. Molotov Cocktail.

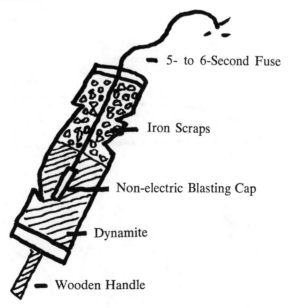

Figure 104. Homemade grenade.

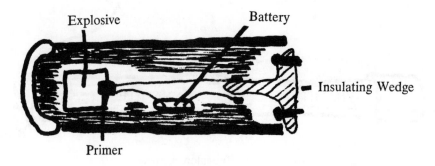

Figure 105. Book trap.

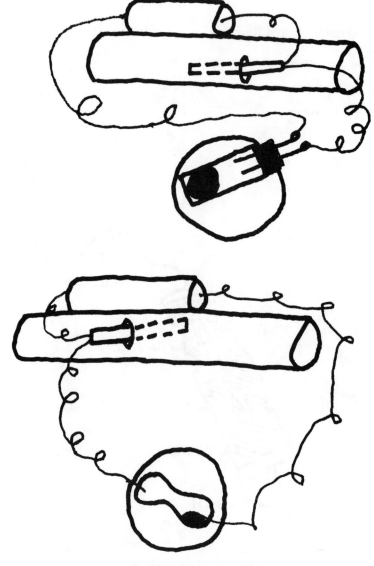

Figure 106. Door-handle traps.

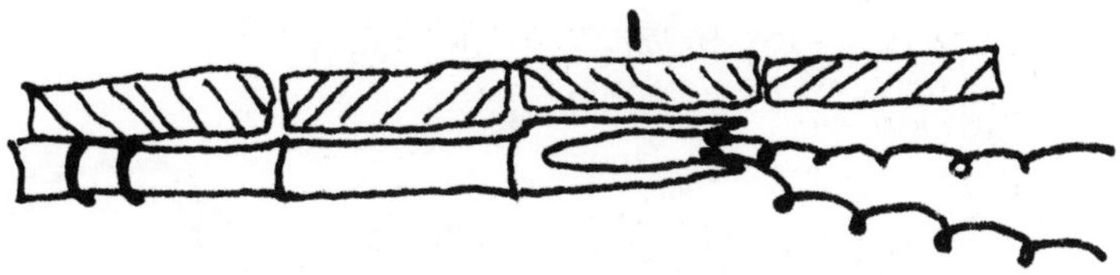

Loose Board

Figure 107. Loose floorboard trap.

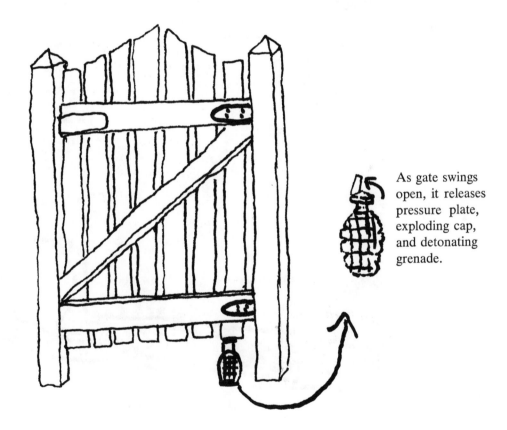

As gate swings open, it releases pressure plate, exploding cap, and detonating grenade.

Figure 108. Pressure-release gate trap.

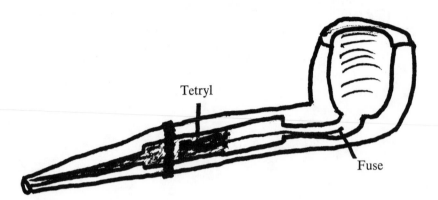

Tetryl

Fuse

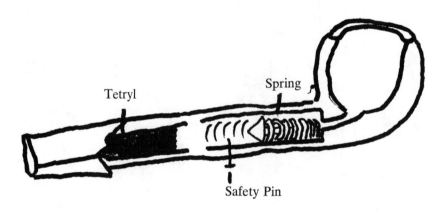

Tetryl

Spring

Safety Pin

Figure 109. Pipe traps.

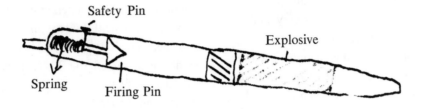

Figure 110. Ball-point pen trap.

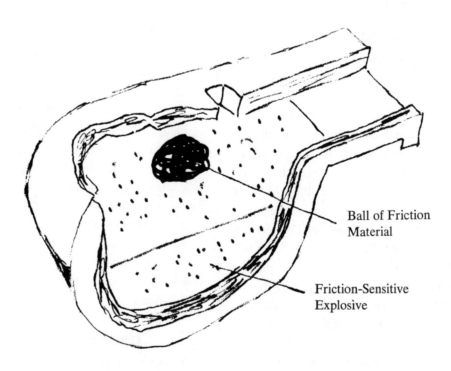

Figure 111. Whistle trap.

is effective, but it has many disadvantages. The procedure is very simple. Take a tin can and fill three-quarters of it with highly compressed gunpowder. Now attach to the top of the can a small magnifying glass, so that the sun's light, when magnified through the glass, will cause the heat necessary to detonate the charge. This works very well, as long as the sun shines, and it doesn't rain.

The alarm-clock detonating method is the most accurate device, in that a person can set the time he wishes the bomb to explode. It is connected in the same fashion as the other electrical-circuit booby traps. Wires are connected to the hammer of the bell and to the bell itself, via the blasting cap, to a dry cell (as shown in Figure 99). The clock should be set before the booby trap is built. When the alarm goes off, the hammer and bell connect completing the electrical circuit and detonating the explosive.

Up to now I have been primarily concerned with detonating devices, rather than the actual application of these bombs and booby traps. In this last section on explosives, I will deal with just a few of the many applications for these booby traps. Each situation calls for different techniques, so use your imagination and your cunning.

Road trap

The first type of application I will discuss is a basic road trap. This incorporates a wire-trip action to complete the electrical circuit. It is extremely simple to make, since all the equipment can be gathered in or around the house. The great advantage to this particular device is that the explosives are detonated when the vehicle is directly over it, so insuring maximum destruction. (See Figure 100.) To construct a road trap, begin by digging three holes across a roadway. Into two of the holes place the explosive charges, and into the third place a regular car battery. Connect the first wire from the negative terminal of the battery via each of the blasting caps, in each charge, to a metal pin on one side of an ordinary clothespin. The second wire should be connected directly from the positive terminal of the battery to the opposite metal pin, located on the same clothespin. The clothespin must be kept open by a small wooden wedge, which is attached to a thin black wire stretched across the roadway. When the semi-invisible wire is pulled, the wooden wedge will fall out of the clothespin, thus closing the clothespin. When the clothespin is closed, the two metal pins will connect and complete the electrical circuit, thus exploding the charges.

Walk trap

In Figure 101 is illustrated what is known as a walk trap. This incorporates the same type of wire-trip action as described in the road trap. The walk trap is not electrically operated, it relies on a percussion detonator. When the wire is pulled, it pulls the safety pin out of the heavy firing pin. The heat created from the detonator's explosion will be sufficient to set off the TNT. This type of booby trap is especially effective in dense undergrowth, where the trip wire cannot be readily seen.

Bangalore torpedo

In Figure 102, the Bangalore torpedo is illustrated. This is nothing more than a few sections of pipe filled with sticks of dynamite, sealed at the ends, and joined in the middle by couplings, thus permitting the torpedo to be of varying lengths. The cap at one end must have a small hole drilled in it, so that a fuse and blasting cap can be inserted. It can be used very effectively to destroy walls, barricades, and steel or iron doors. These are also great weapons against cars, trucks, and even trains. If piping of this sort is not available, you can make a substitute torpedo by taking a stick of dynamite and wrapping it tightly with electric tape and thin copper wire. To be effective, it should have many layers of each.

Molotov cocktail

Figure 103 shows a Molotov Cocktail. This is an incendiary bomb, which bursts into flame on breaking. A quart bottle is filled with two-thirds gasoline and one-third oil. A fuse is made of an old gasoline-soaked rag, and then stuffed into the mouth of the bottle. The bottle is corked, and the fuse is lit. It is thrown and, when it breaks, it will burst into flame. The enemy will not be able to extinguish the fire with water. These were used with varying degrees of success in the struggle in Hungary. According to reports they can disable a tank.

Homemade hand grenade

A homemade grenade is shown in Figure 104. This is constructed from an empty, clean, condensed-milk can, attached to a wooden handle. It is then filled halfway with a layer of dynamite. In the dynamite is placed a nonelectric blasting cap, with a five- to six-second fuse. The dynamite is then covered with small pieces of iron, until the can is full. Seal the top of the open end closed, leaving a small hole for the fuse.

How to make an anti-personnel grenade

Even more effective than the grenade described above is an anti-personnel grenade. This is constructed by taking a piece of pipe and closing it at one end, either by soldering or by screwing a cap on it. The pipe is packed tightly with dynamite, and sealed at the other end, leaving a small hole for the detonator, which is made in the following manner. A piece of one-eighth-inch tubing is fastened to the end of a piece of fuse, which in turn is attached to a detonating cap. On the other end of the fuse, a bit of cotton, saturated with chlorate of potassium and common sugar, is placed, followed by another piece of cotton and a little vial of sulfuric acid. (This vial must be hermetically sealed, to prevent leakage.) Finally, a piece of wood or iron, which can be easily moved, is packed in the remaining empty space. The piece of wood is placed there, so that when the pipe is moved the piece of iron or wood will fall against the vial of sulfuric acid and break it. Once the sulfuric acid contacts the potassium chlorate, the chemical reaction will cause a very hot flame, which will ignite the fuse and cause the explosion. If this type of device is placed in a roadway, or directly in the path of the enemy army, there is a good chance it will be set off—either by a kick or by curiosity.

Book trap

Figure 105 depicts a book trap. To construct this, you will need a large book, perhaps a thousand pages. The book should be hollowed out, leaving the edges intact. In this hollow place, put a dry cell battery and your explosive, and connect the wires. Fix two metal contact points to the edges of the book, and separate them with a wooden wedge, which is attached to the rear wall of the bookcase. This must be accomplished in such a manner that, when the book is removed from the shelf, the metal contact points will touch and complete the electrical circuit, thus causing the detonation of the explosive charge.

Door-handle traps

Two basic methods of booby-trapping door handles are illustrated in Figure 106. The first employs a short test tube, a cork, two needles, three wires, one electric blasting cap, one metal ball bearing, and one stick of dynamite. The two needles are pushed through the cork to an equal length, and the ball bearing is placed within the tube. The test tube is corked, and taped to the inside of a door handle. The wires are then connected from the eyes of the two needles to the battery, with one wire going via the blasting cap. Next, the battery and stick of dynamite are taped to the back of the door. When the handle is turned, the ball bearing will roll and touch both points of the needles, thus completing the electrical circuit and exploding the dynamite.

The second door-handle trap is much the same, except it uses a mercury thermostat switch, rather than a ball bearing.

Loose floorboard trap

The loose floorboard trap (Figure 107) utilizes the same principles as the Book Trap, in that it relies on two metal contact points touching to complete the electrical circuit. Beneath the loose floorboard are two strips of pliable metal or bamboo, each with a metal contact point, which will touch when pressure is brought down on the loose floorboard.

Gate trap

Illustrated in Figure 108 is the utilization of a regulation military grenade in a booby trap. This is an extremely simple, effective, and relatively safe booby trap. To cock the booby trap, pull the pin on a regular tension release grenade, and place beneath a swinging gate, or anywhere that will supply the pressure necessary. When the gate is moved (either opened or closed), the pressure will be released and the grenade detonated.

Chimney trap

An extremely simple but effective booby trap can be placed in a fireplace in a matter of seconds. Take three or four sticks of dynamite and tape them together. Attach a nonelectrical blasting cap, with a three- or four-foot fuse. Now tape the dynamite about five feet up on the inside of the chimney, leaving the fuse hanging loose downward. The end of the fuse should be about a foot or so up the chimney so that it is out of sight. When a fire is lit, the heat generated will ignite the fuse, and it will explode the charge, further up the chimney. This works extremely well, since most of the tamping is supplied by the very structure of the chimney.

Lamp trap

A personnel booby trap can be made by taking any oil or kerosene lamp and draining it of all the fuel. Now replace the oil with high-octane gasoline. When lit, this will cause a massive incendiary explosion. A candle can also be booby-trapped, by stuffing a small amount of lead azide or tetryl pellets into the wax, near the wick. The explosives will detonate from the flame of the candle.

Car trap

It is an extremely simple procedure to booby-trap a car. It has many advantages, the most important being that you do not have to carry your own power supply, but rather use the ignition system of the car itself. Wires are run from the electrical blasting cap to points along the electrical ignition system, and attached with alligator clips. When the key is turned, it will complete the ignition system, and thus explode the bomb. A good place to hide explosives is in the hollow cavity behind the dashboard, since then the full force of the explosion will be directed at the individuals in the front seat.

Pipe trap

There are basically two methods of booby-trapping pipes. The first is very similar to the chimney trap, except the intent is to blow off the smoker's head. A small amount of tetryl or lead azide is placed in the mouthpiece of the pipe, and a fuse is attached, which leads through the rest of the pipe to a point about one-quarter-inch beneath the bowl (Figure 109). When the smoker lights the pipe, the fuse will be lit, and burn down untouched, until it detonates the explosives in the mouthpiece, and blows the smoker's head off.

The second method (illustrated in Figure 109) is a little more complex but just as effective. A very sensitive explosive is placed in the mouthpiece, as before, except an activated firing pin is placed in the stem of the pipe. The smoker will attempt to light the pipe and find he cannot suck through it. Believing the stem to be blocked with tar or nicotine, he will unscrew the threaded joint. The act of unscrewing will release the firing pin, and detonate the explosives.

Pen trap

An ordinary plastic or metal retractable ball-point pen can be turned into a lethal weapon in a matter of minutes. The refill ink cartridge is removed, and in its place is put a small amount of tetryl. Above the charge is placed a firing pin, similar to the one used in the second method of the pipe trap. This firing pin will be held under pressure created by the pen's own spring. The tension is released by reversing the firing-pin motion. When the user snaps the plunger at the end of the pen, the firing pin is released and goes crashing in the tetryl, and detonates it. (See Figure 110.)

Whistle trap and other handy devices

A booby trap that has an effect similar to the one created by the pipe trap, is the whistle booby trap. It is constructed by separating the metal or plastic sides into their natural halves. This can be accomplished by steaming. Now, fill each half one-fourth full of an extremely friction-sensitive explosive. Before gluing the two halves together, include a small ball made of a rough sandpaper-like substance. When the whistle is blown, the ball will bounce around inside the shell, creating enough friction heat to set off the explosive charge.

An interesting booby trap can be constructed by using a bottle, full of a highly sensitive liquid explosive, which will detonate on the extraction of the cork. The cork is designed with a friction element that pulls through a sensitive explosive. When this booby trap explodes, it does extensive damage, due to the fragmentation of the glass.

An extremely simple device for setting a time-delay fire is a book of matches, with a lighted cigarette stuck in it. This is then left upon combustible material. The cigarette, as it burns down, will light the matches, and they in turn will generate the heat necessary to ignite the other larger combustible material.

Another incendiary time-delay device is constructed out of a candle, friction matches, and several rags soaked either in gasoline or kerosene. The candle is placed upright in the center of the bundle of matches. The soaked rags are placed around the base of the matches. As the candle burns down, it will ignite the matches, and they will ignite the rags. One can usually expect about a fifteen-minute delay with this device.

Cacodyal

To conclude this chapter, I will present the most horrendous recipe I could find. Since it is not feasible to make napalm in your kitchen, you will have to be satisfied with cacodyal. This is made by chemically extracting all the oxygen from alcohol, and then replacing it, under laboratory controls, with metal arsenic. The formula for alcohol is $C_4 H_5 O$, whereas for cacodyal it is $C_4 H_5 AR$. Now, this new substance, cacodyal, possesses spontaneous inflammability, the moment it is exposed to the air. Therefore it can be put into a bottle and used like a Molotov Cocktail. If it is thrown, it will explode on impact, but this is not its real advantage. When it explodes, a dense white smoke is given off. This is white arsenic, a deadly poison. One inhalation will probably cause death in a matter of seconds.

Postscript

This is the section I had hoped would not be necessary. When I began the book, I said to myself that there was a relatively good chance that we might have more degrees of real freedom by the time the book was finished. Well, finished it is, and Vietnam is still there, Cambodia has been added, the corporations are still polluting, and the government is still lying. Since we can still legally call ourselves oppressed people, I find this last section on legal crap necessary.

It is amazing with so many so-called "intelligent" people running about that we still have a state, a government, a bunch of archaic laws, and a multitude of psychotics willing to enforce them. If people depend on the state to make laws, to prevent themselves from doing what they really want to do, then I say that these people are nuts. I mean to say, if I really want to do something, I don't particularly care if it's legal, illegal, moral, immoral, or amoral. I want to do it, so I do it. The only laws a man can truly respect are the ones he makes for himself.

Have you noticed that the people who actually make the laws, the people in power, never make laws for themselves? They pass legislation for the other people, who don't want the laws to begin with. This government is a vicious bureaucratic cycle, with the people in power denying they have the power, passing legislation to protect their power, and conveniently losing any legislation which does not conform to their own particular brand of megalomania, in one of their many advisory committees.

I do not want laws that protect me from myself. Does it sound absurd? If I wish to ride a motorcycle without a helmet, it is my absolute right to do so. If I wish to be a fool, it is my right, since the only person who could be hurt by my action is me. If I want to sleep with men, or take LSD, or march naked across Sheep Meadow, or do perverse things to my dog, then by what right does the government stop me?

Robert Heinlein, in a recent book *The Moon Is a Harsh Mistress,* talks about an idea for taxation which I think could be extremely functional. It is that the people in power—the senators, congressmen, presidents, *et al*—should pay all the taxes themselves. Since these officials are making laws nobody wants anyway, why shouldn't the people keep the government as financially weak as possible?

Since the revolution hasn't taken place yet, I have included here some basic common-sense legal advice.

I was busted about two years ago at a demonstration. The charges were trumped up and finally dropped, but the affair cost me five hundred bucks in legal expenses. That five hundred I couldn't afford. I had to borrow it from friends but, whatever it cost, it was worth it. It showed exactly where the legal system of this country was at. Ninety percent of the guys in jail with me were black, and Spanish, because they couldn't dig up the outrageous bails. I sincerely hope that, if and when they ever get out, they will still be able to see the injustice with the same clarity and passionate hatred.

Prison does strange things to men. Although its purpose is to break the free spirit of a man, in many cases it just adds fuel to the fire that has never been and never will be extinguished.

> The wheel of the law turns
> without pause.
>
> After rain, good weather.
> In the wink of an eye.
>
> The universe throws off
> its muddy clothes.

For ten thousand miles
the landscape

spreads out like a beautiful brocade.
Light Breezes. Smiling flowers.

High in the trees, amongst
the sparkling leaves

all the birds sing at once.
Men and animals rise up reborn.

What could be more natural?
After sorrow, comes happiness.

—Ho Chi Minh
Written in prison

The cop is a phenomenon, unto himself. He is a paranoiac. He is a megalomaniac. He can be a sadist. He can be vicious and cruel. He can be nice and sweet, especially if he wants something. He can break the laws that he pretends to be enforcing, with impunity. He is very sensitive to being called names, and tends to react the only way he knows how. He is armed to the teeth, with clubs, chemicals, gases, firearms, and the most frightening weapon of all, righteous indignation. He tends to be stupid, and uneducated, and very aware of his shortcomings, although he doesn't appreciate people's comments on them. He travels in packs or gangs, and feels a certain degree of security when he is with his own kind. His word is taken without question in all courts, and he relies on this.

When unarmed and confronted by a police officer, you must take all these factors into consideration, before deciding what course of action you intend to follow. Most individual confrontations between police and individuals take place in the street. If you are black, Puerto Rican, or white with long hair, you can expect this. Cops have the *legal* right to stop and frisk any person, in suspicious circumstances. Suspicious circumstances are solely the cop's interpretation. He can always bust you for something like disturbing the peace, or disorderly conduct, and then throw in a resisting-arrest charge.

I can fully appreciate the fury and anger that a person can feel when put through a humiliating experience by a cop, but I would recommend strongly that a person maintain his cool, and in no circumstances lose his temper. If you lose your temper, you are playing right into the cop's hands.

The cop will probably ask you a bunch of questions: Name? Address? What you are doing? Where you are going? Etc. I would suggest that you answer all his questions, although you are not legally bound to. In no circumstances should you answer any questions about drugs truthfully (unless you have none and have never used them). By refusing to answer questions, you will antagonize the cop, and probably get yourself busted for loitering, or refusing to obey a policeman's orders. Be polite and concise, but do not give any information that is not asked for, and in no circumstances use anyone else's name. It is a good idea to refer to the cop as "officer," since it helps his ego, and enhances your chances of staying out of jail.

Cops may go further than just harassment. They may actually assault you. In these circumstances, you still have no legal right to defend yourself. In these conditions stay calm, if possible. Do not attempt to defend yourself other than just to cover your groin and head. If you see an opportunity to grab a nearby weapon, and are reasonably sure that you can be successful, then defend yourself, but never forget that the cop has a gun, and he has used it, and will use it.

When confronted on the street by the police, a common emotion for a person to feel is fear. There is nothing wrong with this. In fact, it's quite healthy, but do not show it to the cop. If the cop realizes you are afraid of him, he will take full advantage of the situation and play on your fear. This doesn't mean to act belligerently, and, for God's sake, do not be a high school or college lawyer, and explain to the cop what he can and cannot do. He can do anything, he's got the gun.

As I have stated before, I hate demonstrations. I feel they must be sponsored by the government to give the cops a heyday. But some demonstrations are necessary, although the reason for this escapes me at the moment. When taking part in a demonstration, you have opened yourself up to brutality and arrest, and you must understand this. Do not go to a peace rally thinking about peace. Peace is won, and respect is earned. At all mass street meetings, use common sense. In no circumstances carry drugs, cherry bombs, stink bombs, spray paint, or any object that might be considered a concealed weapon. These include penknives and nail files. I have always made it a policy never to take my wallet or any identification, but this does risk arrest for not possessing a draft card.

If you are going to a demonstration that you think might

be violent—this means all demonstrations—do not wear jewelry. Women should not wear skirts, and everyone should wear helmets, and carry a gas mask. If you smoke, carry an extra pack of cigarettes with you, as it is a real bitch getting cigarettes in jail.

One of the most threatening aspects of any demonstration is the plain-clothes cops. Over the past few years they have proved more and more successful, and accordingly their numbers have increased. Plainclothes cops are not plainclothed, they are in disguise. Generally they try to grow long hair and beards but, if you have any perception at all, it is not hard to pick them out. If you are performing an illegal act, be especially careful and aware of who is standing behind you.

Believe it or not, if you are arrested and attempt to resist, and the original charge you were arrested for is thrown out of court, you still can be jailed for resisting arrest. So, when resisting arrest or making an attempt to escape, be pretty sure that you have a good chance of success, and never forget the gun. Many persons have managed to escape from their arresting officers during demonstrations, with help from their brothers and sisters creating confusion.

Remember the cop doesn't have to use the phrase, "You are under arrest." He may just grab you. This act in itself will hold up in court as a legal arrest. The cop also has the prerogative of not arresting you; he may just detain you for questioning. Detainment can last as long as the cop likes, but usually it does not last more than several hours. If you are held for questioning, you are treated the same way as if you were arrested, but you have none of the legal rights you have if you are under arrest.

If you are arrested, do not talk. The more you say, the more you will incriminate yourself, and probably other people as well. You have the right to remain silent, and by talking or trying to find out what you are charged with, you may make a confession, without even realizing that you have done so.

There are three things you should do as soon as you are arrested:

1. Shout out your name, so that somebody knows you have been busted—not that he will do anything about it, but it helps your peace of mind.

2. Try to remember anyone who saw you busted, since they may be useful as witnesses.

3. Get and memorize the cop's badge number and name. If a different cop shows up in court, and you can prove it, there is a good chance that the charges will be dismissed.

At the police station, you will be booked. This is a form-filling-out time, where they will persist in asking every incriminating question possible, and you, of course, should answer none of them. Although you are supposed to have the right to call an attorney before being questioned, don't count on it. In fact, don't count on anything at all. If you are lucky enough to be allowed to call a lawyer, do so immediately. If you don't know a lawyer, and are busted in New York City call any of the organizations listed below and explain your situation. If you are communicating with your parents, call them at once. Parents can get you out of jams faster than any lawyer.

National Lawyers Guild—227-0385, 227-1078, 962-5440

Emergency Civil Liberties Committee—683-8120

New York Civil Liberties Union—929-6076

Mobilization for Youth Legal Services—777-5250

Part of being booked is the arresting officer's filling out a Vera form. This is a test to see if you qualify for a summons. If you do, you will be released immediately and given a date to appear in court. Vera summonses are only given for nondrug-related misdemeanors. To be eligible for Vera, you must have someone verify your address and occupation, by phone, to the arresting officer. The police will also check your previous record. This is an extremely easy system to beat, if you have good friends. I was arrested in Brooklyn, for disorderly conduct and disturbing the peace. About a week before the bust, a friend and I had worked out a series of aliases and phony addresses, for just such occasions. The arresting officer called my friend, and asked him if he was indeed my father. After he had verified my phoney name, address, and occupation, I was released with a summons, never to appear again.

Vera works on a point system. If you manage to verify your existence and accumulate the correct number of points, you will be released. The actual scale of points appears a few paragraphs below.

After you are booked, if you don't rate Vera, you will be taken to a larger city jail. In New York City, it is 100 Centre Street, better known as the Tombs. The Tombs is a large prison, without windows. It houses about twice as many people as it is supposed to. This incredible overcrowding has resulted in bureaucracy. These impersonal bureaucratic systems are the really frightening aspect of any large city jail. Everything is performed like clockwork, except if you get lost. What if someone loses your card, and you don't have any friends on the outside? Absurd? No, this isn't absurd. It has happened many times: A guy gets lost in the Tombs, and he's found a year or so later. He was originally charged with disorderly conduct, which has a usual maximum sentence of 30 to 60 days. When he is found, he has already spent a year in jail.

If you are under 21, in New York City you have a special treat in store for you—either Atlantic Ave., or Rikers Island. Either one of these places is many times worse than the Tombs. The prison officials have a great deal of difficulty understanding why the suicide rate is so high in these locations. I have a great deal of difficulty understanding the prison officials.

When you are put into a big-city jail, you will probably be frightened, lonely, humiliated, and completely drained of any spirit. This is normal. Talk to the fellow prisoners, write, play cards, read, doodle, do anything to keep your mind occupied, but above all do not verbalize your misfortune to your fellow prisoners. Each one of them has had similar situations, and is sick of thinking about it.

Vera Point System:

To be released with a summons a defendant needs:

1. A New York area address where he can be reached.

2. A total of five points from the following categories.

PRIOR RECORD

2 No convictions.

1 One misdemeanor conviction.

0 Two misdemeanor convictions or one felony conviction.

—1 Three or more misdemeanor convictions or two felony convictions.

EMPLOYMENT

3 Present job one year or more.

2 Present job four months, or present and prior job six months.

1 An on-and-off job in either of the above two lines. Or a current job.

Or unemployed three months or less, with nine months or more on prior job.

Or receiving unemployment compensation, or welfare, or supported by family.

FAMILY TIES (in New York Area)

3 Lives with or has contact with other family members.

2 Lives with family or has contact with family.

1 Lives with nonfamily person and gives this person as reference.

RESIDENCE (in New York area, not on-and-off)

3 Present address for one year or more.

2 Present residence six months, or present and prior one year.

1 Present residence four months, or present and prior six months.

TIME IN NEW YORK CITY

1 Ten years or more.

Depending on the time of day that you are arrested, the time will be set for your arraignment. If you are busted late at night, the chances are very good you will be held overnight. (A word of advice: If you get the choice between the upper and lower bunks in a cell, choose the lower. Prisons do not turn off their lights at night, and I spent a sleepless night, without a mattress, with a five-hundred-watt bulb shining directly into my eyes.)

The arraignment is nothing more than the judge telling you what you are charged with, and setting bail for you. You should have a lawyer present, since, if you don't, the judge will assign a moron from the Legal Aid Society. If you can't get a lawyer on your own, accept one from the Legal Aid Society, but do not let the guy make any deals for you. Legal Aid lawyers are notorious for wheeling and dealing themselves out of work, and you into jail. It is better to use a lawyer, rather than to attempt to defend yourself, because the lawyer knows all the legal hocus-pocus that might reduce your bail. Judges get pissed-off when defendants try to defend themselves. I was once called "a dirty layman," when trying to defend myself in a civil case, by some old asshole judge.

At the arraignment you will be required to plead guilty

or not guilty to any violation. Never plead guilty to a violation. If necessary, you can change your plea later. If you are charged with a misdemeanor, you will be given an opportunity to plead, but you are not required to do so. Do not plead on a misdemeanor. You will not be allowed to plead on a felony.

In most circumstances, if the judge does not release you on your own recognizance (without bail), he will set a figure and often a cash alternative. In other words, if your bail is set at $500, he may only require a small percentage, say $50 in cash. This is good, since if you have to go to a bondsman it is a big hassle, and he will require incredible amounts of security, such as automobiles, title deeds to houses or property, bank books, etc.

The best advice possible on any legal matter is (1) maintain your cool and temper, (2) keep your mouth shut, (3) get a good lawyer and call your family, and (4) never forget what you have been through. Allow the fear and loneliness, and hatred to build inside you, rather than diminish with time. Allow your passions to fertilize the seeds of constructive revolution. Allow your love of freedom to overcome the false values placed on human life. For the only method to communicate with the enemy is to speak on his own level, using his own terms. Freedom is based on respect, and respect must be earned by the spilling of blood.

Bibliography

Books

Firearm Silencers, U.S. Combat Bookshelf.

Che Guevara on Guerrilla Warfare, Che Guevara, Vintage Books.

Explosions and Demolitions, U.S. Combat Bookshelf.

Hand to Hand Combat, U.S. Combat Bookshelf.

The Bust Book, Students for a Democratic Society.

Handbook of Revolutionary Warfare, Kwame Nkrumah, International Publishers.

The Guerrilla and How to Fight Him, Praeger Publishers.

Revolution for the Hell of It, Abbie Hoffman, Dial Press.

Fuck the System, The Yippees.

Submachine Guns Caliber .45, M3, and M3A1, U.S. Combat Bookshelf.

Essays from the Minister of Defense Huey Newton, Black Panther Party.

Allied Electronics Catalogue, Allied Electronics, Inc.

Continental Telephone Catalogue, Continental Telephone Supply Co.

Right of Revolution, Truman Nelson, Beacon Press.

Coup D'Etat: A Practical Handbook, Edward Luttwak, Knopf Publishers.

Explorer Scout Manual, Boy Scouts of America.

The Turn-On Book, Barnel Enterprises.

Hashish Cookbook, Panama Rose, Gnaoua Press.

Alice B. Toklas Cookbook, Alice B. Toklas, Anchor Books.

How to Stay Alive in the Woods, Bradford Angier, Collier Books.

Pot: A Handbook of Marihuana, John Rosevear, University Books Inc.

Air Conditioned Nightmare, Henry Miller, Grove Press.

Quotations from Chairman Mao Tse Tung, Mao Tse Tung, Foreign Language Press.

Booby Traps, U.S. Combat Bookshelf.

150 Questions on Guerrilla Warfare, Panther Publishers.

Axioms of Kwame Nkrumah, Kwame Nkrumah, International Publishers.

Prison Diary, Ho Chi Minh, China Publishers.

Police Manual on Non-Lethal Weapons, Police Department.

Minuteman Manual, The Minutemen.

Homemade Bombs and Explosives, Joseph Stoffel, Thomas and Thomas Publishers.

U.S. Army Field Manual for Physical Security, Office of Government Publications.

Some Dare Call It Treason, Liberty Bell Press.

Soul on Ice, Eldridge Cleaver, Dial Press.

Post Prison Writings, Eldridge Cleaver, Random House.

Who Rules America? William Domhoff, Spectrum Books.

Communist Manifesto, Marx and Engels, International Publishers.

Confessions of an Irish Rebel, Brendan Behan, Lancer Books.

Escape and Evasion, U.S. Combat Bookshelf.

Guerrilla Days in Ireland, Tom Barry, Anvil Books.

Drugs A to Z, Richard R. Lingeman, McGraw-Hill Publishing Company.

Artaud Anthology, Antonin Artaud, City Lights Books.

Woodstock Nation, Abbie Hoffman, Random House.

Do It, Jerry Rubin, Simon and Schuster.

Urban Guerrilla, Martin Oppenheimer, Quadrangle Books.

Ho Chi Minh on Revolution, Ho Chi Minh, New American Library.

Puppet Masters, Robert Heinlein, New American Library.

The Moon Is a Harsh Mistress, Robert Heinlein, Berkley Publishers.

The Pot Book, Mota West of San Francisco.

How to Grow Your Own, A Mikus Book.

Low-High Boom-Modern Explosives, Philip Danisevich, A Bridgeview Gun Sale Book.

Shooters Bible, Follett Publishing Co.

Gun Digest, Follett Publishing Co.

Fundamentals of Small Arms, U.S. Combat Bookshelf.

Electronic Invasion, Robert M. Brown, Rider Publications.

Magazines and Newspapers

East Village Other, 105 2nd Avenue, New York, N.Y. 10003.

Berkeley Barb, 2042 University Avenue, Berkeley, California, 94704.

Berkeley Tribe, P.O. Box 9043, Berkeley, California 94709.

Rat, 241 E. 14th Street, New York, N.Y.

The Seed, 2628 North Halstead, Chicago, Illinois 60614.

The Panther Paper, Ministry of Information, Box 2967, San Francisco, California.

The Militant, 873 Broadway, New York, N.Y.

New York Free Press, 200 West 72nd Street, New York.

Movement, 330 Grove Street, California 94102.

Corpus, 14 Cooper Square, New York, N.Y. 10003.

Great Speckled Bird, 187 14th Street, Atlanta, Georgia.

International Times, 27 Endell Street London, WC2, England.

L.A. Free Press, 7813 Beverly Boulevard, Los Angeles, California 90036.

New York Review of Sex and Politics, 80 5th Avenue, New York, N.Y. 10011.

Old Mole, 2 Brookline, Cambridge, Massachusetts.

Om, c/o Roger Priest, U.S. Navy, P.O. Box 1033, Washington, D.C.

Orpheus, Bin 1832, Phoenix, Arizona 85001.

Other Scenes, Box 8, Village Station, New York, N.Y. 10014.

Oz, Princedale Road, London, W11, England.

Philadelphia Free Press, 1237 Vine Street, Philadelphia, Pennsylvania.

The Rag, 2200 Guadalupe, Austin, Texas 78705.

The Sage, P.O. Box 1741, Santa Fe, New Mexico 87501.

San Diego Free Press, 751 Turquoise Street, San Diego, California 92109.

Space City News, 1217 Wichita, Houston, Texas 77004.

Spokane Natural, Box 1276, Spokane, Washington 99201.

View from the Bottom, 532 State Street, New Haven, Connecticut.

Washington Free Press, 1522 Connecticut Avenue, Washington, D.C.